T0319758

Autos, Smog and Pollution Control

Autos, Smog and Pollution Control

The Politics of Air Quality Management in California

Wyn Grant

Professor of Politics
University of Warwick, UK

Edward Elgar
Aldershot, UK • Brookfield, US

Published by
Edward Elgar Publishing Limited
Gower House
Croft Road
Aldershot
Hants GU11 3HR
UK

Edward Elgar Publishing Company
Old Post Road
Brookfield
Vermont 05036
US

British Library Cataloguing in Publication Data
Grant, Wyn
    Autos, Smog and Pollution Control:
    Politics of Air Quality Management in
    California
    I. Title
    363.7384

Library of Congress Cataloguing in Publication Data
Grant, Wyn.
    Autos, smog, and pollution control: the politics of air quality
    management in California / Wyn Grant.
        p.   cm.
    Includes bibliographical references and index.
    1. Air quality management—Government policy—California.
    2. Automobiles—California—Motors—Exhaust gas.   I. Title.
    HC107.C23073   1996
    363.73'87—dc20   95-13483
                                                                  CIP

ISBN 1 85278 927 1

Printed and bound in Great Britain by
Biddles Ltd, Guildford and King's Lynn

Contents

Tables

Preface

This book is the result of research funded by the Economic and Social Research Council as part of the transport and the environment programme coordinated by Dr David Banister. I would like to express my gratitude to Dr Banister for his support and for his very effective management of the programme. Managing a research programme is not an easy task. For me the programme enabled me to bring together my interest in Californian politics and my growing interest in environmental politics.

I would like to thank all the individuals in California who gave up their time to answer my questions and who provided me with a considerable amount of very helpful documentation. The California State Library in Sacramento was also a very useful source of material, and I would like to thank the staff for their helpfulness in the face of budgetary cutbacks. I am grateful to the students at Warwick who have taken my course in California Government and Politics, sustaining my old fashioned belief in the fruitful interaction between research and teaching.

The University of Warwick continues to provide a supportive environment in which it is possible to combine the roles of a managing professor and a research professor. Within the department, I would like to thank Professors Barry Buzan and Jim Bulpitt for their support and assistance in my management duties.

Maggie Grant has shown her usual tolerance during the writing of yet another book. Sophia, Ros and Milly were also a great source of support; as a manager at Post Haste couriers, Ros kept me reminded of the central role of transport in a modern economy.

Wyn Grant

1. Introduction

Motor cars are a central feature of 20th century life, not least in California where an 'auto culture' was facilitated by the freeway and expressed in a dispersed pattern of land use. The manufacture, distribution and maintenance of motor vehicles is a core activity of a modern
economy, and taxes on transport are an important source of revenue for
governments. The ability to get in one's car and drive where one wants
and when one wants is generally regarded as a key entitlement of the
modern citizen. Acquisition of one's first car is a rite of passage into
adulthood. The prevalence of the 'road movie' in American cinema is
no accident. The freedom to get up and go somewhere else on impulse
is a central element of the American dream, part of the ability to 'start
over again' when things go wrong. Take away mobility, and you have
taken away one of the key features of an open society. 'Individual
transportation has been as much a part of [the] American utopian ideal
as the house with its backyard, or as the nuclear family' (Rieff, 1991,
p. 45).

Yet the car is not unequivocally celebrated in the way that it once was.
The construction of new roads is opposed by protesters who are sometimes successful. Even in California, voters have supported the spending
of large sums of public money on new rail systems. This increased public
concern reflects a greater sensitivity to environmental issues, enhanced in
the case of transport by the diversity of its environmental impacts which
include noise, accident risk, solid wastes, impacts on land use and air
pollution (Button and Rothengatter, 1993, pp. 21–4; OECD, 1992, pp. 18–
20). Concern about the local impact of automobile-generated air pollution has been present in cities such as Los Angeles for over 50 years, but
the debate has been given an additional impetus in the 1980s and 1990s
by concerns about 'global warming'. Developing robust theoretical models to measure and predict climate change is not an easy task, but, 'there
is mounting, although some would argue not yet conclusive, evidence
that high levels of CO_2 in the atmosphere, by preventing heat escaping
from the planet, will lead to global climate changes' (Button and

Rothengatter, 1993, p. 360). Motor vehicles make a significant contribution to carbon dioxide emissions. 'Estimates suggest that about 15 per cent of the world's total man-made emissions of CO_2 are generated by motor vehicles and in some OECD countries the figure may reach 40 per cent' (OECD, 1992, p. 19).

A central problem for political decision-makers as the 21st century approaches is finding some balance between the benefits of the motor vehicle and its costs. They are not helped by the fact that the electorate, as so often, makes contradictory demands on 'the politicians' who are then blamed when they fail to make a satisfactory reconciliation between them. Voters place a high value on environmental quality, but they also want to retain the benefits of a lifestyle in which unrestricted mobility is a key element. In California, 'the polls keep saying that people want their health protected, they want air quality not to be fouled and polluted' (interview, Sacramento, 30 March 1993). The same respondent noted: 'The single most frequent item that [legislators] hear from their constituents about relates to the constituent's car'. He concluded:

> It's now getting to the point that air pollution is not going to be addressed simply by technological refits on stationary source emissions, it's going to have to entail some changes in lifestyle and changes in development habits … To enact that type of legislation is not politically favourable, it's very easy to say we'll put on some control technology because we want clean air back, to say we're going to try to get you out of your car or going to try to change development patterns, that's no no in this state.

Formulating policies that attempt to strike a balance between the benefits of motor vehicle transport and its environmental costs is not an easy task, but it is relatively easy compared to the task of implementing such policies in an effective way. An underlying problem is that, 'the individual is confronted with choices only on a piecemeal basis and has to take as a fixture the relevant conditions of use. Thus the choice is not between private motor transport and public transport, but between buying an auto and putting up with the existing bus service' (Hirsch, 1977, p. 90). The central paradox can be stated thus: government transport policies generally have a relatively marginal or incremental impact on the choices faced by consumers. If, however, government attempted to make radical changes in conditions of use (for example, allowing cars to be driven on alternate days on the basis of their number plates), it would encounter substantial resistance from the electorate.

It is therefore not surprising that government intervention in the sector has been extensive but often unsuccessful. 'Many of the current environmental problems, therefore, are not due to traditional market failures but are the by-products, albeit often accidental, of deliberate policy initiatives' (Banister and Button, 1993, p. 6). As one policy specialist in California commented in interview: 'If you look back at the various transportation management options that have been considered, the impact of those transportation management measures has been very, very disappointing. That means the consumer doesn't want to change his lifestyle in almost any way when it comes to a car' (interview, Sacramento, 25 March 1993). Policy failure is thus a recurrent problem in the sector, but continued policy failure will not only lead to ever increasing local pollution and congestion costs, but also to global impacts on sea levels and agricultural activity.

One of the central arguments of this book is that governments, even where the political context is favourable to environmentally friendly policy initiatives, may adopt inappropriate policies. In part, this is because there is a tendency to adopt policies which show an immediate and visible impact in terms of 'bringing home the bacon' to the legislator's district, rather than less dramatic and more prosaic policies which may have a greater long-term effect. There is, however, a more general problem of implementation deficit even where the policies adopted are appropriate. Weale (1992) argues that pollution control policies have been particularly prone to suffer from problems of implementation deficit, in part because of the reliance on traditional administrative regulatory strategies. In particular: 'Regulators are often faced with a choice between negotiating compliance and enforcing standards. There are strong psychological pressures to negotiate compliance, which itself has a number of different moral and social judgements involved' (Weale, 1992, p. 17).

In short, devising an optimal pollution policy is not just a matter of choosing the most effective course of action, given the current state of technical knowledge; it is also a question of selecting the political design that gives the best chance of securing the desired set of outcomes. This should not be taken to imply the advocacy of some rigid 'plan' that will be put into effect regardless of the opposition or difficulties it encounters. Good design implies a clarity about objectives combined with a willingness to be flexible about the means of achieving those objectives, taking into account systematic monitoring of the extent to which programme goals are being achieved.

In this book, air pollution policy is considered in relation to California. Why California? First, because it has faced an air pollution problem, especially in the Los Angeles basin, for nearly 50 years and has considerable experience in policy development and implementation. Second, if policy measures can succeed in an economy and culture which is as auto-oriented as that of California, they may have some chance of success elsewhere. Third, quite apart from California's displacement in the world economy (it would be the sixth or seventh largest economy in the world if it were an independent state), it also has considerable political displacement, particularly in terms of innovative, agenda-setting policies. Whether in terms of tax-cutting policies in the 1970s, environmental policies in the 1980s, or term limits for legislators in the 1990s, California has often pioneered policies that have then been adopted elsewhere. In the US, the role of California has often been seen as 'analogous to that of West Germany in the EC in terms of raising environmental issues' (Grant, 1989, p. 211). Many Americans look, 'to California as Americans have done so often in their dreams, as the place where the American future might possibly be working itself out' (Rieff, 1991, p. 23). It may, of course, be the case that those who go to California in search of the future now find that they have seen the future and it is not working (Davie, 1972, p. 5). Matters, however, have changed since the early 1970s when it could be reported that: 'Few Los Angelenos object to the dominance of the automobile' (Davie, 1972, p. 73).

It should also be noted that political scientists have placed an increasing emphasis on the effectiveness of policy-making and implementation at the state level, reflecting such developments as the reform of state legislatures and the increasing professionalism of state bureaucracies (Ringquist, 1993, pp. 65–6). 'Potomac' fever, which suggests that, 'almost everything of importance happens in Washington DC' (Sabatier, 1993a, p. 15) is being quelled by the antidote of a new emphasis on what happens at the state and local level.

THE POLITICAL SCIENCE CONTRIBUTION TO TRANSPORT STUDIES

The participants in the Economic and Social Research Council (ESRC) transport and the environment programme were drawn largely from three disciplinary backgrounds: economics, geography and land use (or town and country) planning. Each of these disciplines has a clear contribution to make to the discussion of the interrelationship between transport and the environment. As far as economics is concerned, there is evidently a miniature forecasting industry which attempts to predict the volume and composition of future traffic levels, information which is of clear value in the Department of Transport in providing a basis on which it can construct its road-building programme. More generally, economists can suggest ways in which the price mechanism can be used to achieve environmental policy objectives in a way that is more effective than 'command and control' regulation in achieving specified goals, imposing fewer transaction costs, and having fewer distorting effects on the operation of market mechanisms. Geographers and land use planners can enhance our understanding of the spatial factors which influence traffic patterns. They can ask questions such as how can planning controls be used to affect traffic generation in a way that minimizes additional environmental costs arising from new developments? This emphasis in the transport and environment programme on a variety of interdisciplinary approaches attacking a common problem area is consistent with what may tentatively be termed the 'Warwick view' of political science. Along with other features such as an emphasis on the importance of theory and methodology, the 'Warwick view' subscribed to by some members of the Department of Politics and International Studies emphasizes politics as a 'junction subject' open to, and benefiting from, a wide variety of disciplinary perspectives.

What can political scientists contribute to the debate? Transport has for many centuries been perceived as a central function of a polity. As Hobbes comments (1651, p. 160): 'The nutrition of a commonwealth consisteth in the *plenty*, and *distribution* of *materials* conducing to life: in concoction or *preparation*; and, when concoted, in the *conveyance* of it, by convenient conduits, to the public use'. Contemporary political scientists have written about transport, often in connection with pressure group studies focused on the 'roads lobby' (Dudley, 1983). Contributing to a policy debate, however, involves more than tracing how decisions are made or not made: it also requires suggesting how they could be made more effectively.

Much of the current debate centres on how economics can be used to incorporate the costs imposed by external bads such as pollution, not charged to anyone, into the price mechanism so that it can reflect the full social costs of production and use. The underlying assumption is that the price mechanism can have an immediate and wide-ranging impact on behaviour, while still leaving the choice between alternative courses of action to the individual consumer rather than imposing on her the decisions of an expensive and inefficient bureaucracy. There is certainly scope for a shift from 'command and control' regulation to greater use of the price mechanism, but this does not remove from the agenda the problem of good policy design. 'Economists, for instance, are particularly good (or at least think they are) at defining optimal solutions but often less good at mapping out the appropriate path to these solutions. By nature most people are risk adverse and prefer immediate benefits to future benefits' (Banister and Button, 1993, p. 7). This raises questions about the compatibility of a democratic system of government with persuading citizens to look beyond their own immediate needs and wants, and it is here that political philosophy becomes relevant.

A conception of democracy that might appeal to economists is one that enables a clear preference ordering to appear in relation to alternative policy options. Thus:

> ... the elected government determines what should be the objectives of economic policy in the light of its adopted social welfare function. It is assumed that the government can list the objectives, and also specify the rates of trade-off between any two objectives; in other words, that a well-defined social objectives function can be provided by the government (Grant and Nath, 1984, p. 11).

Thus: 'In welfarist or preference-based theories, the basic aims of democratic institutions are to elicit individual preferences and to provide procedures for regulating them when they conflict so that the greatest degree of overall preference satisfaction is achieved' (Hurley, 1989, p. 323). In California, the existence of a system of direct democracy facilitates this process to some extent. For example, voters could declare a preference for a system of road pricing and the conditions (for example, new roads, levels of road congestion) under which such a system of pricing should come into effect.

A rather more demanding conception of democracy is a cognitive one which requires citizens, 'to express not their own preferences, but rather their well-considered beliefs about what can be done' (Hurley, 1989, p. 323). As Susan Hurley is the first to recognize, such demands are unrealistic, but may nevertheless be worthwhile as goals which one attempts to attain in a democratic polity. It may be that voting is not the best way to achieve thoughtful and reasoned opinions. Hirsch argues that the market provides consumers with a series of incremental decisions, so that as public transport deteriorates, more people travel by car, and public transport suffers a further deterioration:

> The choice is posed at each stage in a dynamic process; there is no chance of selection between the states at either end of that process. By contrast, the political mechanism through which preferences between alternative states could in principle be posed, has not yet developed a satisfactory system for such decision (Hirsch, 1977, p. 18).

Is there any conceivable political arrangement which could provide a choice between alternative end states? Party-based elections bundle a range of choices, and are also affected (particularly in California) by personality issues. California has an extensive system of direct democracy. Yet even in referendum votes where citizens are provided (as they are in California) with extensive information about the merits and demerits of the alternatives, the costs of acquiring the information greatly exceed the likelihood of one's vote affecting the outcome. Citizen-based pressure groups may, however, be able to advance and test out new ideas, while open hearings before legislative committees also provide a forum for evaluating alternative courses of action and removing those which are inappropriate from the policy agenda.

Theoretical concerns about the nature of democracy, the distribution of power within democracies, and the implications of such distributions for questions of equity and social justice, will be kept in mind throughout this volume, even if they are not always evident in an explicit way. If political science is led solely by empirical concerns, political scientists may fall into the trap of becoming commentators on current events – 'inside dopesters' – without the sources available to journalists.

Another question which needs to be addressed is whether there is anything distinctive about environmental politics as an area of enquiry compared to any other arena of political activity. Weale (1992, pp. 5–9) identifies a number of distinctive characteristics of pollution control policy which are represented in Table 1.1. In this table, the policy characteristics identified by Weale are compared in general terms with air pollution control policies in California. One point that emerges is that policies to promote public transport as an alternative to the use of the car have some different characteristics from air pollution policies seeking directly to restrain emissions from mobile sources. Policies to build new underground or light rapid transit lines, or open up passenger services on freight lines, confer benefits on identifiable constituencies,

Table 1.1   Distinctive characteristics of pollution control policies

Characteristics identified by Weale (1992)	Air pollution policies in California	Rail and light rapid transit policies in California
Public goods	Meets public goods criterion of non-exclusion	Some citizens excluded from benefits
Pollution control does not use public spending as primary instrument	Correct, large element of self-funding in policies	Substantial public capital and current expenditure
Policy has a large technical core	Policy development highly reliant on scientific discoveries	Some technical expertise, but policy debate open to outsiders
Level of complexity can be high	Often the case, e.g., alternative fuels debate	Some complexities, but fewer than in pollution policy
Boundaries of problem not confined to particular political system	Correct, federal and global debate	Policy benefits more local in character
Cuts across established policy sectors, difficult to establish leverage on traditional policy sectors	Does encounter difficulties in attempts to influence land use policy	Also encounters difficulties in terms of land use patterns

involve spending public money, and pose fewer technical complexities than air pollution policies. They are therefore particularly attractive to politicians seeking to demonstrate that they are 'doing something' about the environment, particularly when opening the line may involve the chance to ride on a special train and make speeches from the back platform in the style of Harry Truman. The structure of this book therefore treats decisions about the development of rail transit separately from those about attempts to reduce emissions from motor vehicles.

IS THAT A POLICY COMMUNITY I HEAR CALLING?

The ability to sketch map the policy community is part of the tool kit of the modern political scientist. As neo-Marxists have retreated into the more obscure aspects of discussion about the nature of post-Fordism, and as corporatists have admitted that they were wrong to challenge the pluralist orthodoxy without separating themselves from it, the field of what is sometimes called 'mainstream' political science has been left free for the neo-pluralist model of the policy community, although a possible alternative, the advocacy coalition framework, is discussed below.

The debate in recent years about the notion of a policy community has suggested that the mainstream of British political science is rather sluggish and shallow, with much disagreement about what may be properly termed as a policy community as distinct from a policy network. As Judge notes (1993, p. 121): 'As more researchers joined the empirical field, so adjectival proliferation came to characterise the discussion of the concept, so replicating the same process that had occurred in the previous decade over corporatism'. Dowding (1994a) goes further in his attack, criticizing the whole policy community approach as representative of an informal descriptive empiricism characteristic of British political science which failed to address deeper questions which could only be approached through a theory of power.

Rhodes and Marsh have responded to Dowding's attack, while not claiming to, 'rebut every inaccuracy in his critique, only the most wayward' (Rhodes and Marsh, 1994, p. 2). No attempt is made here to referee this dispute which led to a 'clash of the titans' at the 1994 conference of the UK Political Studies Association. Rather, attention is focused on the limited but defensible claims made by Rhodes and Marsh for what they term the 'policy networks' approach. (They use 'policy networks' as a generic term, with policy communities being a cohesive type of policy network displaying certain characteristics.) What the Rhodes–Marsh model helps to explain are the bargaining games which occur between government, interest groups and other agencies. In this book, the reader will encounter many empirical examples of such bargaining games, for example, over the 'smog check' issue. In their model, policy change is the result not only of endogenous but also of exogenous factors: thus, in California, it is necessary to consider not only the state-level bargaining game, but also the actions of the federal government. The Rhodes–Marsh model, 'treats networks as political structures which both constrain and facilitate policy actors and policy outcomes' (Rhodes and Marsh, 1994, p. 9). They are not claiming to be able to explain the distribution of power in society. 'The concept is a tool for analysing the policy process and intermediation and, like any tool, it only does the job for which it was designed' (Rhodes and Marsh, 1994, p. 10).

As a working definition, policy communities will be regarded as, 'characterized by a limited number of participants, frequent interaction, continuity, value consensus, resource dependence, positive sum games, and regulation of members' (Rhodes and Marsh, 1992, p. 23). In practice, value consensus may be limited to decision-making procedures or ultimate goals specified in a rather general way which can be interpreted differently according to the interests of particular participants in the policy community. Issue networks, in contrast, 'are characterized by a large number of participants with a limited degree of interdependence. Stability and continuity are at a premium, and the structure tends to be atomistic' (Rhodes and Marsh, 1992, p. 14).

The semantic debate will not be pursued here. Rather, the notion of policy community will be treated as a useful heuristic device which opens up interesting questions about power and democracy, although the normative issues the debate opens up have been relatively neglected. As Marsh reminds us (1992, p. 199):

> After all, we are concerned with the basic questions of power and interest. As such we need to ask three separate yet related questions. Who rules? How do they rule? In whose interest do they rule? The policy community/ policy network literature is locked into the first two questions and, given its origins in pluralist thought, can tend to imply the outcome of the policy process is broadly in the national interest. The policy network/policy community classifications may be useful, but not if they avoid the broader questions.

One issue that needs to be disposed of is whether the policy community model or its equivalent can be deployed in the United States. Many of the characteristic features of American politics may tend to produce relatively unstable issue networks rather than policy communities which intuitively seem to fit better with a European tradition of politics with such features as disciplined political parties and the centralization of government functions in departments rather than their dispersion across a number of special purpose agencies and fragmented functional jurisdictions. It might be argued that many of the distinctive attributes of the American system of government such as checks and balances, multiple points of access and a predilection for open government act against the formation of relatively exclusive policy oligopolies. In many areas of American politics, this is undoubtedly the case. However, particularly where exclusive property rights are involved, well-developed policy communities can form in the United States. The American literature on subgovernments conveys a notion of stable networks engaged in regular policy-making networks that is consistent with the idea of a policy community (Jordan, 1990, p. 331). The term has, however, been used differently in the US from Britain. In the United States: 'The core sense is that policy communities consist of a combination of policy professionals who shape policy agendas through professional consensus' (Jordan, Maloney and McLaughlin, 1992, p. 2).

There are two features of the policy community debate which are of particular value in highlighting features of the decision-making process which may have an influence on the kind of policy that is formed and the way in which it is implemented. First, there is the notion originally emphasized by Jordan and Richardson that policy communities represent a vertical segmentation of the decision-making process. The policy map is divided up into a series of compartments which contain their own set of actors addressing their own particular agendas. This is particularly significant in relation to environmental policies because of the way in which they cut across well-established policy sectors. Thus, 'policy actors responsible for the environment confront the political problem of how to gain ... leverage on other traditionally more powerful actors ... the problems of confronting the entrenched practices of sectors that impinge upon the environment can be considerable' (Weale, 1992, p. 9). In California, the land use policy community has been able to obtain a clause in the Clean Air Act which prohibits public actors in the air quality policy community from intruding into land use decisions.

The other important feature is the issue of inclusion and exclusion. 'Social closure is a process by which a group is formed on the basis of criteria that are employed by members of the group to exclude others who might want to join' (Cawson, Morgan, Webber, Holmes and Stevens, 1990, p. 28). Policy communities are not clubs from which potential members can be blackballed, but some of them are relatively exclusive, and use a variety of legal and procedural devices to confine the policy debate to an agenda which suits an established set of interests. Thus water policies in California benefited the engineering firms which built the dams and the unionized labour that helped to build them; the irrigation farmers who got cheap water; the real estate developers who were able to expand cities on the basis of assured supplies of water; and the politicians who got financial support from these interests to ensure their re-election (Reisner, 1986, p. 503). Until the 1970s, environmental costs were largely ignored. The air pollution policy community in California has developed more recently, and has a range of public consultation duties imposed on it by law, but this does not mean that issues of inclusion and exclusion do not arise.

Even bearing in mind that the policy community is a diagnostic device for understanding policy processes rather than a living entity, there is a problem about recognizing a policy community when it is encountered. Indeed, it may be that we are too ready to recognize them because they are such useful constructs for bringing order to a disparate research topic. One respondent commented in interview: 'I'll be interested to see how you map the policy community'. There is no intention to provide a functional equivalent of the useful map of political Sacramento that the *California Journal* provides for the 'political visitors' that fill the downtown hotels Monday to Friday when the legislature is in session. What the idea of the policy community does do is help an exploration of the way in which the policy debate is defined, structured and moved forward.

In order to structure the discussion of policy communities in subsequent chapters, it is intended to deploy three criteria developed for the identification of a policy community in the context of the ESRC government and industry relations programme (Grant, Paterson and Whitston, 1988, pp. 55–8):

1. *Differentiation.* The policy community should have identifiable boundaries, a sense of policy identity, and in some cases perhaps even a shared image or self-perception.
2. *Specialization.* The community should have specialized organizations and policy-making institutions of its own.

3. *Interaction between members of the community.* Any emphasis on interpersonal relations is contentious (Rhodes and Marsh, 1992, p. 17). Data on interaction patterns are often incomplete or unreliable. Without straying outside accepted orthodoxies, one can, nevertheless, make a distinction between, 'frequent, high-quality interaction of all groups on all matters related to the policy issue' (the policy community form) and contacts which, 'fluctuate in frequency and intensity' (the issue networks form) (Rhodes and Marsh, 1992, p. 251).

THE ADVOCACY COALITION FRAMEWORK

An alternative, although not necessarily mutually exclusive, analytical framework to that of the policy community model is provided by Sabatier's advocacy coalition approach (Sabatier, 1988, 1991, 1993a, 1993b; Sabatier and Jenkins-Smith, 1993). Sabatier's work is influenced by a social psychology tradition, and is concerned with such issues as the structure of belief systems. Whereas the policy community approach is essentially concerned with the institutionalization of interests, Sabatier's work emphasizes knowledge rather than interests. 'An advocacy coalition consists of actors from many public and private organizations at all levels of government who share a set of basic beliefs ... and who seek to manipulate the rules of various governmental institutions to achieve those goals over time' (Sabatier, 1991, pp. 151–3). Coalition composition and belief systems are relatively stable over time. When changes occur in the core aspects of a policy, they, 'are usually the result of peturbations in noncognitive factors external to the subsystem, such as macroeconomic conditions or the rise of a new systemic governing coalition' (Sabatier, 1993a, pp. 19–20). Long-term policy changes are seen as the result of the interaction of three sets of factors: the interaction of competing advocacy coalitions within a policy subsystem/community; changes external to the subsystem such as energy price changes; and the effects of state system parameters such as federalism (Sabatier, 1993b, p. 18).

This approach has a number of merits compared to the policy community approach. It emphasizes the role of analysis in policy adoption, seeking to end the division of policy studies into two distinct literatures, 'one that focuses on the interplay of self-interested policy actors pursuing rational strategies in pursuit of predetermined goals ... and another that elaborates the processes by which analysis and learning are integrated into policy making' (Sabatier, 1993b, p. 8). It advocates expanding, 'the list of subsystem actors beyond the traditional iron triangles to include the generators and disseminators of ideas' (Sabatier, 1993a, p. 35). This is particularly important in an area such as air pollution policy (which Sabatier has studied extensively), where judgements about what is technically feasible are an important element of the policy debate. The framework also emphasizes the need to distinguish between relatively stable policy parameters and those dynamic factors that serve as major stimuli to policy change. The policy community approach has been relatively useful in explaining policy inertia or incremental change, but less satisfactory in explaining how policies experience non-incremental changes.

In his discussion of Sabatier's work, Dowding reviews the four defining features of the advocacy coalition approach: the need for a time perspective of at least a decade to understand policy change; the need to concentrate on the policy network; the need to understand change through an intergovernmental framework; and the conceptualization of public policies as belief systems which Dowding sees as the distinctive feature of the Sabatier approach. Dowding acknowledges that the 'epistemic communities' literature emphasizes the importance of expert advice in foreign policy, but maintains that: 'The advocacy coalition literature has a more developed account of belief systems, which are thought to be composed of a set of core beliefs which will remain unchallenged ... and a set of policy beliefs about how best to protect one's core beliefs' (Dowding, 1994b, p. 10).

Although Sabatier thinks that the beliefs/interests distinction can be overstated, he agrees that the innovation offered in his work is to make, 'it much easier to introduce the role of ideas and technical innovation into the policy process in a coherent fashion' (personal communication, 3 November 1994). He also emphasizes the importance of the distinction between deep core and policy core versus secondary aspects (personal communication, 6 October 1994). Deep core beliefs, 'define a person's underlying philosophy'; near (policy) core beliefs concern the strategies for achieving the beliefs in a policy area; and secondary beliefs are made up of, 'a multitude of instrumental decisions and information searches necessary to implement the policy core in a specific policy area' (Sabatier, 1993a, p. 30). Change is easiest in relation to secondary aspects and most difficult in relation to core beliefs, where something akin to a religious conversion is required. Sabatier notes in relation to the air pollution problem in the United States that while some issues since 1970 have involved core disputes, 'most policy making has focused on secondary aspects' (Sabatier, 1993a, p. 32). A contemporary example discussed in this book is the smog check dispute in California.

In his work on air pollution policy, Sabatier has identified two major policy coalitions: the Clean Air Coalition of environmentalists and their allies which regards air pollution as a serious problem which requires regulatory action; and an Economic Feasibility Coalition dominated by industrial sources of air pollution and the energy companies, seeing the problem as less serious and advocating technologically feasible solutions and the use of economic incentives (Sabatier, 1993a, pp. 26–7). Sabatier considers whether there is a third Economic Efficiency Coalition, but decides that, 'most economists traditionally have mirrored the views of the Economic Feasibility Coalition' (Sabatier, 1993a, p. 38). These categorizations can be applied to the subsequent analysis, although particular interests may cut across them: for example, electricity utilities may support electric vehicle programmes.

One methodological problem which Sabatier acknowledges is that, 'belief systems are normally highly correlated with self-interest and the causation is reciprocal' (Sabatier, 1993a, p. 28). He prefers to use belief systems as a focus rather than interests because, 'beliefs are more inclusive and more verifiable than interests' (Sabatier, 1993a, p. 28). This assertion is at least open to question. It is also important to remember that relevant technical information may be given little attention by policy-makers if it is not backed by well-organized political interests. For example, 'methanol had no real congressional champions; consequently, there are few provisions specifically requiring its use. The lesson is clear: if a powerful economic and political interest can be harnessed to environmental goals, inclusion of the relevant provisions is virtually guaranteed' (Bryner, 1993, p. 140). Indeed, Dowding draws attention to the way in which ideas emerging from an advocacy coalition can be misused by other actors with different goals such as saving money (Dowding, 1994b, p. 11).

For someone who comes from an intellectual background which has emphasized the identification and analysis of interests, Sabatier's approach offers a refreshing challenge. One of its insights is to distinguish between the policy subsystem which includes all the actors active in a policy area (that is, the policy community) and specific coalitions which are those subsets of actors who share policy core beliefs. The advocacy coalition framework, 'chooses advocacy coalitions – that is, sets of actors from both public and private institutions at various levels of government who share critical aspects of a belief system – as the principal vehicle for aggregating individuals into a manageable number of units' (Sabatier, 1993a, p. 36).

There is a clear risk that an interests-based approach may neglect the importance of technical debates over issues, and the role of policy-oriented learning. However, as Jenkins-Smith and Sabatier note (1993, p. 45): 'Policy-oriented learning occurs in the context of a *political* process where people compete over the authoritative allocation of values and over the ability to use the instruments of government ... This process is not a disinterested search for "truth"'. One way of conceptualizing the different approaches on offer is to revert to Kingdon's (1984) notion of policy-making as three largely unrelated 'streams': a problem stream, consisting of information about past attempts to solve real world problems; a policy stream/community made up of various policy analysts; and a political stream made up of elections, legislative power struggles and so on. In Kingdon's approach, when these three streams come together, a window of opportunity occurs to develop an acceptable, technically feasible policy proposal that politicians can adopt and approve.

Dowding provides a good summary of the distinctive contribution of Sabatier's approach:

> The advocacy coalition framework has generated enormous interest because it reintroduces the concept of ideas and their origins in the study of policy change. By concentrating on beliefs as a generator of policy change they force attention away from seeing public policy simply as a battle between groups (Dowding, 1994b, p. 11).

IMPLEMENTATION ANALYSIS

Political scientists have regarded implementation analysis as a key element of assessing policy effectiveness for over 20 years. The interest in political science in implementation problems was largely stimulated by a study of policy application in California, in terms of the work of the Economic Development Administration in Oakland. In this study, implementation was defined, 'as a process of interaction between the setting of goals and actions geared to achieving them' (Pressman and Wildavsky, 1973, p. xv). They emphasized that: 'The separation of policy design from implementation is fatal. It is no better than mindless implementation without a sense of direction' (Pressman and Wildavsky, 1973, p. xvii). A number of stages in the implementation process can be identified, such as translating legislation into a set of regulations; securing adequate budgetary funds to carry out the specified tasks; appointing and training personnel; taking enforcement action; and monitoring the policy implementation process to ensure that both intermediate performance goals and the ultimate policy goal are achieved. It should be noted, however, that among those analysts who take a 'bottom up' approach, focusing on interactions among actors at the operational level rather than on a policy decision, 'the familiar stages of formulation, implementation and reformulation tended to disappear' (Sabatier, 1986, p. 22).

A substantial implementation literature has developed, although the proliferation of models has not assisted the achievement of parsimony: 'One cannot predict which variables are likely to be most important and under what circumstances' (Lester and Bowman, 1989, p. 732). Rose argues (1993, p. 91) that, 'the approach is a weakness insofar as it redirects a search away from innovation to familiar and easily implemented programs'. There is something in this criticism: there is the risk of trying to fix what went wrong with the last policy package, rather than trying to anticipate the rather different problems likely to be encountered in implementing the new policy package. It is important to be aware of the limits of what implementation analysis can offer. It does not provide a set of prescriptions about how a policy initiative should be designed and implemented. Rather, it can be treated as a means of identifying some of the likely obstacles that may arise in putting a policy into effect, and of learning from past achievements and errors.

It is necessary to shop rather selectively among the models available to pull out those that might be helpful in identifying the questions that need to be asked about implementation in this analysis. Sabatier and Mazmanian (1980) have developed an influential model of the implementation process which, in terms of its independent variables, focuses attention first on the need to analyse the tractability of the problem being addressed in terms of the availability of valid technical theory and technology; the diversity of target-group behaviour; and the extent of behavioural change required. Attention is then paid to the ability of the statute to structure implementation in terms, for example, of clear and consistent objectives, financial resources and the recruitment of implementing officials. Non-statutory variables affecting implementation include media support, public support, attitudes and resources of constituency groups, and the commitment and leadership skills of implementing officials. One finding to emerge from subsequent research is, 'the importance of selecting implementing institutions supportive of the new program' and the creation of, 'new agencies as a specific strategy' (Sabatier, 1986, p. 27). 'There is also some evidence that interest group support may be more critical in the US than in many European countries' (Sabatier, 1986, p. 28).

It is also useful to distinguish between broad implementation strategies, with one of the central discriminating questions being that of how much discretion is allowed to the implementing agency. Ingram and Schneider (1990) distinguish four broad approaches:

1. The strong statute approach where implementers are, 'supposed to reproduce faithfully statutory designs' (Ingram and Schneider, 1990, p. 74). Clarity of objectives may be desirable, but may be difficult to achieve and may inhibit adjustments in policy to take account of the reactions of target populations. Ingram and Schneider's discussion of this approach points out that it is based on an assumption that implementing agencies are impediments to policy achievement rather than potential sources of value added.

2. 'The Wilsonian approach is the same as the strong statute orientation in relation to goal specificity, but it grants wide discretion to administrative agencies on other matters, including organizational structure, specification of target populations, rules, tools and selection of causal theories' (Ingram and Schneider, 1990, p. 77). Considerable emphasis is placed on accountability in assessing successful implementation which is assumed to be a sufficient check on manipulation of the rules.

3. The grass roots approach is very much a 'bottom up' rather than a 'top down' perspective. 'Discretion over all the elements of policy logic, rather than being worked through in the statute, should be allocated to the lowest level implementor or to target populations themselves' (Ingram and Schneider, 1990, p. 79). This approach may facilitate the building of coalitions of support for a programme and the reconciliation of conflicting interests, but it may also lead to substantial diversity in policy outcomes.

4. The support-building approach places less emphasis on goal achievement and more on values and participation patterns and the

reconciliation of conflicting interests. 'The underlying assumption of the support building approach is that the political resolution of conflict overshadows substance in policy' (Ingram and Schneider, 1990, p. 81).

One point that should be emphasized is that the same implementation strategy may not be desirable across all aspects of air quality management policy. 'The superior ability of US air pollution authorities to regulate automotive emissions than to reduce vehicle miles travelled can be attributed to a greater understanding of, and control over, the factors involved' (Sabatier, 1986, p. 27). It is also important not to exaggerate the impact of policy design and implementation compared with other exogenous factors over which air quality policy-makers have no control. For example, air pollution figures in the Los Angeles basin at the end of the 1980s and beginning of the 1990s were favourably affected by meterological factors and by a reduction in work-related trips as a consequence of the recession. This particular example underlines the importance of taking a suitably long time period when examining the effectiveness of implementation efforts. 'Numerous studies have shown that ambitious programs that appeared after a few years to be abject failures received more favorable evaluations when seen in a longer time frame; conversely, initial successes may evaporate over time' (Sabatier, 1993a, p. 16).

The analysis in subsequent chapters will need to take into account a range of factors such as changing perceptions of the air quality problem; new technological responses to it; and the actors involved in the policy process and their particular perceptions and interests. It is important not to lose sight of the fact that decisions on air quality management issues are ultimately taken and implemented in a political context. This may lead to 'quick fix' solutions which are innovative in content, but pay insufficient attention to implementation design. As Wachs comments (1990, p. 249): 'The recent changes in policy have ... been evaluated hastily, primarily on the basis of their political feasibility, and nearly without regard to their likely technical consequences'.

A NOTE ON RESEARCH METHODS

The principal research method used was semi-structured interviews conducted with state civil servants, air quality management district

officials, legislative aides and lobbyists in California. Initial respondents were identified through the existing literature and the use of publications such as the *California Journal* roster. The interviews were also
used as a means of obtaining various types of documentary material
which were supplemented by materials obtained from the California
State Library in Sacramento. The writer also attended legislative committee meetings and floor meetings of the Assembly and Senate in
Sacramento, while two public interest organizations set up round-table
discussions for him.

Semi-structured interviews have been used by the author as a research technique for over 20 years, and are seen as a particularly
appropriate means of studying political phenomena at the decision-
making (as distinct from electoral) level, where respondents and their
comments do not have equal weight and their responses cannot sensi-
bly be quantified. The ground covered in the interviews depended on
the particular respondent: different questions were put to a technical
specialist on alternative fuels compared to a legislative aide. With all
respondents, however, an attempt was made to establish their estima-
tion of the nature and seriousness of the air quality problem in California; what they thought about the effectiveness of the measures being
taken to tackle it; and who they thought the key actors in the policy
process were and their opinion of their effectiveness. The interviews
were recorded and transcribed afterwards. Quotations throughout the
book are taken from the transcripts.

2. The air pollution problem

The problem of air pollution in California is perceived primarily in terms of its local impact on health and, to a lesser extent, visibility. 'All of the attainment is based on health standards, that's the driving force behind the Air Resources Board' (interview, California Air Resources Board, 30 March 1993). The contribution of emissions from cars to global warming is not seen as a principal concern. The idea that addressing concerns about global warming might be one of the main objectives of air pollution policy was responded to in interviews with reactions that varied from bafflement to an acknowledgement that the balance of policy concerns might be different in Europe from the United States. For example, one state employee argued in interview that there was a scepticism in the political system about climate change. California was not ready to advance the global climate issue. Asked about the issue of global climatic change, an Air Resources Board official responded: 'That's so interesting that you ask because there have been people from Japan, from Canada, who have asked us the same question, and there is not a whole lot that is based on the global climate change issue' (interview, California Air Resources Board, 30 March 1993). An Air Quality Management District official pointed out: 'We all realize that global warming is linked to transportation, but from a formal agency point of view, and in terms of the California Clean Air Act, global warming is not something we work on or deal with' (interview, Bay Area Air Quality Management District, 12 August 1994). Looking at the problem in a broad comparative context between the United States and Europe, an environmental lobbyist commented:

> Europe generally has been more aggressive on global warming ... Part of our political problem is the coal states. Under our constitution they have a disproportionate influence, small states with extractive industries ... we have for political reasons and economic reasons simply not been able to really revive the global warming issue in a meaningful fashion (interview, Sacramento, 9 September 1993).

Californians have good reason to be preoccupied about their own local air pollution problems. A combination of geographical features and very high levels of auto ownership and use gives them some of the worst air in the United States, especially in Los Angeles but also in other locations such as the Central Valley. The air of the South Coast remains the dirtiest in the nation. Ozone levels, although cut by half, are still more than two and a half times the level judged to be healthy. The South Coast is the only area in the nation with unhealthy levels of nitrogen dioxide. Unhealthy levels of carbon dioxide occur more often on the South Coast than anywhere in the United States. According to the Air Resources Board, three-quarters of the nation's health problem from excessive ozone is concentrated in the greater Los Angeles area alone.

Evidence of the health effects of smog comes from experiments on animals, controlled testing of humans in laboratory or field settings, the results of accidental human exposure and epidemiological research. Whether, of course, studies that have shown that ozone damages the lungs of animals can be applied to human beings is a matter of some disagreement. The California Air Resources Board considers, however, that its research has established that air pollution aggravates cardiovascular and respiratory illnesses; adds stress to the cardiovascular system, forcing the heart and lungs to work harder in order to provide oxygen; speeds up the natural ageing process of the lung; damages cells in the airways of the respiratory system; damages the lungs even after systems of minor irritation disappear; and contributes to the development of diseases including bronchitis and emphysema.

There is some preliminary evidence from Air Resources Board research that a degree of permanent lung damage may occur in adults aged 14 to 25 who are thought to have been life-long South Coast residents. A pilot study of the lungs of young accident and homicide victims found that nearly of all the lungs examined had some form of chronic bronchitis and 76 per cent showed some degree of inflammation. 'In addition, about one-third of the subjects had some degree of chronic interstitial pneumonia, a form of the disease found deep within lung tissue' (California Air Resources Board, 1991, p. 4). The working days lost to pollution in Southern California have been estimated at $10 billion a year (Kirlin, 1990, p. 164).

THE CONSTITUENTS OF AIR POLLUTION

The United States establishes acceptable levels of concentration in the outside air for six pollutants: ozone, carbon monoxide, particulate matter, nitrogen dioxide, sulphur dioxide and lead. 'The pollutants differ considerably in terms of their sources, levels, health impacts, and the control measures that have been developed to reduce their concentration in the air' (Bryner, 1993, p. 42). Each needs to be considered in turn in terms of its characteristics, health impact and methods of control.

Mention of ozone causes some confusion to the person who is not an expert on air pollution. Why is concern expressed about ozone holes in the upper atmosphere at the same time as it is seen as a problem at lower levels? 'At low levels, ozone is a noxious pollutant. In the stratosphere, however, ozone provides a protective layer that absorbs most of the ultraviolet rays from the sun, thereby shielding life on earth from their harmful effects' (Bryner, 1993, p. 52). Ozone is the chief component of urban smog and is California's most persistent and widespread air quality problem. A colourless, odourless gas, it is not emitted directly into the air from an identifiable source, but forms in the air when hydrocarbons (also known as reactive organic gases) and nitrogen oxides (from motor vehicles and industrial sources) react in sunlight.

The lungs are ozone's main target. It is a strong irritant that can cause constriction of the airways, forcing the respiratory system to work harder to provide oxygen. It makes breathing more difficult during work and exercise for healthy people, but may pose its worst threat to those who already suffer from respiratory diseases such as asthma, emphysema and chronic bronchitis. In the South Coast basin, it is estimated that about 10 per cent of the population, or 1.2 million people, suffer from such diseases. 'Ozone has been one of the most difficult pollutants to regulate ... Gains in the use of cleaner technologies and processes have been offset by growth in the number of sources' (Bryner, 1993, p. 53).

Carbon monoxide is an invisible, colourless, odourless gas that is the by-product of the incomplete combustion of organic material, primarily from motor vehicle exhausts. The highest concentrations are found in areas with congested or high volumes of traffic and during the winter months. Carbon monoxide emissions in a confined area, liked a closed garage, can kill. Outdoor carbon monoxide levels are relatively low, but people with heart ailments are still at risk from low-level exposure. There is increasing evidence of the health risk posed by carbon monoxide. 'Carbon monoxide reduces attention span, problem-solving ability, sensory ability, and visual acuity' (Bryner, 1993, p. 49).

Particulate matter is made up of mixtures of man-made and natural substances, coming from a variety of industrial and mobile sources, and may be emitted directly or formed in the air. Although all particles can pose a potential health problem, concern is focused on microscopic, invisible particles which are seen as the greatest health threat. These particles are less than ten microns in diameter, about one-fifth the size of a human hair, and are known as PM10. They are especially harmful because they can reach the deepest recesses of the lung without being captured by the natural cleansing action of the respiratory system. Short-term exposures can lead to coughing and minor throat irritation. Longer-term exposures can lead to increased bronchial disease and an increased risk of death from heart and lung disease. Moreover, the main ingredients of visible smog are airborne particles, combined with moisture. One respondent thought that PM10 was likely to acquire a greater significance in air pollution policy in the future:

> Our emphasis I think will shift, we'll become more focused on reducing PM10 emissions, much more so than we have in the past ... scientific studies [show] that PM10 is more of a health concern than [we have realized] in the past. I think probably at some point in the not too distant future we'll likely see the federal PM10 standard revisited ... It's certainly also going to be a much more difficult problem to deal with. We think that PM10 is going to be a much tougher longer-term problem for us, that's primarily because it's linked much more closely to vehicle miles travelled than emissions of carbon monoxide or volatile organic compounds (interview, Bay Area Air Quality Management District, 12 August 1994).

Nitrogen dioxide, a toxic reddish-brown gas, is a by-product of all combustion, with motor vehicles being the most important source on the South Coast. It is one of the pollutants known generically as nitrogen oxides, which are a major component of urban smog. Nitrogen dioxide is responsible for smog's reddish-brown haze. In the winter, when the photochemistry that forms ozone is at its lowest, nitrogen dioxide concentrations remain at high levels. At higher concentrations, nitrogen dioxide can damage crops such as beans and tomatoes. 'Relatively little is known about the long-term effects of nitrogen dioxide at current ambient air quality levels' (Bryner, 1993, p. 79).

Sulphur dioxide is an invisible gas with a strong smell produced primarily by the combustion of coal, fuel oil and diesel oil. It poses a particular health hazard for asthmatics, but is not a significant problem in California. Sulphur dioxide concentrations have been reduced to levels well below federal and state standards.

Lead concentrations have also met federal and state standards since 1983. Lead particles small enough to be inhaled into the lungs are readily absorbed into the blood and circulated throughout the body, with the brain being the main target. At relatively low levels, lead exposure can result in a permanent decrease in the IQ of children. 'The most dramatic change has been the reduction in lead emissions as a result of the phasing out of leaded gasoline' (Bryner, 1993, p. 46). Descriptions of the reliance of the British Government on a tax induced price differential to reduce leaded petrol consumption were greeted with some incredulity by Californian respondents.

THE GEOGRAPHY OF POLLUTION

The Los Angeles basin has a particularly severe air pollution problem because of its topography: a basin surrounded on the landward side by mountains, combined with prevailing onshore winds and long hours of sunlight producing the photochemical reactions that lead to smog formation. As hot air moves in towards the coast from the Pacific Ocean, the lowest layer in the mass is cooled by cold coastal currents. This cooler layer of air, which is denser than the warm air above, cannot rise. In 1542, Cabrillo observed that smoke from Indian camp fires rose only a few hundred feet and then spread out at the base of the mountains. Air pollution is thus often trapped close to the ground under an inversion layer of warm air, while the mountains slow the smog's outward escape. Some of the polluted air does escape, however, and has been detected as far away as the Grand Canyon. Ozone levels are typically lowest along the coast and increase during the day as sea breezes blow pollutants inland. In contrast: 'The North Coast has good air quality because of the climate (low temperatures, fewer days of sunshine and more of wind) but also benefits from the terrain (mountains don't capture and hold pollution) and the lack of development' (Hall, 1993, pp. 38–9). In the Bay Area, natural ventilation normally disperses most of the pollution, although relatively unusual hot conditions produce ozone alerts, as happened in August 1994.

The greatest number of smoggy days in the United States outside of Los Angeles foul the southern two-thirds of the Central Valley, while in the northern part of the Valley, the state capital of Sacramento has ranked for years among the ten most persistently smoggy cities in the United States. The Central Valley has been compared to a banana split dish filled with thin brown soup when viewed from the crests of neighbouring mountains. Ocean breezes blow in from the coast through the Carquinez Strait (the eastern terminus of the northeastern arm of San Francisco Bay) pushing smog up against the foothills and to the north and south. High pressure holds the air down creating an inversion layer which forms a lid on the Valley's air, particularly between May and September. Pollution is caught between the Sierra Nevada and the coastal mountain ranges, while the Valley is sealed at its south end by the Tehachapis. These geographical features create a 450 mile long trough where the wind often blows in circles, swirling pollutants around rather than blowing them away and providing a natural smog incubator. Driving down through the foothills on the interstate on a hot summer's day, one glimpses the high rise buildings of Sacramento peeping through a murky haze in the distance.

One might think that Californians have the option of getting above the smog in the mountains at weekends. The mountains, however, have their own air pollution problems. Health damage caused by carbon monoxide is a bigger problem at high altitudes where the air is less dense, making the consequences of a reduced oxygen supply worse. Hence there is a special carbon monoxide standard for the Lake Tahoe basin at 6 000 feet. The combination of heavy car traffic and the extensive use of wood-burning stoves is creating air pollution problems in the mountains in the winter. Thermal inversions in the winter months seal in pollutants and, if the weather stays calm, concentrations can build to very high levels. In the Northern Sierra Air Quality Management District: 'On calm winter days, Truckee suffocates beneath a noxious blue-gray haze of woodsmoke, road dust and automobile fumes' (*Sacramento Bee*, 13 December 1993). Between November 1992 and March 1993, Truckee exceeded the California standard for particulates on 55 days and Mammoth Lakes on 63 days. Both towns are major ski resorts. Concentrations of fine particulates in the winter can be higher than in Los Angeles or Sacramento, so escaping to the mountains in the hope of finding clean air is not necessarily an option for Californians.

THE EXTENT OF THE PROBLEM

Air quality has improved substantially in the Los Angeles basin. The highest hourly ozone concentrations are three times greater than the state's health standard (0.099 parts per million/hour) but only half of the levels measured in the late 1960s, when levels of 0.50 ppm and higher were recorded. Emissions of smog-forming hydrocarbons and nitrogen oxides were cut by 27 per cent and carbon monoxide by 40 per cent during the 1980s. By the year 2000, these emissions are expected to be half of current levels.

The pollutant standards index (psi) was developed by the federal Environmental Protection Agency (EPA) as a simplified method of forecasting, reporting and comparing air quality conditions. For example, the federal ozone standard of 0.12 ppm for one hour (less stringent than the state standard) converts into a psi reading of 100. The California clean air standard is 75 psi, and the federal standard 100 psi. At 130 psi, sensitive people are advised to avoid all outdoor activity, and others are advised to avoid prolonged vigorous outdoor activities. At 200 psi – a Stage I smog episode – sensitive people are advised to go indoors, and others to avoid vigorous outdoor activities. At 275 psi – a Stage II smog episode – all vigorous physical activity should stop. At 400 psi – a Stage III smog episode, last called in 1974 – everyone is advised to stay inside.

The Los Angeles basin enjoyed in 1990–93 the cleanest consecutive years in a 40 year history of air quality monitoring, although that still left the air the dirtiest in the nation. In 1991 the South Coast exceeded the state standard on 183 days, and there were Stage I smog alerts on 47 days. This figure was reduced to 41 days in 1992 and to 24 in 1993, but this improvement was in part the consequence of special climatic factors. An unusually strong three year El Nino pattern (a warm Pacific Ocean current that affects climate patterns) produced more turbulent weather and less stagnant air in Los Angeles than usual. In 1994 there were only two Stage I alerts in Riverside County, one of the smoggiest areas.

There has been a steady downward trend in ozone levels for over 20 years. The South Coast has managed a reduction in peak ozone levels of nearly 75 per cent since the worst days of the mid-1950s. The number of Stage I smog episodes have been cut by more than half since the 1970s, and there have been no Stage II smog episodes, common more than a decade ago, in the late 1980s and early 1990s. Even so, the

Table 2.1   Number of days per year with unhealthy air

(ozone concentration of greater than 0.9 parts per hundred million or
more for at least 1 hour per day)

Basin	1980	1988	1992
South Coast	210	216	191
San Joaquin Valley	124	154	124
Sacramento Valley	73	98	74
San Francisco Bay	47	41	23
Mountain counties	n/a	39	54

Source: California Air Resources Board data.

*Table 2.2   Number of days state ozone standard exceeded at selected
air quality monitoring stations in the South Coast basin,
1992*

Station	Number of days standard exceeded
Long Beach	19
Los Angeles	57
Pasadena	128
Crestline	160
Glendora	164

Source: South Coast Air Quality Management District data.

air was still unhealthy for over half the year in 1992, and ozone levels
are not expected to fall within air quality standards until at least the
year 2010. Moreover, as air quality in the Los Angeles basin has improved, these gains have not been matched elsewhere in the state (Table 2.1). There are also considerable variations in air quality within the
Los Angeles area, reflecting the way in which pollution is blown inland
against the mountains (Table 2.2).

A number of factors have helped the reduction of air pollution in the
South Coast basin. The early emphasis was on controlling dust and
fumes emitted by manufacturing industry which operated on a much
more substantial scale in the Los Angeles area in the earlier post-war

period than is the case in the 1990s It also stopped the use of home incinerators and burning on public dumps. 'These moves reduced dustfall, which in some areas had been as much as 100 tons per square mile per month, by two-thirds, bringing it back to about the level that existed in 1940 before smog became a serious problem in the community' (Haagen-Smit, 1964, pp. 27–8). The tightening of auto emission controls, such as the adoption of catalytic converters, which convert hazardous exhaust gases into ones which cause less harm, made a substantial contribution to reducing auto-related emissions: 'A 96-per cent reduction of the carbon monoxide and hydrocarbons and a 76-per cent reduction of the nitrogen oxides given off by car engines' (Nadis and MacKenzie, 1993, p. 56). The recent substantial decline of defence employment may have affected commuting patterns in a way that tends to reduce automobile emissions, given that defence workers have tended to commute longer distances than other workers (Law, Wolch and Takahashi, 1993).

THE EARLY DEVELOPMENT OF AIR POLLUTION CONTROL IN LOS ANGELES

The early development of air pollution control in Los Angeles was based on a combination of public concern about the deterioration of air quality and the availability of new scientific evidence about the sources of air pollution. What distinguished this early period of air pollution control from current efforts was a facile optimism about how easily the problem could be resolved. It was felt that once the problem had been identified, and a 'supremo' appointed to implement solutions, blue skies would be restored to Los Angeles. In this early period, the emphasis was on the control of stationary sources of pollution, in part because they were a more significant part of the problem then, in part because the automobile industry at first tried to deny that vehicle emissions were a significant problem.

With the outbreak of the Second World War, industrialization increased rapidly in Los Angeles. One of the new plants was a butadiene plant involved in the production of synthetic rubber essential to the war effort. In the summer of 1943 Los Angeles experienced a series of severe smog attacks which caused eye and throat irritation, and in which the butadiene plant was soon identified as the main culprit. On 27 July 1943, the *Los Angeles Times* reported:

> With the entire downtown area engulfed by a low-hanging cloud of acrid smoke yesterday morning, city health authorities and police officials began investigations to determine the source of the latest 'gas attack' that left thousands of Angelenos with irritated eyes, noses and throats. Yesterday's annoyance was at least the fourth such 'attack' of recent date, and by far the worst. Visibility was cut to three blocks in some sections of the business district. Office workers found the noxious fumes almost unbearable.

The extent of concern in Los Angeles was such that, despite the importance of the plant to the war effort, the City Council instructed the City Attorney to take whatever legal steps were necessary to close the plant until such time as proper pollution abatement devices were installed. The plant did close down for a while in October. After the federal rubber director had flown from Washington and stressed the importance of the plant to the war effort, while promising abatement measures, the City Council withdrew its injunction and production resumed. However, during the plant closure, it had been observed that smog had persisted, indicating that the butadiene plant was far from being the sole source of the problem.

In November 1944 Los Angeles City created a Bureau of Air Pollution Control. This body had inadequate resources to tackle the problem which was getting worse. 'By 1947 there were recorded in downtown Los Angeles 57 days in which visibility fell below one mile; in 1941 there had only been seven' (Briennes, 1975, pp. 102–3). The *Los Angeles Times*, working under the influence of the proprietor's wife, 'Buff' Chandler, played a major role in mobilizing public concern about the air pollution problem. Real estate and tourism interests were concerned about the economic consequences of persistent air pollution. The railroads and the oil industry had a different agenda, but sufficient concessions were made to them to persuade them to drop their opposition to Assembly Bill 1 sponsored by Los Angeles County which led to the creation of the Los Angeles Air Pollution Control District in 1947. By 1954 the District had 117 employees and a budget of $700,000.

The early emphasis was very much on stationary sources, with relatively little attention given to automobile emissions. This encouraged a belief that the problem could be resolved relatively quickly by tackling the problems caused by clearly identifiable plants. When the first chief of the Air Pollution Control District, Dr Louis C. McCabe, arrived in Los Angeles, the *Times* wrote up his visit in their most vivid prose, referring to smokestacks that 'poured forth', incinerators that 'fumed', foundries that 'erupted' and steel plants that 'belched'. The report was accompanied by a dramatic photograph of McCabe looking at a paving plant pouring out a dark cloud of smoke, labelled 'what makes his job tough'. The whole tone was similar to that of homicide reports of the same period, with references to McCabe 'invading' pollution's 'stronghold'.

The Los Angeles smog problem was much more complicated than the smoke control problem in St Louis, a city whose progress in attaining cleaner air had been boosted by the *Times*. When blue skies did not appear again over Los Angeles, emphasis on the role of the automobile increased, a development enhanced by new scientific research on the formation of photochemical smog. In 1950, Arie Haagen-Smit of the California Institute of Technology, 'proposed a theoretical mechanism for smog formation in which automobile exhaust and sunlight play central roles. His findings were hotly contested by the oil and auto industries' (Nadis and MacKenzie, 1993, p. 21).

Faced with increased evidence of the contribution of automobiles to smog formation, the Automobile Manufacturers' Association created a Vehicle Combustion Products Subcommittee whose members were sent to Los Angeles to see the problem for themselves. 'Seven of the nation's top automotive engineers arrived on the Santa Fe Super Chief yesterday to begin an intensive two week study of the contribution of automobile exhaust fumes to LA smog' (*Los Angeles Times*, 26 January 1954). They were still trying to claim that the real problem was garbage incineration not automobiles and, at the welcoming dinner, the leader of the auto industry delegation set fire to some crumpled papers in a fruit can, claiming, 'that's where your smog is coming from'. This stunt seems to have been a measure of the auto delegation's desperation, and the visit does seem to have convinced them that the auto industry had a new problem it had to face (Briennes, 1975, p. 201). A reluctance to change its ways continued to characterize the reaction of the industry in the 1980s and 1990s

What was happening was the formation of 'advocacy coalitions' as outlined by Sabatier. Scientifically based ideas began to play a much more important role in the decision-making process. 'A new emphasis on scientific research and highly trained investigators began altering the status of smog workers; they became respected professionals, distinct from dog catchers, garbage collectors, and the old style smoke inspectors' (Briennes, 1975, p. 205). The staff of the Air Pollution Control District continued to expand, reaching 467 by 1957 (Briennes, 1975, p. 250).

The public was, however, disappointed with the lack of any percep-
tible improvement in air quality, leading to a rather bizarre experiment
in 'command and control' regulation. Captain Louis J. Fuller, who had
been in charge of the motor cycle division of the Los Angeles Police
Department, was brought in as the 'smog sheriff'. His adherence to
police department thinking was apparent when he declared: 'In order to
have clean air somebody's going to get hurt and somebody's going to
have to pay for it' (Briennes, 1975, p. 252). Specially marked patrol
cars cruised the streets, targeting diesel trucks which were unpopular
with motorists anyway. In public relations terms, the campaign was a
great success because it dealt with very visible pollution sources, but
its impact on the underlying problem was negligible. Rather more
significant was the banning in 1957 of the practice of burning rubbish
in backyard incinerators.

The state government became increasingly involved in air pollution,
first through a Motor Vehicle Pollution Control Board established in
1960, and then through an Air Resources Board with broader powers
established in 1967. The Lewis Air Quality Management Act in 1976
brought together Los Angeles, Orange and Riverside Counties and the
non-desert portion of San Bernadino Counties in the South Coast Air
Quality Management District, creating an air quality management
authority for the whole Los Angeles basin. Breaking the control of LA
county supervisors was a major purpose of the bill. According to the
bill's author: 'The main thing the bill will do is free us from what I
consider the rather archaic attitude of Los Angeles county toward air
pollution control' (*Los Angeles Times*, 3 July 1976). As is so often the
case with institutional reforms, progress was disappointing. 'For a host
of reasons, plans proposed in 1979 and 1982 were never implemented
to the intended extent. Some blame a lax air-district board' (Waldman,
1990, p. 79). James Lents, the chief executive appointed in 1986, re-
called:

> The unstated position of the agency between 1977 (its first year of exist-
> ence) and 1986 was 'we will try to improve the air quality, but Los Angeles
> is never going to have clean air.' In 1987, however, we decided that would
> no longer be the case, that it is our mandate to have air in this basin that is
> healthy to breathe (quoted in Waldman, 1991, p. 92).

Since the late 1980s, a reinvigorated Air Quality Management District
has adopted a new air quality management plan that sets targets for the
attainment of federal and state health standards, although only after

2010 in the case of state standards for ozone and total suspended particulates. The plans to attain these targets are discussed in later chapters.

THE CURRENT PROBLEM

Mobile sources (principally cars and trucks, but also planes, trains, ships and construction equipment) account for 64 per cent of smog precursors in the South Coast air basin, a figure that rises to over 70 per cent in the Central Valley. Modern cars are far less polluting than those of 25 years ago, and much of the pollution from cars comes from so-called 'gross emitters' which has led to a number of policy proposals to tackle this problem (see Chapter 5).

Exhaust emissions, the consequence of the incomplete combustion of petrol or other fuels, result both from starting the engine (cold start) and driving the vehicle (running exhaust). Emissions control equipment works better when the engine and equipment are warm, so that 'cold starts generally cause about five times more emissions of reactive organic gases than hot starts' (Sacramento Air Quality Management District, 1991, p. V-2.3). For an average seven mile trip from a cold start, 60 per cent of all hydrocarbon emissions occur in less than one mile of driving, with a further 17 per cent occurring during the hot soak cycles at the end of the trip. 'These figures show that it is more important to reduce the total number of trips than to reduce the length of trips' (Sacramento Air Quality Management District, 1991, p. V-2.4). This has clear implications for land use policy, for example in terms of the need to reduce trips to shopping malls by making more local facilities available which could be safely reduced on foot or by bicycle. A rapid transit policy which leads commuters to use generous car parking facilities at transit stations may have less impact on air pollution than desired because it generates a large number of relatively short, highly polluting trips.

Congestion can also increase pollution. For example, slowing a ten mile trip from 55 miles an hour to 25 miles an hour adds four grams of hydrocarbon emissions, an amount that becomes significant when multiplied by a large number of slow-moving vehicles on a multi-lane freeway, although congestion is not as significant a factor as trip length. Reducing congestion may, of course, lead to a short-term reduction in air pollution which is then offset by other motorists deciding to use the vacated space on the highway.

Technological advances such as pre-heating catalytic converters may reduce the impact of cold start emissions. However, any technological progress in controlling automobile emissions is always in danger of being outpaced by the growth in population and of the number of car miles travelled:

> In the South Coast, for example, population is projected to grow 30 percent between 1987 and 2010, but the number of vehicles driven will increase by twice that, or by more than 60 percent. This means that pollution per mile driven has to drop by 60 percent *just to stay even* with the 1987 pollution level ... From 1987 to 2010, the average resident of the South Coast is expected to increase the number of miles traveled in a private vehicle each day by 25 percent (Hall, 1993, p. 40).

An even larger increase in population, of the order of 50 per cent, is anticipated for Sacramento by 2010. The number of vehicles in use is expected to match the growth in population, as will daily vehicle trips, but because the metropolitan area will be much more spread out, daily vehicle miles travelled are anticipated to increase by three-quarters (see Table 2.3).

Table 2.3   The consequences of urban growth in Sacramento

	1987	2010	Increase (%)
Population	947,000	1,415,000	49
On-road vehicles in use	751,497	1,104,738	47
Daily vehicle trips	3,392,808	4,979,849	47
Daily vehicle miles travelled	21,116,000	37,140,000	76

Source: Sacramento 1991 Air Quality Attainment Plan.

The general increase in vehicle use in part reflects changes in the structure of the labour force. 'The intensification of vehicle ownership and usage can be traced in part to the sharp increase in households having more than one person working outside the home, as more women entered the job market' (Downs, 1992, p. 11). In a two person household, two cars may be used to travel in different directions to workplaces. An older child may use a third car to travel to school or college, while if there are younger children, travelling to and from the child care facility may add considerably to the total miles travelled. It should be emphasized, however, that: 'In the Los Angeles area, an estimated 57 per cent of all peak hour trips and 70 per cent of all daily trips are *not* work-related' (Nivola and Crandall, 1993, p. 19).

The 'Gross Emitter' Problem

The available evidence suggests that a high proportion of total emissions from cars and trucks comes from old and/or poorly maintained vehicles. 'The older car is not necessarily a gross emitter, but because it's prior to 1982 it's not going to have a sophisticated control technology' (interview, Bay Area Air Quality Management District, 12 August 1994). Whether they are older vehicles, or newer vehicles which have not been properly maintained: 'Something like ten per cent of the worst emitting vehicles contribute more than half of the total source emission inventory' (interview, South Coast Air Quality Management District, 1 April 1993). Twenty per cent of the vehicles on the road emit 80 per cent of the smog-forming hydrocarbons (*Sacramento Bee*, 17 November 1993). There are clear policy implications which can be drawn from the large proportion of air pollution resulting from 'gross emitters'. For example, 'the emission reductions that would occur by scrapping old cars are much more cost-effective than the stationary polluters installing more pollution control equipment' (interview, South Coast Air Quality Management District, 1 April 1993). In Chapter 4, there is a discussion of a complex and controversial dispute between the federal and state authorities over the efficacy of California's 'smog check' programme under which the exhaust systems of vehicles are inspected and, if necessary, repaired every two years.

Interview respondents stressed that even relatively new cars could be gross emitters if there was an equipment failure or they were not properly maintained. However, older cars, 'tend to pollute from five to twenty times higher than newer vehicles that are properly functioning' (interview, South Coast Air Quality Management District, 1 April 1993). As Table 2.4 shows, the older the vehicle, the higher the level of pollutants that tends to be spewed out, although this is somewhat offset by lower annual mileage for the older vehicles. This problem is exacerbated by the fact that the average age of cars in California is higher than elsewhere in the United States:

Table 2.4   Exhaust emission rates for vehicles by age in 1991

Model–Year Group	Emission rates (grams per mile)		
	Hydrocarbons	CO	NO$_x$
Pre-1975	8.16	66.42	3.13
1975–1979	2.84	31.91	2.80
1980 and later	0.89	10.90	1.04
Fleet average	1.58	16.90	1.38

Source: California Inspection and Maintenance Review Committee, Fourth Report to the Legislature, original data from Air Resources Board.

> We're not like the East Coast where we have heavy snows and don't salt the roads and vehicles tend to last a long time here on the west coast. Thus, we have a car culture ... people treat these machines with great love and care, far beyond what they deserve in a lot of cases and so they last a long time (interview, Senate aide, Sacramento, 26 March 1993).

Classic cars aside, older cars tend to be driven by the poorer members of the population so, 'people who drive those cars do not have a lot of economic means and therefore the repairs are probably done less frequently' (interview, Senate aide, Sacramento, 26 March 1993). The gross emitter question thus raises distributional issues which complicate the development of policy solutions to this problem. The alternative policy solutions, and the political and other problems associated with them, will be analysed in Chapter 5.

Land Use Patterns and Automobile Use

At an early stage of its history, Los Angeles and other parts of California developed dispersed land use patterns which encouraged reliance on the automobile. Levels of automobile ownership in relation to the population grew rapidly even in the inter-war period. Reliance on the automobile for work and leisure activities has reinforced by more recent developments such as the emergence of 'edge cities' which generate complex solo commuting. For example, in a study of Pleasanton, a suburban office centre near the junction of two freeways 35 miles east of downtown San Francisco, Cervero found, 'that the drive-alone automobile was, by far, the most prevalent means of commuting among Pleasanton workers' (Cervero, 1989, p. 157).

The development of Los Angeles as a dispersed community predates the extensive availability of the automobile. Halberstam emphasizes the role of the Chandler family, publishers of the *Los Angeles Times*: 'The city is horizontal rather than vertical because they were rich in land, and horizontal span was good for them, good for real estate' (Halberstam, 1979, p. 95). Real estate interests continue to be a significant factor in the metropolitan pattern of development. Davis claims (1990, p. 132) that, 'land development is still Southern California's most lucrative large industry'. Problems of land scarcity, and political resistance to growth, 'has resulted in the creation of a vast lobbying and campaign finance network' (Davis, 1990, p. 133).

Streetcars and inter-urban railways had a significant impact on the pattern of development. 'Los Angeles ... grew at a time when the railways could spread its residents across the countryside, resulting in much lower urban densities' (Bottles, 1987, p. 32). The development of the freeways simply reinforced an existing dependence on the automobile. It is interesting to compare how two books published on Los Angeles in 1967 and 1991 treat the role of the freeways in the city. Both give the freeways a lot of space: they are central and recurrent themes of the books. The tone in *Los Angeles: The Ultimate City* is one of celebration: a picture of the freeways is on the cover. 'Los Angeles is an autopia ... the freedom lies in driving oneself ... the power to whizz off in the direction of one's choice' (Rand, 1967, p. 52). Smog is admitted to be a problem, but the reaction is ambivalent: 'Smog is LA's great curse and the great expression of its auto culture' (Rand, 1967, p. 64). Readers are assured, however, that Los Angeles is coping with these problems by leading what is termed, 'the technological assault on the environment' so that we can still celebrate Los Angeles, 'as the climax of modern urban mechanization' (Rand, 1967, p. 67).

Just as Rand offers a celebration of modernity, Rieff's account of *Los Angeles: Capital of the Third World* is postmodernist in tone. The freeways are now part of the problem, not part of the solution. City residents have to debate whether to go 'surface' to avoid congestion on the freeways, something with which they have had to become familiar since some of the busiest freeways were destroyed in the 1994 earthquake. Yet driving remains central to living in Los Angeles:

Driving, after all, was one of the main points of living in Los Angeles, not only because it was spread out, and had, in fact, been designed for the automobile, but also because the freeway system was just what John Gregory Dunne had called it: 'More an idea than a roadway' (Rieff, 1991, p. 34).

The Deterioration of Transit Systems

As the population became more dispersed, and a smaller proportion of the population worked downtown, transit systems deteriorated. The Pacific Electric Railway was an inter-urban transport system that once covered the entire Los Angeles basin, operating over one thousand miles of track by the 1920s. Passenger service was almost entirely discontinued in 1950 with the last 'big red car' running on the Long Beach line in 1961. According to some accounts this decline was accelerated by a conspiracy by motor industry interests. National City Lines was owned by General Motors (GM) along with oil companies, tyre companies and other auto interests. 'In 1949, a federal jury convicted GM and the other companies of conspiring to replace electric transportation systems with buses and to monopolize the sale of buses' (Nadis and MacKenzie, 1993, p. 5).

Taking a dissenting view, Bottles (1987) argues that the real problem was that the service provided by the inter-urban lines was inadequate and inefficient so that customers turned in increasing numbers to the automobile. One of the ironies of the situation is that large sums of public money are now being spent on re-creating various forms of rail-based transit in Los Angeles, although it has to be admitted that even a comprehensive rail-based transit system would find it very difficult to accommodate more than a small proportion of the complex journeys undertaken in the Los Angeles basin.

There is an extensive bus system in Los Angeles and other major Californian cities, and it might seem to offer a more cost-effective way of expanding public transport than building more rail lines. The buses do, however, have a serious image problem which is in part related to their use by poorer members of the community from ethnic minority groups. Rieff notes (1991, p. 119):

> During the time I spent in LA, I met no one on the Westside who had been on an RTD bus more than once or twice in their lives ... The RTD buses are slow, their air-conditioning often breaks down, and even if they take you in the general vicinity of where you are going, that proximity is relative. More often that, you still have to walk another mile or two to get to the actual

street address. And there can be few experiences more disconcerting than walking along a wide LA street without the reassuring jangle of car keys in your pocket.

The research interviews yielded evidence of concern about the quality of the bus system, and the problems faced by individuals without a car in Southern California:

> In downtown Los Angeles we don't have enough transit to serve employers, it's not uncommon for you to have to stand on a bus, or to have one or two buses pass you by because they're too full. On the other hand, when you come out to the Diamond Bar area, you're looking at forty minute to one hour headways and that means when you go out and stand on the street corner, you wonder if the bus just left or if it's just around the corner ... One of the stigmas that we have here in Southern California is that the public bus is kind of thought to be second rate transportation for only the poor folks ... a couple of years ago RTD had a series of incidents where bus drivers went beserk and ran off the highway, people would come in and shoot up users, two buses would collide at forty miles an hour and kill half the people on it. It just seemed that there was a whole problem with that and it really scared people away from public transit. I think we're finally getting beyond that now with the advent of metro link and the foothill transit and light rail. It's getting a better public perception (interview, Diamond Bar, 1 April 1993).

Bottles concludes (1987, p. 254) that: 'No matter how much social critics and urban planners push for rapid-rail systems, it is unlikely that urban residents will give up the freedom and convenience afforded by the automobile'. No one, of course, expects Americans to give up the automobile, but rather to use it in more socially acceptable ways. One way in which behaviour could be affected would be to raise the cost of using a car in terms of gasoline prices and parking charges. The cost of driving in real terms in the United States is decreasing. 'The price of gasoline today in real terms is at a 50-year low. In 1940, in today's dollars, a gallon of gasoline cost $1.57 ... In June [1993] the price at the pump was $1.18 ... Gasoline in the United States is the biggest bargain in the world' (*Sacramento Bee*, 2 October 1993). The available evidence suggests that drivers are particularly likely to cut leisure trips in response to a fuel price increase, although car pooling for commuting has also increased at times when prices have risen rapidly (Nivola and Crandall, 1993, p. 11). Free parking spaces are encouraged by the tax regime. 'Employers provide parking privileges to workers partly because the Internal Revenue

Service does not tax this fringe benefit' (Nivola and Crandall, 1993, p. 44).

The various policy options available to reduce both the level of car use, and the air polluting effects of a given level of use, will be reviewed in later chapters. However, according to Kunstler, the real problem may have been incorrectly defined. The focus on air pollution is distracting attention from the real underlying problem:

> In LA the very pattern of the city is the underlying problem, and the city is stuck with it. It is stuck with sprawling low-density single-family house monoculture communities, with its long commutes and the addiction to gas ... So, unable to deal with the city's inherent structural problems, Angelenos are addressing the enduring problem of their famous *smog*. This effort is not going to save their fantasy city, but it will be an instructive exercise in making some of the sacrifices that the future will certainly require of all industrial peoples (Kunstler, 1993, p. 213).

Nobody believes in Disney's 'Autopia' any more, but they are uncertain about how to move towards an alternative vision. The political dice are stacked against fundamental change:

> A society which averages almost two registered passenger vehicles for every household may generate broader opposition to higher fuel costs than a society with only two-thirds as many vehicles per household (the West European average). And the comparatively low voter turnout [in the United States] probably magnifies the political consequences. Voter participation rises with family income, as does the number of cars (Nivola and Crandall, 1993, p. 23).

Ways of Evading Change

Faced with difficult choices, government agencies tend to back down. In response to a court order obtained by environmental groups the EPA was required to develop federal implementation plans for the South Coast, Ventura and Sacramento air quality management districts to bring them into line with national standards. (For a further discussion, see Chapter 4.) The EPA offered Sacramento a six year extension from 1999 to 2005 (justified by reclassifying Sacramento as a 'severe' rather than 'serious' air pollution region) in exchange for supposedly tougher controls on commuting and business expansion. The EPA argued that they could see no way that the Sacramento region could meet the 1999 deadline without imposing a radical and unprecedented restriction –

prohibiting motorists from driving for one day a week. A spokesman for the Sierra Club Legal Defense Fund complained: 'Six more years of dirty air. It's another way for the EPA to relieve itself of the politically difficult choice of imposing meaningful restrictions' (*Sacramento Bee*, 14 January 1994).

There are real political and technological problems in achieving even federal, let alone more stringent state, clean air targets. The cost of attainment in the three federal implementation plan areas is estimated at between $4 and $6 billion dollars over a 16 year period (EPA, 1994, p. 2). On the South Coast in particular, there are doubts about whether the targets can be achieved given current technology. The EPA notes (1994, p. 13):

> The overwhelming reductions needed for ozone attainment in the South Coast appear to require that each individual pollution source within the FIP area eventually abate its emissions almost completely. For practically every controllable source category, this ultimate degree of control is beyond a level now forseeable with existing technology and control techniques.

Although there are no easy routes to cleaner air, there is a temptation to resort too readily to a symbolic politics which promises change some day without hurting anyone with political clout in the present. One form of such politics is to set target attainment dates that are so far in the future that none of the present decision-makers will be around to be held accountable when they are not reached. For example, in 1971 the Los Angeles County Air Pollution District promised air quality up to Californian state standards by 1990 (Environmental Quality Laboratory, 1972, p. 19). Now the successor organization is promising clean air sometime after 2010. Progress may be promised on the basis of technologies which do not exist, or which have not been fully tested in everyday driving conditions, or which are too expensive to be commercially feasible. Building expensive subway systems provides visible evidence of a policy outcome which gives local politicians good publicity while the tab is picked up largely by the federal government. Technological innovations may provide short-term gains, but really air pollution is about how people work and live, and how far they are prepared to change their lifestyles in the interests of cleaner air.

3. The policy community

The state of California often behaves as if it was an independent nation. State propaganda claims that California is the sixth largest economy in the world. The state is separated from the rest of the United States (apart from the other Pacific states) by large tracts of mountain and desert. Newspaper stories in California often refer to 'the United States' as if it was a foreign country. California has its own representative offices in London, Frankfurt and Tokyo. The trappings of state authority are apparent in fly pasts by the state's air units at major funerals, or in references to the Governor's wife as 'the first lady'. While the California constitution acknowledges the supremacy of the United States constitution, Article 1, Section 24 (adopted in 1974) states that: 'Rights guaranteed by this Constitution are not dependent on those guaranteed by the United States Constitution'. This, 'declaration undoubtedly served to galvanize the development of a body of California law independent of the federal Constitution' (Grodin, Massey and Cunningham, 1993, p. 22). This reflects a trend which has led California and other states to experience, 'a renascence of the independent state constitution' (Grodin, Massey and Cunningham, 1993, p. 21). This trend is reinforced in the case of California by a number of distinctive features of its political process which are a reflection of the progressive reforms carried out in the first three decades of the century: weak political parties; an extensive system of direct democracy; and a merit-based civil service. In 1990, the voters of California placed limits on the terms that could be served by their legislators, a development with important implications for the conduct of state politics.

One should not, of course, push the notion of distinctiveness too far. California is part of a federal system of government where the national government can provide substantial financial and political rewards and penalties. California politicians often have ambitions to serve at the federal level, in some cases as president. However, as the largest state in the union, California does not just have to respond to a federal agenda, it can also help to set that agenda. The pattern of federal–state interaction can be highly complex and unpredictable, a theme developed in the examination in Chapter 5 of the smog check issue.

Political life in California is focused on the state capital of Sacramento, some 90 miles from San Francisco. The majority of electors live in Southern California, in particular in the 'Southland' metropolis based on Los Angeles, but effectively stretching to San Diego. Tensions between north and south are a recurrent feature of state politics, and have led to some popular support for plans to split the state. Although many legislators have lived in Sacramento, this may change with term limits, but in any event legislators have always had to devote a considerable portion of their time to tending their districts.

Sacramento is a political hothouse of legislators, legislative staffers, lobbyists and bureaucrats. At the weekends, the hotels empty out, and the state Capitol is left to tourists enjoying guided tours of its restored splendour. During the week, however, and particularly from Monday to Thursday, the corridors of the capitol (and the coffee houses located near it) are buzzing with political conversation. The atmosphere becomes particularly frenetic in the last weeks of the legislative year in August and September when the two houses of the legislature are in almost continuous session. However, one should not forget that much of the development of policy, and certainly its execution, is in the hands of the civil servants located in (apart from a few neo-classical buildings) rather bland modern offices dotted around downtown. There are over a quarter of a million of them, and although many of them are carrying out the routine functions of motor vehicle licensing and benefit provision carried out by governments everywhere, some of them, such as the 880 at the Air Resources Board or the 476 at the Energy Commission, are concerned with matters directly relevant to air pollution policy.

MAPPING THE POLICY COMMUNITY

Who are the key actors involved in the formulation and implementation of air pollution policy in the state of California? This was a question put to interview respondents and a considerable degree of consensus emerged in the replies. They do, of course, refer to the period when the research interviews were carried out (1993–94) and term limits mean that some of the key actors in the legislature will soon disappear from the political scene. The principal actors identified were:

1. The legislature:
a) Senators Robert Presley, Quentin Kopp and Herschel Rosenthal; and Assemblymen Byron Sher and Richard Katz.
b) The Assembly Natural Resources Committee.
c) The Senate Energy and Public Utilities Committee and the Senate Transportation Committee.
2. The executive:
a) The Governor and the Governor's Office.
b) The Air Resources Board.
c) The California Energy Commission.
d) The Public Utilities Commission.
3. The Air Quality Management Districts, especially those for the South Coast, Sacramento and the Bay Area. The Southern California Association of Governments is also involved in the management of air quality policy.
4. The 'third house' (lobbyists):
a) Business, especially the oil companies.
b) The energy utilities.
c) The environmental and public health lobby.

One important point to note about air pollution policy in California is that it has been developed in a relatively bipartisan atmosphere in which there is consensus about goals, if not about the methods by which they are to be achieved. A legislative aide commented in interview:

> I think that part of the success both of California and the federal level is that for the most part we have kept air quality policy in a bipartisan fashion. In this particular area, as opposed to others, we haven't seen the pitched battles between the [Republican] administration and the Democratic controlled legislature. I think that's because everyone decided to have a sort of moderate path to follow in the expectation of a consensus. I think there's been a fairly good working relationship both with [Republican Governors] Deukmejian and Wilson on these air quality issues. Again I think that means that some of the more zealous legislators like Sher have tempered their goals. On the other hand, I think that some of the more zealous [business] groups that would like to roll back requirements have been prevented from doing so (interview, Sacramento, 8 September 1993).

A senior official of the state's Air Resources Board emphasized in interview the extent to which air pollution policy has been developed in a bipartisan context:

People are willing to support health-based air quality standards that are done in a careful, thoughtful, confident manner, and by and large the Air Resources Board has been able to enjoy bipartisan support ... so however the elections go in terms of power in the assembly and senate and whichever party the Governor belongs to we have fared remarkably well (interview, Sacramento, 30 March 1993).

It should not be imagined that consensus generally characterizes California politics. The Governor has been a Republican since 1982, while the legislature was controlled by the Democrats until 1994 when the election results seemed to remove their majority in the Assembly, but they retained a narrow majority in the Senate. Through a series of political manoeuvres, the Democratic speaker, the irrepressible Willie Brown, was able to wrest control of the Assembly back from the Republicans through summer 1995. The parties often split in floor and committee votes, particularly the Republicans who are deeply split on conservative–moderate lines throughout the state. There is a considerable ideological distance between liberal Democrats ('grizzly bears') and conservative Republicans ('cavemen') with both groups well represented in the legislature. Indeed, the 1994 elections increased the left–right polarization by removing a number of moderate Democrats and increasing the strength of conservative Republicans. Floor sessions in the 80 member Assembly towards the end of the legislative year have their share of emotional speeches and angry exchanges between members, while the general hubbub and occasional resort to animal noises means that the Assembly shares more than its decor with the House of Commons. The 40 member Senate, which models its decor on the House of Lords (and has some equally elderly members), generally conducts itself in a more decorous fashion, although even there personal animosities, fuelled by greater partisanship, have intruded in the 1990s.

The more consensual character of the air pollution policy community compared with other policy communities in California may be illustrated by the contrast with water policy. Sabatier has commented: 'In terms of the number of actors involved and the complexity of the conflicts, California air pollution is a simple matter compared to California water' (personal communication, 6 October 1994). Much of California is semi-arid, and the intensive, large-scale agriculture of the state is substantially dependent on irrigation and water for dairy and beef herds. The federal and state governments have spent huge sums of money to construct an elaborate system of dams, aqueducts, pumping stations and ditches to transfer water from the north of the state (and from out of state) to intensive agriculture in the Central Valley and to the metropolis of the south (which still retains a significant share of dry lot dairy farming and other agricultural activities). Farmers have paid a subsidized price for their water which is well below the cost of its provision, or indeed its market price. Their position is protected by entrenched property rights, but their privileges have attracted increasing political criticism, both from cities which have suffered from water shortages and from environmentalists who are worried about the effect of large-scale water transfers on areas such as the Sacramento delta. A policy deadlock has increasingly developed which has made it difficult even to make incremental improvements to the existing water distribution system:

> Three basic problems repeatedly appear in the heated politics of water: the apparent goals of the different interest groups seem to be diametrically opposed; there is little trust among the parties, and the leaderships of the groups have little real authority to negotiate because their constituents are more entrenched than the leaders (Macdonald, 1993, p. 89).

In air pollution policy, better air quality is a shared goal; the various participants in the policy process generally respect and trust one another; and flexible negotiations are possible.

THE LEGISLATURE

The legislature of the state of California is the site of considerable legislative activity, even more so since the introduction of term limits. Members of the Assembly have six years in which to make a political impression, and members of the Senate eight years. Members of the Assembly face re-election every two years, compared with four year terms in the Senate, so Assembly members in particular are engaged in a continuous political campaign. Hence there are considerable incentives to introduce legislative measures which benefit constituents, which attract media attention or which satisfy the needs of some interest which may be a source of campaign donations. In the 1992–93 session, the legislature passed 1 113 measures, although some of these were subsequently vetoed by the Governor. In any legislative year, a number of measures relating to air quality issues will be under consideration. Members of the legislature can be expected to receive a considerable amount of correspondence and messages from their constituents about auto-related issues. 'The single most frequent item they hear from their constituents about relates to the constituent's car, whether it's the highway patrol, the department of motor vehicles, the review of automotive repair' (interview, legislative aide, Sacramento, 30 March 1993).

Committees play a crucial role in processing legislation in both houses, and all measures have to be reported out of committees on to the floor to progress any further. Committee chairs are therefore in a position of considerable influence. In the Assembly, most air quality measures are considered by the Natural Resources Committee. There is no equivalent committee in the Senate and the existence of the committee in the Assembly reflects the influence of its chair in the early 1990s, Byron Sher, a Stanford University law professor representing Palo Alto who was the author of the state's landmark clean air measure, the 1988 Clean Air Act (usually referred to as 'the Sher Act'). Indeed, one Senate legislative aide commented in interview: 'I'm not sure there's anyone comparable to Sher over here in terms of the Clean Air Act'. A number of respondents emphasized the influence of Sher on air quality legislation:

> The chairmen of the committees in our system have a tremendous responsibility and opportunity to shape and direct the flow of legislation. The Assembly Natural Resources Committee functions as the bulwark to protect not just the South Coast and Air Resources Board, but other agencies from the perils of regulatory backlash (interview, environmental lobbyist, Sacramento, 9 September 1993).

> There's one person who does stand out head and shoulders above the rest and that's a man called Byron Sher (interview, executive agency, 30 March 1993).

> That committee [Natural Resources] is really the guardian of environmental policy for the state ... I'm sure that [Sher] has his personal stamp on that committee (interview, intergovernmental affairs officer, South Coast Air Quality Management District, Diamond Bar, 1 April 1993).

Byron Sher and the Natural Resources Committee have been regarded as the key players on air quality issues in the Assembly. However, the power sharing agreements agreed in 1995 after the election of a deadlocked Assembly in 1994 left Sher in a much less effective role for his last two years in the Assembly.

The Assembly Transportation Committee has been less focused on air quality issues directly and more on transit issues which, of course, have significant implications for air quality. The committee was chaired at the time of the study by Richard Katz, a graphic artist and printer representing a seat in the central San Fernando valley in the Los Angeles metropolitan area. Katz ran unsuccessfully for Mayor of Los Angeles in 1993. A profile of Katz notes that as chair of Assembly Transportation, 'he has wielded his gavel adroitly, firmly and sometimes even arrogantly'. A believer in the craft of compromise, Katz is able to deliver policy changes:

> Katz seems turned-on by his wheeler-dealer/problem-solver image around the Capitol. ... Katz has made his mark and put his deals together – in transportation, enough so that he has become a recognized leader in the field. For instance, he put together a 10-year, $20 billion transportation master plan in 1990, which included a major land-use planning and environmental strategy (*California Journal Weekly*, 20 September 1993, p. 4).

Katz has taken a prominent role in relation to clean fuel issues and was seen by some respondents as an effective supporter of efforts to improve air quality:

> The Assembly Transportation Committee seems to me to be far more environmentally concerned and aware than does the Senate committee which is much more conservative; cost seems to really affect that committee more than policy. They may love your policy, and still kill your bill because of a cost issue. They're much less willing to help you identify a way to pay for something (interview, South Coast Air Quality Management District, 1 April 1993).

It is not surprising that the Senate is seen as more conservative than the Assembly. As the natural career progression is from Assembly to Senate, middle-aged to elderly white males of a conservative disposition still predominate in the Senate. Senator Ralph Dills, who was born in 1910, first entered the Assembly in 1938, and has chaired the powerful Government Organization Committee since 1970. Dills, 'has helped bury anti-smog bills, incurring the wrath of environmentalists, who are left wondering why the bills went to his committee in the first place' (California Political Almanac, 1993–94, p. 136). Dills was not the oldest member of the Senate in the early 1990s, a distinction held by Alfred Alquist who was born in 1908. The exceptions to this general pattern, such as Tom Hayden, a radical environmental activist, and Diane Watson, a combative African American representing South-Central Los Angeles, often find themselves isolated.

The Senate has, however, included among its members policy brokers who have been prepared to facilitate clean air legislation. The key player in the early 1990s was Robert Presley, an army veteran and former sheriff's deputy who became a local legend as a detective and was elected to represent a seat in Riverside County in the greater Los Angeles area in 1974. The geography of his district is important in understanding his political role in air quality legislation. As one respondent commented in interview:

> The Riverside–San Bernadino area, they're a conservative area, but they've always had the most severe pollution in the basin so they have generally been more supportive, so the Inland Empire [a name for the area devised by boosters] tends to be a little better on air pollution than its politics would otherwise dictate (interview, environmental lobbyist, 9 September 1993).

Presley's political advisers urged him not to get involved in air quality issues on the grounds that it was a vote loser, but he proved them wrong. He is on record as stating that his 1982 smog control act was the most difficult bill he ever carried, and he went on to reorganize and strengthen the South Coast Air Quality Management District and to take an active part in promoting other air quality measures. As chair of the Senate Appropriations Committee, which considers all measures with financial implications, he has been able to push for the funding of air quality programmes. By 1993 he was widely talked about as a possible new leader of the Senate (president *pro tem*), but instead left the Senate to fight unsuccessfully for a seat on the state's Board of Equalization.

Quentin Kopp, the chair of the Senate Transportation Committee, who sits for a San Francisco seat, is one of the two independent members in the Senate, although he generally votes with the Democrats on major issues:

> Although Kopp may be politically unattached, he is far from unhinged. He is more of an institutional iconcoclast – an irreverent insider … And it's irreverence that influences his legislation and political maneuvring. Never one to retreat from rankling the status quo, Kopp borders on being contrary (*California Journal Weekly*, 19 July 1993).

Viewers watching Kopp's weekly commentary on KTVU-TV in Oakland will have heard him booming away on smog check among other issues. A legislative aide working with him commented in interview, 'he's very active, more active than you can imagine, seven days a week, all day long, all evening. And transportation has been his background for the longest time'.

The Energy and Public Utilities Committee has played a significant role in clean air issues in the Senate, for example holding hearings on the electric vehicles issue. A legislative aide working for the Senate Transportation Committee estimated, however, that 80 per cent of bills connected with air quality issues went to the Transportation Committee, with bills that had implications for the electrical utility industry being directed to Energy and Public Utilities. The principal consultant to the Energy and Public Utilities Committee explained the committee's role in the following terms:

> We tend to focus on air quality in the context of energy policy. The chairman of this committee, Herschel Rosenthal, is from Los Angeles and has a strong interest in air quality because of the pollution. His focus, and this committee's perspective, has been less on the Clean Air Act and more on cleaner fuels in two contexts, one is traditionally a focus on stationary sources, a lot of work with utilities and refineries ... More recently ... the committee has been promoting the development of electric vehicles, the use of compressed natural gas as fuel, and to some extent, flexible fuelled vehicles using methanol, providing incentives to complement the mandate that the state has (interview, Sacramento, 8 September 1993).

There are a number of points during the legislative process at which a bill can be defeated or stalled. A bill will have to pass two floor votes in each house; at least two policy committees in each house, perhaps a reference to another policy committee; and to finance committees in each house if the bill has fiscal implications. If the house of origin does not accept second house amendments, the bill has to go to a conference committee. If the conference committee cannot agree, the bill dies, but if a conference report is produced, both houses have to vote on it. If the report is adopted by both houses, the bill goes to the Governor for signature or veto. It should also be noted that a bill needs a majority vote to pass (21 votes in the Senate, 41 in the Assembly), so a bill can be defeated by abstentions. This threshold increases to two-thirds for an urgency bill or a bill with fiscal implications. In practice, the legislative process can only work through an elaborate process of bargaining or compromise. Bills are heavily amended during their passage through the legislature, so that, for example, SB 629 of 1993, which originally started off as a bill on airport noise at San Francisco International Airport, became a bill on the smog check programme with pages of crossings out and new passages inserted in italics. Over time, a body of legislation is built up so that, for example, the 1993 edition of the *California Air Pollution Control Laws* ran to 431 pages.

It is difficult to predict the impact of the introduction of term limits on the legislative process. Term limits will not prevent members of the Assembly moving to the Senate, giving them a total legislative career of 14 years, but this option will not be open to all members of the Assembly given the larger size of the lower house. Already some prominent members of both houses have announced their departure, either to run for statewide executive posts, or for Congress, or to take up posts in business or education. Of the key players in air quality, Presley left in 1994; Katz and Sher have 1996 term limits (although both would be credible candidates for the Senate); Kopp can remain until 1998, when he will be 70; and Rosenthal's term limit is also 1998 when he will be 80 years old. The depletion of experienced legislators may increase the influence of lobbyists who can offer expert advice: hardly what was intended by term limits which, according to the constitutional amendment which introduced them, were intended to restore a system of representative government undermined by incumbency.

THE EXECUTIVE

The Governor is a key player in the political system of California. He can influence the legislative process through recommending legislation, preparing and submitting to the legislature the annual state budget and vetoing bills, a power which can only be overriden by a two-thirds vote of each house of the legislature. In addition, the Governor may reduce or eliminate particular lines in the state budget. This line item veto is a power not enjoyed by the president at the national level. The Governor's office is a small but high powered operation which exerts subtle and not so subtle pressure on the legislature. In one conversation which took place in a lobbyist's office between two lobbyists with the researcher present, one lobbyist reported that he had been threatened by the Governor's office on a particular bill: 'They're going to get more active on the block'. After one lobbyist had commented resignedly, 'this is politics', it was decided to dispatch two lobbyists to the Capitol to get more intelligence so that a counter strategy could be developed.

Since 1983, California has had Republican Governors: the conservative George Deukmejian from 1983 to 1991, and the ostensibly more moderate Pete Wilson from 1991 who has been talked of as a future

Republican candidate for president, or perhaps more likely for vice-president. Wilson faced a tough re-election campaign in 1994, but after being over 20 points behind in 1993, surged ahead to overtake Kathleen Brown who was seeking to become the third member of her family to serve as Governor of California. Kathleen Brown's economic plan called for California, 'to become the international hub of green technology development, manufacture and export' (Friends of Kathleen Brown, 1994, p. 22). She pledged to commit the state to purchase clean fuel vehicles and to create a market-based incentive programme to stimulate the manufacture and purchase of cleaner cars that exceeded minimum legal requirements. Assessing the position in 1993, a senior legislative aide commented in interview:

> To some extent environmental and air quality progress has been a function of the executive branch. So it'll be a significant factor whether Governor Wilson is re-elected or whether he is succeeded by a Democrat. He has had an adequate environmental programme, air quality programme, particularly in terms of defending existing programmes at a time of recession, but I don't think we've seen any really ambitious undertakings in terms of becoming more zealous in the area of air quality or energy policy. I think that with a Democratic Governor with a tendency to be more responsive to the environmental groups and some of the other issues there might be a more far-reaching programme. And I think the legislative process tends to reflect on the executive branch on how far it's willing to go.

The Air Resources Board

The Air Resources Board is the state agency that has primary responsibility for protecting air quality in California. This responsibility includes the establishment of air quality standards, the administration of air pollution research studies, and the development and implementation of the State Implementation Plan for the attainment of federal clean air standards. The relevant legislation states that the Air Resources Board is responsible, 'for control of emissions from motor vehicles and shall coordinate, encourage and review the efforts of all levels of government as they affect air quality' (*California Air Pollution Control Laws*, 1993, p. 11). As well as providing financial help and technical assistance to local air pollution control agencies, the Board operates its own statewide enforcement programme.

California established a Bureau of Air Sanitation to identify air pollution levels that could endanger public health in 1955, and a Motor Vehicle Pollution Control Board in 1959. These two bodies were combined to create the Air Resources Board in 1967. The Board is governed by a board of nine members appointed by the Governor with the consent of the Senate, a full-time chair and eight part-time members, four representing air control districts (including one each from the South Coast, Bay Area and San Diego) and four with professional expertise. The board is backed by an executive staff which numbered 880 in 1993. The total budget of the Air Resources Board in 1992–93 was just over $100 million, of which just under $53 million was spent on mobile source programmes. Part of its budget comes from 'user fees', ranging from permits paid by polluters to the six dollars each car owner pays for a smog check certificate. This means that Board workers have carried on being paid when the state's budget problems have led to its employees being paid in i.o.us. 'The arrangement also insulates the agency from legislative pressure' (*New York Times*, 13 September 1992).

During Jerry Brown's first term in office (1975–79) the Air Resources Board became involved in controversy under, 'the aggressive leadership of Tom Quinn' (Harvey, 1991, p. 283). The Board intervened on the South Coast, claiming that local regulators 'were soft on smog' (Harvey, 1991, p. 283). The South Coast district complained of, 'regulation by one-upmanship and shoot-from-hip press releases' (Lazzareschi, 1977, p. 226). 'Warfare between the state and the South Coast Air Quality Management District continued well into the eighties' (Harvey, 1991, p. 284). There is always a potential for conflict between the Board and local air quality management boards, as the state's clean air legislation gives the Board a reserve power, after holding a public hearing, to find that a district is not taking 'reasonable action' to enforce rules to achieve state air quality standards, after which the Board may exercise any of the district's powers (*California Air Pollution Control Laws*, 1993, p. 157). The Board is prepared to use these powers:

> We've used it on Kern County ... but generally local folks will try and avoid having us come and do that, so it's more because we have the power that we can usually secure the necessary legal compliance, but in some cases they don't act [and] the law is sufficiently clear and specific enough' (interview, Air Resources Board, 30 March 1993).

In relation to the oil companies and auto manufacturers, the Air Resources Board sees itself as having a technology forcing role:

We purposefully push technology as part of our regulatory programme and that's what we do with clean cars, clean fuels. We've approached it from a systems standpoint because we kept getting the argument by the auto makers, we're not going to do this until we get the fuel, and the fuel folks are saying we're not going to do this unless there's the cars (interview, Air Resources Board, 30 March 1993).

During discussions in Sacramento in September 1993 it was suggested that the Air Resources Board is, 'facing a lot of political ill wind now'. In November 1993, it was announced that the chairwoman of the board, Jannane Sharpless, was to resign after nearly nine years in the post. Rumours about her departure had been, 'fueled by controversy over the state's smog check program and a recent squabble between ARB and those who use diesel fuel. Diesel users ... were honked off at new ARB-devised clean-air regulations and made their displeasure known to ... GOP legislators, who increased pressure on Wilson to sack Sharpless' (*California Journal Weekly*, 22 November 1993). There may also have been conflict between the Board and the agency which coordinates it and other environmental boards, the California Environmental Protection Agency (Cal/EPA): 'There is an ongoing power struggle between the Cal/EPA and the boards it coordinates' (*California Journal Weekly*, 13 December 1993). It has been suggested that Governor Wilson would like to make the Air Resources Board a department of the EPA, giving him more power over the stand the Board takes over key regulations opposed by the auto-related industries (*California Journal Weekly*, 13 December 1993). Sharpless was replaced by Jacqueline Shafer, but the state Senate refused to confirm her appointment, in part because of the unpopularity with environmentalists of the head of Cal/ EPA, James Strock. John Dunlap, an experienced air quality expert, was nominated by Governor Wilson as chairman in 1994.

These upheavals should not distract attention from the high regard in which the Air Resources Board is held throughout the United States. 'The board lays down the toughest regulations, forces the biggest changes, and generally blazes the path for everyone else, including the United States Environmental Protection Agency' (*New York Times*, 13 September 1992). The environmental commissioner in New York state has argued that the Board's, 'mobile source program is more competently staffed than [the] EPA's' (*New York Times*, 13 September 1992). Within the state, the Board's success is attributed by its own officials to taking a balanced, consensus-building approach that resonates with public opinion:

The environmental ethic is strong enough in California that generally what we propose is thoughtfully balanced between protecting the environment and recognizing ... the economic situation ... we do go out and we build consensus and we do bring ... around the table the major players and keep working at what we can feasibly do ... the polls keep saying that people want their health protected, they want air quality not be fouled and polluted. We've been able to demonstrate that we can do that and in a competent way (interview, Sacramento, 30 March 1993).

The California Energy Commission

The California Energy Commission (CEC) was established in 1974 after the first oil shock to address the energy issues facing the state. It had a budget of $84 million and 476 employees in 1992–93. The CEC is the state's principal energy planning and policy-making organization, responsible for ensuring a reliable and affordable energy supply. As part of its mandate, the CEC encourages the development and use of alternative fuels to help ensure energy diversity and improve air quality. The Transportation Technology and Fuels Office assesses and demonstrates the market potential of new transport technologies and fuels, entering into public–private partnerships, for example with oil companies to make methanol available at filling stations. In general, as a senior CEC official emphasized: 'We only get involved in the air quality issues in so far as they involve energy' (interview, Sacramento, 25 March 1993).

A legislative aide noted in interview, 'the evolution of the clean fuel legislative process is that it originally started many years ago after the oil crisis as a fuel security and diversity issue. And in the eighties it became more of an air quality issue that drove it' (interview, Sacramento, 8 September 1993). This development in policy emphasis put the Air Resources Board more at the centre of the political stage than the CEC, and Governor Wilson has proposed abolishing the CEC. In December 1993, the Governor announced a proposal to absorb the Energy Commission into the Department of Conservation to create a new Department of Energy and Conservation, a change thought likely to lead to the loss of 300–400 jobs. Welcoming the announcement, the press secretary for the Republican minority leader in the Assembly commented: 'The Energy Commission has outlived its original purpose. It was brought in during the energy crisis. It's a dinosaur' (*Sacramento Bee*, 2 December 1993).

The CEC has, however, shown itself adept at adjusting to new circumstances, while still emphasizing the continued importance of its original policy concerns. Asked about the primary drive behind their policies, a CEC respondent replied:

> Early on it was really, at least in the transportation sector, a concern about our energy security ... And when the concern about energy security waned it became clear to us that the environmental considerations still had much appeal and merit and we built essentially an alternative fuels programme which has now emphasized the environmental considerations, although we feel that the energy diversity and energy security reasons are still very, very valid and in themselves worth pursuing, but in actuality those areas are not easy to quantify in terms of economic benefit (interview, Sacramento, 25 March 1993).

The CEC has become more drawn into the air quality policy community in recent years. In part this is a reflection of the greater maturity of the policy community which is now interconnected with a greater range of policy networks. New regulations developed by the South Coast Air Quality Management District affected the availability and output of power plants, leading to intensive consultations between the CEC and the District:

> We were really caught a bit by surprise, by the same token we found that the Air Quality Management District was virtually unaware of the energy implications of the air quality regulations, so we've spent a good deal of the last three years in working groups between the staffs of the two agencies trying to improve our understanding and what they're going to do and also trying to get them to take into account the energy implications (interview, Sacramento, 30 March 1993).

Public Utilities Commission

The Public Utilities Commission (PUC) operates under Article XII of the Californian constitution. This, 'provides the commission with a wide latitude to perform both administrative and judicial functions. The California courts have long recognized the unusual status of the commission ... the commission is expected to undertake investigations of fact and initiate its own proceedings' (Grodin, Massey and Cunningham, 1993, p. 205). In particular the PUC is responsible for providing the public with the lowest reasonable rates for utilities and transport services, and ensuring that the services provided are adequate and safe. It thus performs a similar role to regulatory bodies at the federal level. It has been suggested that the PUC's annual budget of $80 million and staff of 1 165 in 1993 reflects the existence of unduly cumbersome processes. Along with his proposed reforms to the CEC, Governor Wilson suggested that the size and scope of the PUC's activities could be reduced.

An important link with clean air policy is provided by Senate Bill 2103 (Rosenthal and Leonard) which requires the PUC to evaluate and implement policies to promote the development of equipment and infrastructure needed to facilitate the use of electric power and natural gas to fuel low emission vehicles. This task is carried out in cooperation with the other actors in the policy community: indeed, the list provided in Senate Bill 2103 fits very well with the map of the policy community used here. The sums provided by the utilities from the payments collected from their ratepayers are not insignificant, amounting to $50 million in 1993 (PUC, 1993, p. 1). There are limits to what the PUC can achieve as it, 'has jurisdiction over only two of many fuels that will be competing for the emerging market share' (PUC, 1993, p. 5). The PUC has therefore emphasized working closely with the other actors in the policy community.

Senate Bill 2103 requires the PUC to ensure that the costs of LEV programmes are passed on to ratepayers only if these programmes are in the best interest of ratepayers. The difficulty is to decide what constitutes the best interest of ratepayers. So far these issues have been addressed on a case by case basis, but the PUC is seeking to develop a long-term policy. In general, there are two alternative views of what constitutes ratepayer interest:

> A broad view of ratepayer interest would necessitate the consideration of the marginal environmental benefits of utility LEV programs, as well as the direct costs of those programs, and those due to increased electricity and gas development. A conventional view of ratepayer interest would not incorporate societal interests such as air quality and energy security (PUC, 1993, p. 6).

In April 1994 the Division of Ratepayer Advocates of the PUC published a report that was highly critical of plans advanced by the utilities to have their customers fund $581 million in programmes to promote the use of electric and natural gas vehicles. The report expressed particular concern about the subsidization of car purchases. The PUC project manager accepted that the utilities should be involved to some extent, for example, by using electric and natural gas powered cars in their fleets. There was, however, no justification in promoting a market that yielded a profit for the utilities' shareholders. Some analysts argue that as electric cars are more likely to be bought by the better off, rebate incentive programmes involved a subsidy of the well off by low income utility customers.

The utility companies argue that they are in a good position to promote the development of natural gas and electricity and vehicle fuels, and that ratepayers serve as a good proxy for the general service area population. It was therefore not surprising that a utilities lobbyist in interview designated the PUC as an 'extremely important' actor because, 'they have ultimate jurisdiction on what utilities can do in this area' (interview, Sacramento, 26 March 1993). The utilities are opposed by ratepayer advocate groups such as Californians Against Utility Company Abuse and competing alternative fuel suppliers, although these are not as well organized as electricity and natural gas utilities for reasons discussed in the section on lobbying below. The opponents of using utility funds to promote LEVs argue that this approach constitutes, 'an involuntary levy on ratepayers, who, because of the monopolistic nature of utility service, are unable to obtain services from another source and thereby avoid such a levy' (PUC, 1993, p. 8).

These issues have yet to be resolved, but the PUC has become an increasingly important actor in the air quality management debate, although its principal responsibilities lie elsewhere. One indication of a change of focus for the PUC towards this area is the appointment of Daniel Fessler as its head in 1993. 'He's very proelectric vehicles and he thinks it would be good for the Governor to jump on this electric vehicle programme' (interview, Sacramento, 26 March 1993).

THE AIR QUALITY MANAGEMENT DISTRICTS

The adoption and enforcement of rules to achieve federal and state air quality standards is the responsibility of air pollution control districts of which there are 33 in California. These can be counties, in which case the board of supervisors governs the district, or groupings of counties such as the San Joaquin Valley Unified District. The state legislation makes special arrangements for the nine counties in the Bay Area, with the governing board of the Bay Area Air Quality Management District made up of supervisors and city council members of the participating counties. No less than 40 pages of the state legislation are concerned with the South Coast Air Quality Management District which covers all (or portions of) four counties in the Los Angeles basin.

Reflecting its importance, three members of its 14 member board are appointed by the Governor, the Senate Rules Committee and the speaker of the Assembly. At the other end of the spectrum, the Tehama County Air Pollution District is housed in offices the size of a trailer home, while its director is also the county animal control officer, director of weights and measures, and agricultural commissioner.

There has been some criticism of the Air Quality Management Districts for only giving warnings or small fines to stationary polluters. A survey found that Central Valley air pollution officers issued 1 300 notices of violation in 1992, but one in three offenders received a warning, and fines averaged out at $666 (the largest fine was $50,000 against a creamery for operating without required smog controls) (*Sacramento Bee*, 15 November 1993). Presented with these findings, Sierra Club lobbyist John V. White commented: 'We might be better off having a statewide enforcement system for consistency and strength'.

Some individuals involved in air quality management issues consider that the South Coast Air Quality Management District has political legitimacy and accountability problems. In part, this is seen as a consequence of an engineering and research-based philosophy, operationalized through a rather narrowly based analysis of costs and benefits, which does not give sufficient weight to concerns about political credibility and support. In part, the problems arise from the nature of the South Coast Management District as a political structure:

> I think that the District as an institution is problematical because of the sort of smudged accountability that it has in terms of it isn't directly elected, it isn't appointed directly by the Governor, it's this sort of second hand process of county supervisors selecting amongst their own and the cities selecting amongst their own. So when you have an agency with the amount of power and authority and potential public impact, the strains of its political legitimacy arise and I think that the District over the last three or four years really has suffered a loss of its political legitimacy, maybe by doing too much, too far, too fast, maybe by doing not enough well, maybe by simply suffering the slings and arrows that accompany its own job (interview, environmental lobbyist, Sacramento, 9 September 1993).

Observers of air quality management policies in the state contend that the lead in policy development has been taken by the South Coast District and the much smaller Sacramento District:

> I think the two most innovative Districts in the state are the South Coast Air Quality Management District ... and then the Sacramento District, they're

very innovative. Then the other two big districts in the state are the Bay Area Management District and the San Diego Air Quality Management District (interview, utilities lobbyist, Sacramento, 26 March 1993).

The South Coast Air Quality Management District operates on an annual budget of around $100 million, with three-quarters of its funding coming from annual fees that businesses pay based on the volume of air pollutants they emit. However, the recession of the early 1990s reduced industrial production, while new air quality programmes have lowered emissions, leaving the agency with less money. In 1992, it was forced by a budget shortfall to reduce its staff from 1 163 employees to 915, and a further budget shortfall of $7.5 million forecast for 1993–94 led the agency to warn of a further reduction of staff by 120 in 1994. The agency's chief executive, James Lents warned:

> I don't think it's tantamount to us going out of business, but if we're going to live up to our clean air plan, there are a lot more programs we need to put into place and they will probably come into place a lot slower than we would like (*Los Angeles Times*, 4 December 1993).

As well as operating within the framework of federal and state air quality standards, the Air Quality Management Districts have to seek to cooperate with local government authorities with rather different objectives and concerns, particularly in the area of land use policy. Thus in developing its air quality management plan, the South Coast District works in cooperation with the Southern California Association of Governments. This is a voluntary intergovernmental regional organization which nevertheless has a responsibility under state clean air law, 'to coordinate the efforts of the counties and cities in the process of developing and reviewing plan elements which meet the requirements of the plan, state and federal law, and local needs relating to transportation, land use, demographic projections, employment, housing, and other matters of local concern' (California Air Pollution Control Laws, section 40464). This task, along with other responsibilities, has to be achieved by a staff of about 100 who have no enforcement powers and, 'can't even get their constituent cities necessarily to do what they want them to do' (interview, 1 April 1993).

There is political resistance in some parts of the South Coast to the South Coast Air Quality Management District and its plans:

> Some of the members from Orange County are seeking to curtail the powers of the board, especially as it relates to what employers are required

to do ... This is a group of legislators that's very close to the business community and they think that a lot of these prescriptions are onerous for business people (interview, legislative aide, 30 March 1993).

Legislative threats to its standing and programme means that the South Coast District (like other governmental bodies in California) has to maintain its own in-house lobbying operation, as well as contract lobbyists in Sacramento and Washington. In 1993 it paid $103,631 in lobbying fees to the environmental lobbying firm of John V. White Associates out of a total expenditure on lobbying of $198,373 (Secretary of State, 1994, p. 66 and p. 152). Explaining the South Coast District's work in Sacramento, an intergovernmental affairs officer explained in interview:

> For the Sacramento programme we are proactive in terms of trying to clarify certain programmes where perhaps our authority is unclear or we need to make some moderate change, to make either our job easier or for the regulating community. These last few years with the recession coming on, a lot of what we're doing is just damage control. One of the first things people want when their business is in trouble is to get rid of regulation. We've been there sort of standing guard and fending off attacks and being defensive. In fact in 1992 we didn't have any proactive legislation, it was all just standing guard (interview, Diamond Bar, 1 April 1993).

THE THIRD HOUSE

Lobbying is a central feature of the political process in California. Lobbyists, a category which covers both individuals directly employed by firms and associations, and contract lobbyists who hire their services out to a variety of clients, are such an established feature of the political process that they are often referred to as 'the third house'. There were 1 021 registered lobbyists in Sacramento in 1993, with 55 per cent of those with six or more years' experience working for multiple contract firms (Price, 1993, p. 32). Lobbying is big business, with $127.7 million being spent by the employers of lobbyists in 1994 (Secretary of State, 1994). In a political system in which political parties are weak, and in which legislators are constantly having to raise funds for their election campaigns, there are many opportunities for lobbyists to exert influence. Sometimes they go beyond what is lawful: the lobbying community in Sacramento was rocked by the conviction of one of its leading members in 1993 on ten corruption counts. During the trial, it became clear that money had been offered to legislators in return for their assistance in blocking measures opposed by the clients of lobbyists, money in one instance being placed in a trash can in the rest room of a Macdonalds. The outcome of the trial was seen as a, 'direct slap at the comfortable relationship that lobbyists have long enjoyed with legislators' (*California Journal Weekly*, 13 December 1993).

There are three main sets of players involved in lobbying on air quality management policy, leaving aside various executive agencies: business (especially the auto companies and the oil companies); the energy utilities (which have their own special interests in the area of air quality management policy); and the environmental and public health lobby. There was quite a lot of agreement among interview respondents about the main interests involved in air quality management policy:

> I think the groups that are the stakeholders are obviously the manufacturers, the oil companies and the utilities. I think those three interest groups have the greatest influence and the greatest stake. The public health community and the environmental community is also important but that sort of depends on the time of season, it goes up and it goes down (interview, environmental lobbyist, Sacramento, 9 September 1993).

'You have the business community and the energy community, but you also have environmental groups and others' (interview, legislative aide, Sacramento, 8 September 1993).

Business Interests

General business interests are represented by organizations such as the California Manufacturers Association and the California Chamber of Commerce. Both organizations often rank among or near the top ten lobbying employers: $955,037 for the Manufacturers Association and $940,612 for the Chamber of Commerce in 1994. (Figures on lobbying expenditure in this section of the chapter are all taken from Secretary of State, 1994). Business in California shares a general concern about levels of taxation and regulation, reflected in the passage of a package of tax breaks in the 1992–93 legislative session. There has been a wide-ranging and highly publicized debate in the state about whether excessive regulation is driving businesses out of California to less regulated states such as Nevada or New Mexico. The available evidence suggests that some jobs have been lost by outward migration of businesses, to the extent of 708 manufacturing plants relocating or expanding outside

California between 1987 and 1992, leading to the loss of 107,000 jobs. Far greater job losses have resulted from the recession and the downsizing of the aerospace industry following the end of the cold war (Barber, 1993, p. 10). From a business perspective, environmental regulations, 'pose a significant problem – not the standards themselves, but the manner in which they are handled by the myriad of state and local agencies' (Barber, 1993, p. 11). A survey in 1991 by the Business Roundtable discovered that: 'Of environmental regulations, business found air-pollution controls and toxic waste laws the most onerous. Ironically, some companies said poor air quality – especially in the Los Angeles area – was hurting business' (Paquette, 1993, p. 17).

Beyond a general opposition to what is perceived to be excessive taxation and regulation, however, the business community is liable to be divided on air quality management issues. As one respondent noted:

> You have a play within the business community between those who are stationary polluters, the people who may have refineries or factories versus the people that produce the vehicles that run and emit pollution that way. So you have that kind of tension back and forth and sometimes the alliances shift on a particular way (interview, legislative aide, Sacramento, 30 March 1993).

'In fact, many industries would prefer a strong mobile-sources program, and long have argued that the real pollution in California is from automobiles not industry' (*California Journal Weekly*, 13 December 1993). There are also tensions between oil companies and vehicle manufacturers because vehicle manufacturers have called for the burden of cleaning up the air to be shifted to cleaner gasoline which imposes burdens on the oil companies.

The oil companies have always been significant players in California politics. The Western States Petroleum Association usually features among the top ten lobbying employers; it spent $1,356,988 in 1993, giving it a ranking of fourth. A number of individual companies are significant spenders: for example, in 1994 Chevron and its subsidiaries spent $1,172,445; Atlantic Richfield, $978,462; Union Oil, $466,943; and Shell $338,028. As one respondent commented in interview: 'I think one of the stumbling blocks is ... the oil industry which is also a powerful political power and ... there are hurdles they put in the path' (interview, legislative aide, Sacramento, 8 September 1993).

The sophistication of the oil lobby is shown by their deployment of the 'Astroturf' technique: running a campaign which appears to have grass roots support which is in fact artificially created. In an effort to generate support for a bill which would make it more difficult for utilities to spend $600 million to create an infrastructure to charge electric cars, the public relations firm representing the oil companies set up a coalition called 'Californians Against Utility Companies Abuses'. Fifty thousand alarmed Californians who had received letters warning of increases in gas and electric bills sent in 'return' postcards. Some of these were organized by a phone bank to phone legislators' offices, but it was then that the scheme started to go wrong as some of the citizens were not sure whether they were for or against the bill. With the offices of Senate Energy Committee members busy with calls, senators became so angry that they put the bill on hold and left it to die (*California Journal Weekly*, 10 October 1994).

The oil companies are, however, not united on air quality-related issues. ARCO, which is a regional company centred mainly in California, has been at the forefront of developing clean-burning reformulated gasolines. A vice-president of an oil industry consulting firm argued that: 'ARCO appears to have chosen to wear the environmental white hat' (*New York Times*, 21 November 1991). The company runs advertising under the slogan, 'clean fuels for the future'.

In 1991, ARCO announced the development of its third reformulated fuel, EC-X, which would substantially cut unburned and evaporative emissions of hydrocarbons and nitrogen oxide emissions. With sunlight, these three emissions are the main ingredients of smog, and the company claimed that the fuel would cut the ability of a car exhaust to produce ozone by 37 per cent (*New York Times*, 11 July 1991). The new gasoline did not include any proprietary ingredients, and the company was prepared to make the technical details available to anyone who wanted them. It was not prepared actually to sell the new fuel because it would cost 15 to 20 cents more a gallon to produce.

ARCO subsequently argued that proposals by the Air Resources Board to remove from gasoline the components that contribute to smog were not ambitious enough. In this stand, it was supported by the British company, Ultramar, the American operations of which are centred in California. The other oil companies, which do most of their business outside California, had different commercial interests. The Western States Petroleum Association opposed ARCO, arguing that: 'These ideas have a way of spreading very rapidly, and being embraced as state-of-the-art in emissions reductions, regardless of their applicability to any region or place' (*New York Times*, 21 November 1991).

Despite the offer to share technical information, the other companies believed that as ARCO's refineries were among the most modern on the West Coast, it would have a competitive advantage in producing the new fuel. ARCO subsequently disassociated itself from a move by a group of oil companies to block California's gasoline rules through a referendum (*New York Times*, 19 March 1992). Thus even the oil companies are split by different commercial interests and perceptions of their niche in the market place.

The auto companies are clearly unhappy about moving away from their familiar technological base, gasoline fuelled vehicles, and being required to move into areas with unfamiliar technologies and uncertain markets such as electric vehicles:

> I think it's very clear that the automakers are opposed to the entire Air Resources Board low emission vehicle programme, not just the zero-emission requirement, but the whole thing, including all four tiers of increasingly stringent standards and they would just as soon not have to do any of that (interview, utilities lobbyist, Sacramento, 26 March 1993).

> All the auto manufacturers are working behind the scenes and sometimes not that far behind the scenes to try and get the ARB to change its mandate from pure electric vehicle to some kind of hybrid that would allow them to get their range to a point where they'd actually have vehicles they could sell (interview, Air Quality Management District official, 7 September 1993).

Motor vehicle manufacture is not a leading industry in California, and the American Automobile Manufacturers Association is a relatively small spender on lobbying activity ($85,682 in 1993). Larger sums are spent by individual automobile manufacturers, notably Ford ($233,360) and General Motors ($81,698). Dan Walters has commented that the automakers, 'have little political clout in the Capitol – in part because they don't make campaign contributions – so the anti-electric car drive has fallen to oil companies' (*Sacramento Bee*, 20 April 1994). Motor industry representatives at legislative hearings in Sacramento are often specialists flown in from Detroit. It should be noted that each of the major auto companies has extensive dealer networks in the state which can be mobilized in each legislative district. The California Motor Car Dealers Association is a significant force in its own right, spending $397,641 on lobbying in 1993. There is therefore a significant range of business interests likely to want to at least modify or slow down the development of air quality management policy. In particular, 'the battle between the auto industry and clean air advocates over the extent to which cleanup can be achieved through technological controls on tailpipe emissions has dominated the debate over clean air policy for two decades' (Bryner, 1993, p. 132).

The Energy Utilities

One set of business interests has a rather different perspective on air quality management programmes which lead to the development of alternative fuels: the energy utilities (electricity and natural gas). Dan Walters commented as the 1993–94 legislative session gathered momentum: 'It's Big Oil vs. Big Utilities in one of the year's sharpest legislative skirmishes, a struggle over whether California will go ahead with its decision to force automakers into selling thousands of electric cars' (*Sacramento Bee*, 20 April 1994). Cars powered by electricity and natural gas open up for the utilities the prospect of a major new market which they should be able to satisfy without major additional investment. As one respondent commented in interview: 'The utilities have a tremendous market potential in this area in terms of selling the fuels and possibly owning the infrastructure ... California has the largest utilities in our nation with tremendous capital potential' (interview, legislative aide, Sacramento, 8 September 1993).

The energy utilities exert substantial political influence in Sacramento. Pacific Gas and Electric spent $657,618 on lobbying in 1993, while Southern California Edison spent $411,479. Commenting on the natural gas industry, one respondent stated:

> The natural gas utilities are very powerful at the state and the federal level ... you've got industry coordination, so that when federal or state issues come up they have lobbyists full time ... who spend all their time in Congress or at state level, working to make sure that regulations and laws favour the industry (interview, Sacramento, 7 September 1993).

As far as the electrical generation utilities are concerned, all the leading utilities have two or three government relations officers in Sacramento. The five leading utilities have formed themselves into a California Electric Transportation Coalition which supports incentive legislation and the mandate of the Air Resources Board (interview, California Electric Transportation Coalition, 31 March 1993).

Not all the alternative fuels enjoy equal political displacement. Methanol had substantial support in the mid-1980s but: 'The perception that only a liquid fuel was acceptable slowly eroded as the natural gas and electric utility industries began to give more support to natural gas and electric vehicles' (Sperling, DeLuchi and Wang, 1991, p. 20). A number of respondents made the point that methanol producers were less well organized politically than natural gas or electricity:

> Methanol has more of a diverse set of constituents that are not well funded and don't have a lot of infrastructure compared to the gas industry. It's produced by a variety of relatively small chemical companies ... Another aspect is that the methanol industry is the chemical industry and that's how they see themselves, they don't see themselves as fuel suppliers *per se*, and it's an identity thing. They have a hard time re-identifying themselves (interview information, CEC, 25 March 1993).

> If you're just looking at the technical merits of the fuel itself, and there's no politics, no politicians, lobbyists, people with a lot of money, thousand dollar suits, six hundred dollar shoes and all that kind of thing, hanging around, then you just look at the technical merits of the fuel, then methanol becomes very attractive ... Unfortunately, the politics are not gone, they are a big part of the decision-making process (interview, air quality expert, Sacramento, 7 September 1993).

The political weakness of methanol does raise broader issues about the relative strength of ideas and interests in the air quality management arena, and the relative value of the policy community and advocacy coalition approaches. The advocacy coalition approach draws our attention to the importance of belief systems rather than interests: 'advocacy coalitions are *not* simply constellations of interest groups' (Sabatier, 1993a, p. 37); and there is a concern with, 'the generators and disseminators of ideas' (Sabatier, 1993a, p. 35).

One important mechanism for the diffusion of ideas about air quality management is a national organization of air pollution control officers. At a state level, there are close links between three key technical experts on alternative fuels working for the CEC, the South Coast Air Quality Management District, and the Sacramento Air Quality Management District. Three respondents in key bodies stressed the technical merits of methanol, at any rate as a medium-term contributor to air quality management:

> Technically, methanol makes a lot of sense as a transportation fuel. The problem is you've got a fuel that has a lot of technical merit, and no public relations, no market-influencing capability ... they don't have people to influence public opinion, they don't have people to influence public policy,

none of that in place (interview, Sacramento Air Quality Management
District, 7 September 1993).

In the early 1980s [we] determined that methanol looked like a very, very
promising transportation option ... we really began to focus on methanol as
a major transportation alternative (interview, CEC, 25 March 1993).

Methanol is by far the cheapest way to displace one billion barrels of oil a
day (interview, South Coast Air Quality Management District, Diamond
Bar, 1 April 1993).

Ideas advocated by technical experts do have some impact on the
policy process, as is illustrated by projects involving the CEC and the
South Coast Air Quality Management District to run methanol fuelled
demonstration fleets and to ensure that adequate infrastructure is in
place in the form of service stations providing methanol-based fuels.
Nevertheless, it was interesting that at one interview where more than
one technical expert was present, there was a disagreement about why
natural gas was gaining ground as an alternative fuel. One viewpoint
put forward was that: 'The Fuel Gas Research Institute and those folks
representing regulated utilities, they have a lot of money, a lot of gas
and they're really the motivating factor for natural gas and now it's
catching up to methanol'. An alternative view is that methanol is a less
attractive option than was originally supposed because it does not offer
sufficient air quality gains compared with gasoline, and that this perception gradually infiltrated the policy debate.

This specific example leads to two alternative interpretations of how
air quality decisions are made. On the one hand, one has an open
political system with high levels of technical expertise in which there is
a continuing and sophisticated debate about air quality management,
and in which new knowledge influences policy outcomes. On the other
hand, one has a political system in which campaigning is expensive; in
which there is a close link between campaign funds and lobbying; and
in which the back pocket could be seen as the ultimate influence on
policy. The interplay between the two types of politics is both complex
and fascinating, and will be returned to later in this book.

The Environmental and Public Health Lobby

It was noted earlier in this chapter that there has been broad bipartisan
support for air quality management policies in California. This bipartisan consensus has been reinforced by the extent of voter concern about

environmental issues. In the run-up to the 1992 elections, business interests had hoped that a more conservative legislature would favour business concerns over environmental protection:

> Instead, the number of pro-environment members barely changed. Of 38 Assembly members identified as 'allies' by the California League of Conservation Voters, 28 ran for re-election and all of them won. Of nine candidates endorsed by the league for open seats, five won. In the Senate, environmentalists picked up one seat (Paquette, 1993, p. 18).

Whereas in Britain, environmental interest groups are often regarded as policy outsiders, in California they are treated as policy insiders. They are too well resourced, too sophisticated and have too many supporters to be treated otherwise. As one senior legislative aide commented in interview:

> I think there is a very strong segment that we call the environmental community ... the environmental community is very well organized with legislative organizational skills and such ... they know how to play the legislative game ... if you're organized, you can play effectively and they play effectively. Their interests are represented in a structured consistent way (interview, Sacramento, 26 March 1993).

That is not to say that the environmental lobby has an easy task. As one respondent commented: 'You need to have political vision and a political strategy, and you need to have people at every meeting speaking out about this issue, all the time, pushing, pushing, pushing (round-table discussion, American Lung Association, Sacramento, 10 September 1993).

California has, however, experienced a prolonged recession in the early 1990s which has seen unemployment rising to nearly 10 per cent, with levels of over 20 per cent in some areas. A recession on this scale is a new experience in the post-war period for California, a state which is not accustomed to hard times. In its annual scorecard of legislative votes on key environmental bills, the Californian League of Conservation Voters noted in 1994 that for the first time in 20 years there were more bills judged anti-conservation than pro-conservation on the chart. This development reflects national trends in public opinion. A Times-Mirror Center poll of 3 800 adults found that whereas in 1992 67 per cent of the those interviewed said that Americans should be willing to pay higher prices to protect the environment, the number had dropped to 57 per cent by 1994 (*Sacramento Bee*, 21 September 1994).

An Air Quality Management District official commented that he was less optimistic about the passage of relevant legislation than four years earlier:

> In Sacramento the outlook for passage of environmental legislation, for maintaining even existing environmental legislation, is not as good as it was, say in '88, for example. The environmental bills have a much tougher time now than they did in the past. Partly that's a result of the economy, to some extent it's also a result of changing faces in the legislature and the commonly held belief that people are really fed up with anything remotely resembling a new tax (interview, San Francisco, 12 August 1994).

These changed circumstances have led to new perceptions of the trade-off between environmental protection and economic growth:

> Some of the politicians I've talked to have said, maybe we've come to a point that we have to accept a certain level of air quality deterioration because it's only one of the factors that we, representing our constituents, have to consider, and the economy is right at the top of the list now (interview, Sacramento Air Quality Management District, 7 September 1993).

This respondent thought that attitudes to environmental policy varied cyclically, and were bottoming out. Similarly, another respondent commented: 'My experience is that it's a cyclical process to regulation and environmentalism. Right now we're on the downside of it, it's about seven years since the last high water mark of strong public support' (interview, environmental lobbyist, Sacramento, 9 September 1993).

A Senate legislative aide argued perceptively that the focus of the policy process in relation to alternative fuels had changed over the decades. In the 1970s, the emphasis had been on fuel security and diversity; in the 1980s on air quality; and in the 1990s, the focus has shifted to the possibility of creating new jobs through the development of alternative technologies:

> Given the recession in California, that has a major influence. And that actually is a two edged sword. On the one hand, the recession stimulates the legislators to look for economic development opportunities, on the other hand, it tends to be used as an excuse to step back from stringent air quality requirements because of the alleged cost of doing business with stringent requirements. So there's the one effort to preserve the existing standards by making the process more flexible and business friendly, [and] on the other hand, to promote new standards which might drive technology and economic development (interview, legislative aide, Sacramento, 8 September 1993).

There was some measure of agreement among respondents about which the key environmental and public health organizations were. The most frequently mentioned were the Sierra Club, the Natural Resources Defense Council, the Planning and Conservation League and the American Lung Association. Others mentioned included the Environmental Defense Fund and the Union of Concerned Scientists. The Coalition for Clean Air has close links with the Natural Resources Defense Council and the Sierra Club.

With over 155,000 of its 400,000 members in the state, and its national headquarters in San Francisco, the Sierra Club has been described as, 'the largest and most powerful environmental group working in the state' (Culver and Syer, 1988, p. 69). As well as having an extensive, grass roots membership, it also spends substantially on lobbying activities in Sacramento ($278,673 in 1993). Much of its strength is derived from its activist membership. 'Support from the Sierra Club name is the most convincing argument that politicians can use to certify for voters that they are genuine environmentalists' (*California Political Almanac*, 1991–92, p. 402). An activist in another environmental organization took a more sceptical view of their accomplishments:

> I think the Sierra Club has the most recognition. When you say Sierra Club, everyone says 'oh, that's the environmental organization', but if you ask what they have accomplished, 'well, gee, I don't know'. So that's the kind of stigma they have, they don't really seem to accomplish anything, but they've got a very good publicity mechanism (interview, Sacramento, 18 August 1994).

The Sierra Club has recently run into financial problems. It lost $6.8 million between 1990 and 1994, running up debts of $2.9 million. In response, it was planning to make some of its 350 employees redundant. Between 1991 and 1994, more than 100,000 people gave up their memberships and those remaining reduced their contributions. 'Sierra Club executives blamed the problem on the economy and a declining interest in issues like environmentalism' (*Sacramento Bee*, 25 September 1994).

The Planning and Conservation League is a coalition of 120 environmental groups. It is an active lobbyist in Sacramento, spending $179,722 in 1993, but tends to rely quite extensively on using direct democracy. This practice has attracted some criticism from legislators who argue, 'that the League's proposals amount to "Christmas trees", because, they charged, the PCL used bond money to fund the pet projects of various special interests in exchange for those interests' financial support in qualifying and passing the initiative' (*California Journal Weekly*, 12 September 1994). It was thought by some respondents to give more emphasis to land use issues than some of the other groups.

The Natural Resources Defense Council, which is noted for its legal and scientific expertise, was seen as a major player, although its offices are in San Francisco. It works closely with the Clean Air Coalition, an umbrella organization formed to carry out coordinated clean air activities for various citizen's groups. It is headquartered in California in Venice, Los Angeles with an executive director and a staff scientist who produces regular papers on air quality management issues.

The Clean Air Coalition was formed at a national level in the early 1980s to lobby for more effective federal legislation. A range of organizations were involved, including the Sierra Club, the Environmental Defense Fund and the American Lung Association, as well as wildlife organizations, church groups and organized labour (notably the United Steelworkers Union). A particularly significant input was, however, made by lawyers and scientists at the Natural Resources Defense Council (Bryner, 1993, p. 87).

The Environmental Defense Fund principally uses the courts to advance environmental concerns. The Union of Concerned Scientists is a relatively small group, but has been of some significance in agenda-setting, particularly in relation to transport issues. The American Lung Association originally focused on tuberculosis, then shifted its attention to smoking. 'We really have conquered the tobacco issue too. We've broken its back' (interview, American Lung Association, Sacramento, 10 September 1993). A concern with air pollution from vehicles represents a natural extension of the Lung Association's work. 'We are the primary agency that focuses on the health effects of air pollution, whether it be outdoor pollution or indoor air pollution from smoking' (interview, American Lung Association, Sacramento, 10 September 1993). Its activists see the Lung Association as, 'more conservative than the Sierra Club ... but they know that they can come back to us and that we will join forces with them if certain rules of the game are observed. We are known as a more mainstream organization (interview, American Lung Association, Sacramento, 10 September 1993). One consequence of this more conservative stance is that the American Lung Association has been able to reach out to organizations such as the Chamber of Commerce to create a Cleaner Air Partnership in the Sacramento area. It was also evident from interview information that staff in air quality agencies worked through the American Lung Association to act as an advocate and mobilize support on issues of concern to them as a means of influencing board-level decision-makers.

CONCLUSIONS

There is a mature air quality management policy community in California. Institutional development at state and local level is high; there are recognized centres of expertise in the legislature and the active involvement of a range of interest groups. Interviews revealed general agreement among respondents about who are the key actors in the policy process. Participants in the policy community have different perspectives on the means to be used to achieve the goal of cleaner air, but the debate is a well-informed one that takes serious account of relevant technical evidence.

From the perspective of a British observer, the decision-making process is highly fragmented and much more unpredictable than in a polity dominated by a strong executive. On the other hand, participants in the policy process adjust to this by having fewer inhibitions about coalition-building across political divides:

> In the [Bay Area] we try to put together a coalition of other public agencies, especially transportation agencies, for example our metropolitan planning organization which is a code word for the Regional Transportation Agency and some business groups ... and some environmental groups ... if [legislation] is to move forward, the way to move it forward is through putting together these coalitions that involve some quite unusual partners (interview, Bay Area Air Quality Management District, 12 August 1994).

The politics of air quality management in California is not generally confrontational, but this does not mean that policy is driven by a rational, long-term assessment of technological and behavioural policy options and their relative cost-effectiveness. A theme that will be developed in other chapters is that an effective air quality management policy depends to a significant extent on changes in land use policy. However, state clean air legislation states that: 'Nothing in this section constitutes an infringement on the existing authority of counties and cities to plan and control land use, and nothing in this section provides or transfers new authority over such land use to a district'. The boundaries of the air quality management policy community are clearly marked in law to exclude land use policy. 'The plan to achieve healthy air in southern California depends on land use and transportation decisions by local government officials ... who are often reluctant to initiate change' (Hall, 1993, p. 43).

The policy-making process in California may bear all the hallmarks of an open and diverse pluralism, but political scientists are all too aware of the existence of inbuilt biases in pluralist arrangements. 'We typically think of the states as a level of conflict more conducive to business interests, and manufacturing groups do rank among the most influential interest groups in state politics. Environmental groups continue to find it difficult to compete with industrial interests at the state level' (Ringquist, 1993, p. 31). One respondent noted that there were generally five to ten bills a year in the legislature on air quality issues, but: 'In general they tend to go nowhere ... there are little bits and pieces of progress, but in general they're small, isolated and far between' (interview, San Francisco, 12 August 1994).

For all the political difficulties, California has been a global pioneer in the development of air quality management policies. A theme emphasized by many respondents, however, was that there were limits to the extent that technological innovations could keep ahead of the growth in automobile traffic. 'We feel that in order to achieve the standards in the California Clean Air Act, there's no way to do that without radically restructuring how people pay to travel ... however, we do not have the ability to do that here' (interview, San Francisco, 12 August 1994). More radical changes in behaviour might be required, but the political costs of such changes might make them very difficult to secure. In subsequent chapters the policy options available in California will be reviewed.

4. The policy framework

Air quality policy is made at the federal, state and local levels. There is a complex and often conflictual interrelationship between these three levels, further complicated by the fact that none of the levels is a unitary actor and inter-agency disputes and turf fights are common. The federal level passes legislation which imposes requirements and standards on state and local authorities, and provides for the imposition of penalties if these standards are not met. Much of the influence of the federal government derives from its role as a provider of funds for hard pressed state and local governments, and one sanction available at the federal level is to withdraw funds for highway projects if air quality standards are not met. Moreover, 'federal mandates and federal pressure provide state administrators with a lever they can use to pry more money or stronger policy authority from state governors and legislatures' (Ringquist, 1993, pp. 150–51). State- and local-level actors, for example, environmentalists, may attempt to persuade federal agencies to place pressure on other state-level actors. At the state level, California sets standards which go beyond the federal requirements, and which may also be adopted by states elsewhere. Interstate bargaining takes place about whether to adopt California standards. Local Air Quality Management Districts draw up implementation plans, and issue rules and regulations in an effort to achieve their air quality objectives.

FEDERAL LEGISLATION

There are a number of major pieces of legislation at federal level which have a significant impact on air quality policy: the 1970 Clean Air Act (subsequently amended in several years); the 1990 Clean Air Act; the 1991 Intermodal Surface Transportation Act; and the 1992 Energy Policy Act. The 1970 Clean Air Act was a landmark piece of legislation in the effort to clean up America's air, but it was also defective in many respects, and there was a long drawn out battle over the next 20 years to try to remedy those defects:

> The election of George Bush in November 1988 turned out to be the key event in breaking the congressional logjam over clean air. Bush effectively used environmental issues to distance himself from the Reagan administration, since those issues continued to command widespread public support despite President Reagan's hostility to most governmental regulation (Bryner, 1993, pp. 93–4).

Implementation of the 1970 Act was delayed, and its effects reduced, by a series of waivers given to the auto industry in subsequent amending legislation. However: 'One of the successes of the Clean Air Act of 1970 is that it helped to force the development and use of new control technologies such as the catalytic converter for motor vehicles' (Bryner, 1993, p. 131). Under the Act, states were required to produce a State Implementation Plan (SIP) stating how they would meet ambient air quality standards set by the federal EPA. If states failed to produce plans that were approved by the EPA, plans could be imposed on states or particular regions within states. The air quality management plan on the South Coast resulted from the use of this provision by an environmental activist who brought an action in the federal courts, 'charging the administrator of the Environmental Protection Agency with failing to enforce the 1970 Federal Clean Air Act in greater Los Angeles' (Waldman, 1990, p. 80).

The 1990 Clean Air Act is based on the structure of the 1970 Act, but is a highly complex piece of legislation. 'If Title I [on non-attainment] had been passed alone, it would rank as one of the most detailed and complex laws ever enacted by Congress' (Bryner, 1993, p. 123). The Act imposed new, stricter emission standards for motor vehicles and in general 'significantly strengthened' (Ringquist, 1993, p. 51) the provisions of the 1970 legislation. One of the most difficult challenges facing legislators was to balance federal and California standards, higher Californian standards reflecting the fact that: 'Five of the seven areas with the most serious ozone pollution problems in the nation are in California' (Bryner, 1993, p. 150). Before the 1990 Act, only California had been permitted to have higher mobile emissions standards, but the 1990 Act gave states the option of accepting California or federal standards. This development enhanced the importance of California as an agenda-setter in relation to air quality issues.

The 1991 Intermodal Transportation Efficiency Act has been described as, 'an important first step toward more rational transportation planning' (Nadis and MacKenzie, 1993, p. 142). A public transport activist commented in interview on the Act:

> I think that was tremendously important. That was the first time any United States government has shown any vision of what is to come. Whether they actually had any intention of seeing it happen in their lifetime, probably not, but they thought OK, we'll pass this framework and we'll let someone else deal with actually putting it into action (interview, Sacramento, 18 August 1994).

The Act's preamble states that: 'The National Intermodal Transportation System shall consist of all forms of transportation in a unified, interconnected manner, including the transportation systems of the future, to reduce energy consumption and air pollution' (Superintendent of Documents, 1991, 105 Stat. 1914). The Act establishes a surface transportation programme with federal funding for the capital costs of transit projects. The Act provides for the negotiation of full funding grant agreements for the San Francisco Bay Rail Extension Program, and for seven stations and nearly 12 miles of subway extension in Los Angeles. The federal share for a Bay Area Rapid Transit (BART) extension to San Francisco International Airport is set at 75 per cent, while the federal share of the subway extensions in Los Angeles is set at $695 million over the 1993–97 period. Smaller sums of money are provided for improving the Los Angeles–San Diego rail corridor and for improvements relating to the extension of commuter rail service from San Jose through Gilroy to Hollister. Funds are also provided for the preliminary engineering and final design of proposed extensions to the light rail system in Sacramento. In many ways, this is a typical piece of American legislation in which sums of money are split up around the country so that every area with political clout gets a slice of the action. The main deficiency of the Act is that, 'it largely overlooks pricing strategies' failing, 'to give Americans any reason to alter their driving habits, buy alternatively fuelled vehicles, or use more efficient transportation modes' (Nadis and MacKenzie, 1993, pp. 160–61).

The 1992 Energy Policy Act is a wide-ranging measure which includes three sections on alternative fuels and one on electric vehicles. The Act establishes a federal fleet of alternatively fuelled vehicles to reach 10,000 light duty alternative fuelled vehicles in fiscal year 1995. The federal government is authorized to enter into agreements for demonstration projects for alternatively fuelled buses with transit authorities and school districts, setting aside $30 million dollars a year of federal money to fund such programmes. Energy enterprises are required to ensure that their vehicle fleets shall increasingly be made up of alternatively fuelled vehicles, reaching a 90 per cent level of acquisitions by 1999. Less stringent but still demanding requirements are imposed on vehicle fleets outside the energy sector, where 20 per cent of the motor vehicles acquired from 1999 to 2001 have to be powered by alternative fuels, rising to 70 per cent by 2006. Alternative fuels are defined in the Act to include methanol, natural gas and electricity, including the M-85 mixture of methanol with 15 per cent gasoline. It should be noted that there is a discretion given to the federal energy secretary to modify these goals if they are thought not to be economically or technically feasible, giving lobbyists for affected industries an opening at the appropriate time.

There is also provision for an electric motor vehicle commercial demonstration programme to be operated in conjunction with manufacturers and electrical utilities with an appropriation of $50 million over a ten year period. An electric vehicle infrastructure and support systems development programme has been given an allocation of $40 million over five years. While these are not large sums, they do demonstrate a growing federal interest in electric vehicles, while the fleet requirements should help California to achieve its zero- and low-emission vehicle targets.

One omission from the 1990 Clean Air Act was anything relating to global warming, apart from some monitoring of greenhouse gas emissions. The view expressed by American observers was that, 'the scientific consensus concerning the threat posed by CFCs to the ozone layer does not yet exist with regard to global warming' (Bryner, 1993, p. 147). Policy on global warming has developed a new momentum with the advent of the Clinton administration. Clinton reversed the stand of the Bush administration at the Rio summit by committing the United States to reducing emissions to 1990 levels by the year 2000, although it was less clear how this was to be achieved. Clinton's plan, the so-called Clinton Change Action Plan announced in October 1993, relies on voluntary cooperation between federal agencies and industry. Environmental groups were very sceptical about its potential effectiveness. An Environmental Defense Fund greenhouse gases specialist commented: 'The problem is that almost all of the measures are voluntary and there is very little to encourage industry to participate and punish those who don't'. A Greenpeace spokesperson commented: 'It's a repackaging of some old ideas and a few scattered new ones (*Sacramento Bee*, 18 October 1993).

The Federal–State Relationship and Federal Implementation Plans

A failure to meet federal air quality standards can lead to the imposition of a Federal Implementation Plan (FIP). In 1988, following lawsuits originally brought in 1982 by organizations such as the Coalition for Clean Air and the Sierra Club, and subsequent court orders, the EPA disapproved the South Coast ozone and carbon monoxide plans and the Sacramento and Ventura ozone plans (Ventura is to the north of Los Angeles). Following the passage of the 1990 Clean Air Act, the EPA took the view that it would only have to promulgate a FIP if a new set of SIPs designed to meet federal requirements was disapproved. In Coalition for Clean Air, 971 F.2d 219 (9th Cir., 1992) the Ninth Circuit (a federal court) held that despite the 1990 revisions, the EPA was still required to promulgate a FIP within two years of disapproving a SIP. Hence the new section applied retroactively to disapprovals before 1990. The EPA sought and was denied a writ of certiorari to bring the matter before the Supreme Court (113 S.Ct. 1361, 1993). In February 1994, the EPA announced that it was releasing new clean air plans for the South Coast, Ventura and Sacramento. These filled over a thousand pages of the Federal Register in May 1994 (Vol. 59, No. 86, 5 May 1994, 23264-24332).

Apart from illustrating the role of the courts in the decision-making process (albeit it over a 12 year period) this episode also illustrates the reluctance of the EPA to impose solutions on state and local agencies. The documentation issued by the EPA was full of hand-wringing declarations of its reluctance to intervene which it had only done because it had been ordered to do so by the courts. It stated that its goal, 'is to minimize federal intrusion into state and local decision making and implementation authority' while also noting that, 'only prompt action by California officials within the timetables of the CAAA and the court ordered deadlines can significantly diminish the FIP's impact on the state' (EPA, 1994, p. 5). Much was made of, 'the awkwardness of having the federal government undertaking air quality planning for a particular state or locality' (EPA, 1994, p. 10). The EPA considered that state and local agencies should play the lead roles in addressing their own air pollution problems, with the EPA acting as a technical adviser and grant provider and, only as a last resort, as a backstop when state and local responsibilities were not met. In a sentence that drips with reluctance, the EPA admitted: 'It has ... become necessary, both legally and practically, for EPA to play the backstop role at this time' (EPA, 1994, p. 4).

To make things easier for California, the EPA proposed the device of reclassifying Sacramento from a 'serious' to a 'severe' air pollution region which would give it until 2005 instead of 1999 to come into compliance with ozone standards. The FIP did, however, contain some unpleasant surprises for some sections of the community. In particular, it placed substantial restrictions on heavy-duty engines and diesel fuel, with one regulation restricting out-of-state truckers to one stop in the smoggy areas and two in California as a whole. The truckers promptly hired the political consulting firm Woodward/McDowell to protect their interests (*California Journal Weekly*, 18 July 1994). United Parcels Services complained in public hearings that the rules would cost the firm thousands of jobs despite its attempts to develop truck fleets powered by compressed natural gas and air fleets that exceed federal standards ahead of deadlines (*Sacramento Bee* 26 July 1994).

In September 1994 Governor Wilson wrote to President Clinton asking him to delay implementation of the FIP scheduled for February 1995 for at least 18 months to avoid the crippling of freight movements in the state and the loss of 165,000 jobs. In October, he asked the Air Resources Board to initiate a comprehensive economic impact study of the state's counter proposals, noting that this might prevent the state from meeting the November deadline for delivery of the SIP. These moves were in large part political ones made in the context of the election campaign for Governor as a response to heavy criticism of the FIP by business interests. Nevertheless, the EPA acknowledges that its plan would cost the state $4 billion to $6 billion annually for full implementation in 2010. The targets are such that they are almost impossible to achieve:

> While the emission reduction targets in Sacramento and Ventura are formidable, the overwhelming reductions needed for ozone attainment in the South Coast appear to require each individual pollution source within the FIP area eventually abate its emissions almost completely. For practically every source category, this ultimate degree of control is beyond a level now forseeable with existing technology and control techniques (EPA, 1994, p. 13).

The EPA and the state are caught between a rock and a hard place in attempting to enforce federal law in a way required by the courts. Putting to one side the considerable economic cost of the proposals, in many respects both the FIP and the SIP are based on wish lists about what might be technologically feasible in the future. For example, the SIP assumes that cleaner-running engines will go a long way to bringing California into compliance by the turn of the century. It assumes that by 2002 engineers will have designed heavy-duty diesel truck engines that run twice as cleanly as today's diesel engines.

Governor Wilson appeared before a congressional committee in February 1995 to plead California's case, but the EPA indicated that they found the state plan largely acceptable. In particular, the EPA approved a section of the plan which required the statewide use of reformulated (oxygenated) gasoline from 1996. 'The extra dose of oxygen makes combustion more complete thus reducing emissions of carbon monoxide and unburned hydrocarbons' (Nadis and MacKenzie, 1993, p. 62). It was somewhat optimistically claimed that the use of this fuel could reduce emissions from vehicles by as much as thirty per cent. In any event, a federal judge, acting at the EPA's request, postponed implementation of the federal plan until February 1997. It was also thought to be more than likely that the Republican controlled Congress would pass a short piece of legislation exempting the afflicted counties from federal requirements.

In the case of the court-imposed FIP, the EPA office in San Francisco has adopted a cooperative attitude, seeking to work with state executive agencies and legislators to find a solution. As a later case study of the smog check dispute will show, federal–state relations in relation to air pollution can be more complex and conflictual.

Interstate Bargaining

The 1990 Clean Air Act offers states the option of settling for federal standards or the higher California ones. This sets the scene for a complex process of interstate bargaining. Given that summer smog can drift for hundreds of miles, and cars often move across state boundaries, there is a clear incentive for states located in a particular region to cooperate in adopting common regulations. In practice, however, cooperation is made difficult by variations in legislative and rule adoption procedures from one state to another; different balances of political interests from one state to another; the ability of auto and oil industry interests to exploit these differences to split particular states away from an emerging coalition; and the fact that any agreements arrived at may be open to challenge in the courts.

The group of states with the strongest incentive to cooperate are the northeastern states where the ozone problem is at its worst outside California. This region has a population of sixty million and an estimated thirty million cars. Twelve states from Maine to Virginia (plus the District of Columbia) have sought to cooperate, and have made some progress. However, the process has not been without its difficulties which is not surprising when it is considered that some two thousand state legislators are involved in the decision-making process.

Much of the momentum that has been achieved is the result of the efforts of technical experts, reinforcing the notion of the importance of 'advocacy coalitions' in air pollution policy. A particularly important role in the development of policy proposals has been played by a group called the Northeast States for Coordinated Air Use Management, made up of air pollution control officers from New England, New York and New Jersey. In 1989 it coordinated a regional plan to require oil companies to supply low pollution fuel in the summer, overcoming opposition from the oil companies and, initially, from the EPA. It also drew up a report on how the adoption of the California rules could meet the requirements of the 1990 Clean Air Act. Efforts by states to take joint action have also been supported by the State and Territorial Air Pollution Program Administrators and the Association of Local Air Pollution Control Officers. The executive director of both organizations has taken the view that states have to take joint action on their own because there is insufficient guidance from Washington. Waiting for regulations from the EPA was, 'the air-quality equivalent of waiting for Godot' (*New York Times*, 29 April 1992).

A framework for action by the northeastern states has been provided by the interstate Ozone Transportation Commission, an entity established under the Clean Air Act which has the authority to recommend changes to the administrator of the EPA. This process has not been without its delays and difficulties, and it was only in October 1993 that the states decided to draft a formal petition to the EPA asking it to apply California standards in the eastern states. One of the major obstacles has been securing the support of Connecticut, a state located in the centre of the region, where all administrative regulators are subject to veto by a legislative committee, giving state legislators a greater degree of power to block the rule-making process than in other states. An even greater obstacle seems to have been the Governor, Lowell P. Weicker Jnr, who was a maverick Republican senator before being elected Governor of Connecticut as an independent. In November 1991, he announced that the state would not accept strict new standards on automobile emissions, although he also said that he might change his mind in the light of new evidence. If Connecticut adhered to this policy, it would undermine the regional initiative, as a car registered in Connecticut could be bought more cheaply than one in New York as it would not have the additional equipment required to reduce emissions.

The auto manufacturers have responded to the prospect of more stringent air quality regulations in one of the most populated regions of the United States on three fronts. Lobbying efforts at the state level were intensified, but, 'lobbying Washington is often easier than lobbying every capitol building from Annapolis to Augusta' (*New York Times*, 21 July 1991). Secondly, actions have been launched in the courts with mixed results. A federal district court judge in Syracuse, New York, ruled in large part in favour of the car manufacturers who argued that the California rules should not be adopted. However, later in 1993 a federal judge in Boston ruled that Massachusetts could adopt California's emission standards. The contradictory decisions could mean that the federal appeals court will rule on the matter rather sooner than might otherwise have been the case, and they also increase pressure on the parties to come to a negotiated settlement. Thirdly, the auto manufacturers offered that if the northeastern states drop their demands for California rules, they would sell vehicles that are cleaner than federal rules require, although not as clean as California requires. The car makers would phase in cleaner-running gasoline cars between 2001 and 2003, but would not make a proportion of zero-emission or electric vehicles as the California rules require, a development to which the car manufacturers have been strongly resistant on commercial grounds (See Chapter 5).

In February 1994, despite intensive lobbying by domestic automobile manufacturers, the Ozone Transportation Commission, having decided that the auto industry's alternative proposals fell short of desired targets for reducing pollution, voted by nine to four to adopt California's stringent emission standards. The California standards will thus be extended by 1999 to an area accounting in the mid-1990s for one-fifth of the vehicles sold in the nation.

POLICY DEVELOPMENT AND IMPLEMENTATION AT THE STATE AND LOCAL LEVEL

The institutions concerned with the development and implementation of air quality management policy in California have been described in Chapter 3, notably the Air Resources Board and the Air Quality Management Districts. The basic legislative framework for air pollution policy in California is provided by the Sher Act, the 1988 California Clean Air Act. In this section the focus is on the development of plans within the framework of the California legislation by the Air Quality Management Districts on the South Coast and in Sacramento.

They are operations on a very different scale. The South Coast District has nearly a thousand staff and operates from new buildings on a hill near a freeway in one of the parts of the Los Angeles metropolitan area where it is still possible to see cows grazing. The complex incorporates extensive laboratory facilities, and is generally well equipped, leading to some references to it as 'the pollution palace'.

The Sacramento District operates from a rather cramped set of low rise buildings scattered among light industry and offices near a light rail station on the outskirts of Sacramento. It has a staff of about eighty. Whereas the South Coast District has developed and implemented an extensive set of regulations, the Sacramento District was still developing its regulations at the time of the study, anticipating that the first ones would be in place in 1994. 'If you really had to boil down what we do to one descriptor, it would be public education. Everything we do to date has been related to trying to educate and influence somehow or other' (interview, Sacramento Air Quality Management District, 7 September 1993).

Possibly because it has fewer regulatory powers in place, the Sacramento District appears to have relied more on coalition-building in the local community. For example, the District's plan refers to a local citizen's organization, the Cleaner Air Partnership, as a means of, 'increasing the public's awareness of the air pollution problem in Sacramento, as well as providing insight on public attitudes on transportation control programs' (Sacramento Air Quality Management District, 1991, p. I-5.15). There was some evidence from the interviews that the Cleaner Air Partnership was used by District staff to mobilize support in the community in relation to matters being discussed at forthcoming board meetings of the Air Quality District. This evidence of policy sophistication is also reflected in the interesting and innovative policy initiatives to be found in the Sacramento District's plans. Because many of these plans have yet to be tested in practice, the following discussion will nevertheless focus to a considerable extent on the work on the South Coast Air Quality Management District.

The South Coast Air Quality Management Plan

In 1989, after five years of work, the South Coast Air Quality Management District and the Southern California Association of Governments (SCAG) adopted an Air Quality Management Plan designed to achieve federal air quality standards. It was claimed that the plan, 'laid out the most aggressive schedule for new rules seen in the history of air pollution control in Southern California' (Air Quality Plan, 1991, p. ES-1). However, the California Clean Air Act required all polluted air basins in the state to develop new plans to meet state as well as federal standards. Work thus begun on updating the plan, which appeared in a new version in 1991.

The plan is a thick document made up of ten substantial chapters, plus appendices which are even larger, such as that dealing with transportation and land use control measures. In January 1992, the South Coast District issued its rules and regulations amounting to 1500 pages. The regulations specify, for example, when it is permissible to have an open fire to burn Russian thistle, the procedures to be followed for the refuelling of chain saws and the way in which dry cleaning establishments may be operated. There is some willingness to modify these rules in response to public reaction, although some would argue that the District is particularly susceptible to business pressure. Rule 403 relating to fugitive dust from construction required, 'the removal of particulate matter from equipment prior to movement on paved streets', but after affronted hard-hats mounted a candle light vigil at District headquarters, the District granted concessions. The regulations are certainly comprehensive, although enforcing regulations relating to a wide variety of individual sources is another matter. The District has stringently imposed penalties on stationary source polluters, with almost 90 per cent of its budget coming from fines and fees for emissions violations (Waldman, 1991, p. 80). The South Coast District has been criticized for some of the ways it has used its budget, for example buying ten electrically assisted bicycles for the city of Monrovia at $13,943 each (*Sacramento Bee*, 3 February 1994).

Efforts to regulate barbecue grills and lawn mowers attracted national attention, and although open to ridicule, may have served the useful function of bringing home the seriousness of the problems that Southern California faced. The essence of the plan, however, is centred around three phases or tiers, with control measures assigned to each tier on the basis of their control method and implementation date. Tier 1 calls for 132 measures to limit and reduce pollutants from varied sources, although 35 of these may be changed by the adoption of a trading programme. All rules included under Tier 1 are scheduled to be adopted by 1999, and can be accomplished with existing technology. Tier 2 measures are expected to be adopted over the next ten to 15 years, taking the plan into the 21st century. It covers additional pollution reduction measures that rely on breakthrough technologies including ultra-low emission cars and low polluting paints. Tier 3 relies on technology that hasn't yet been fully developed, but is thought to be on the horizon. For example, it is hoped that coatings that dry virtually pollution-free under ultra-violet light will be available by the year 2010.

The Relationship with Business Interests

The South Coast District has been criticized by environmentalists for being over-sensitive to business interests. It has been claimed that, 'there is a large body of evidence that, far from being hard on business, the District has treated business with kid gloves' (Schwartz, 1992, not pagenated). The Coalition for Clean Air claims that this has led to a weakening of air pollution control efforts, and the postponement of rule implementation:

> It seems that business people have nothing to worry about when it comes to the Air District. They aren't enforcing the rules on the books and they're issuing new ones at a glacial pace. Most District Board hearings turn out more than a hundred people from business and local government along with a few representatives from environmental groups. The industry representatives usually testify that passing this or that rule will send Southern California into an economic tailspin. Generally, they get some concessions from the Governing Board (Schwartz, 1992, not pagenated).

The postponement of the rule on pleasure boat refuelling or those on pool heaters or livestock waste may not represent a major dent in the air quality management programme, but a more general consideration is that the South Coast District has to maintain a difficult political balancing act between the requirements of federal and state law, and environmental pressures on the one hand; and business pressures and what is acceptable to public opinion on the other. There are political forces in Southern California that would like to undermine the work of the Air Quality District:

> There is a sort of rebellion growing with some of the more conservative members, especially down in Orange County which is a bastion of conservatism. There are a lot of pieces of legislation now that would restrict or roll back some of the powers of the air districts, especially the [South Coast District]. They think that they've gone too far in their plan ... Some of the members from Orange County are seeking to curtail the powers of the board, especially as it relates to what employers are required to do ... This is a group of legislators that's very close to the business community and they think that a lot of these prescriptions are onerous for the business community (interview, Senate legislative aide, Sacramento, 30 March 1993).

The South Coast District and Local Government

Apart from coping with these political challenges to its authority and operations, the South Coast District faces a structural division of responsibility for implementation between itself and local government. Before explaining this division, some comments are necessary on local government in contemporary California. The state has a confused patchwork of multi purpose and single purpose authorities with overlapping territorial and functional jurisdictions which has been compared to the arrangements that would be devised 'by a child on LSD' (*The Economist*, 13 February 1993). Before the passage of Proposition 13, local government relied on property tax as its main source of revenue, but since then it has become increasingly dependent on subventions by a state government which is itself strapped for cash, and which has transferred the administration of important programmes to local government without fully funding them. Thus during 1993, Los Angeles, for example, 'had a $500 million deficit on its nearly $2 billion budget' (Lamare, 1994, p. 250). Local governments therefore have a predisposition in favour of growth, because it may yield new tax revenues which improve their fiscal position, and they are often interested in using air quality control measures as a new means of raising revenue, so that a secondary policy objective replaces the primary one. Thus in Los Angeles, the Traffic Reduction and Improvement Programme requires developers to pay a fee for each unmitigated afternoon peak hour trip generated by the project, which could be as much as $6 000 per trip (Wachs, 1990, p. 246). Displacement of policy objectives may well occur:

> Cynics have alleged that the real purpose of these programs is to increase revenue flows into public coffers for street, highway and transit programs which have recently experienced fiscal shortages ... If the programs are really motivated by fiscal purposes alone, achievement of the promised congestion reductions may be less important to the framers of the programs than the collection of revenue (Wachs, 1990, p. 255).

Land Use Planning

Local governments are also likely to be very jealous of their prerogatives in the area of land use planning, which is one of the most important tasks they undertake. 'Development plans, zoning cases, urban redevelopment schemes and annexation efforts often stir passionate debate among affected groups ... These issues frequently become highly contentious in California's local politics' (Lamare, 1994, p. 251).

Some of the interests associated with local government, such as developers and marketers of real estate, have a strong stake in further growth, while other groups, such as homeowners' associations, have an interest in slowing down growth and seeing that if growth takes place, it does so in a way that they find acceptable. Despite their importance in Californian politics, homeowners' associations, 'remain largely a *terra incognita*, neglected by urban historians and sociologists alike' (Davis, 1990, p. 160). By pushing for low density developments, homeowners' associations have encouraged a pattern of development that is both inhospitable to public transport and leads to long commutes by car and extensive travel for shopping and recreation. High density developments near train stations in Los Angeles would help to encourage commuting by rail, but this is exactly the kind of development that is likely to be opposed by homeowners' associations.

Historically, local government has been responsible for the implementation of transport and land use measures. 'Successful implementation of the strategies depends on the level of commitment and action by local governments' (Air Quality Plan appendix, 1991, p. I-l). The 1988 Clean Air Act does, however, require the regional government to develop a plan for emissions from transport sources. If the Air Quality District disapproves the plan, it returns it to the regional government for review and, if it is still not satisfied, the District can enforce an alternative plan for transport control, including strategies to reduce vehicle trips, vehicle use, vehicle miles travelled, vehicle idling or traffic congestion.

The Relationship between the South Coast District and the Southern California Association of Governments

In practice, the South Coast Air Management District is involved in a difficult negotiating relationship with SCAG which is based on a formal memorandum of understanding. The difficulties that can arise because of shared responsibilities are illustrated by the management of traffic congestion. Local governments can be certified to undertake congestion management measures such as parking management, traffic flow improvements and high occupancy vehicle lanes. SCAG has to determine that all programmes in the Congestion Management Plan are consistent with the Regional Mobility Plan that it has adopted, and that the programmes of the various counties are compatible with one another. The various measures developed by SCAG which seek to reduce air pollution involve close cooperation with the air quality management district. Hence there are three sets of authorities involved in congestion management: the South Coast Air Quality Management District, SCAG and the cities and counties.

The relationship between the South Coast District and SCAG has not been without its difficulties. SCAG has had to share tasks which were previously its own sole responsibility with the District, although SCAG emphasizes that it is a comprehensive planning agency, while the District is single purpose (Waldman, 1991, p. 81). The memorandum of understanding, 'gives SCAG the lead role in working with local government to implement relevant portions of the plan' (Waldman, 1991, p. 81). Even so, tensions clearly arise in areas of overlapping responsibility. In a letter written on 12 June 1991 to the executive director of the South Coast District, the executive director of SCAG commented:

> Regarding potential overlap, including the District's proposed indirect source rules, the SCAG Executive Committee action is that the District, SCAG and local governments work together to resolve any potential overlap, not that the District automatically 'assume the lead'.

District staff estimate that growth management, with its emphasis on modifying development patterns and land uses, would by 2010 eliminate one-third of the congestion expected from the trend forecast. Respect for the prerogatives of local government in the area of land use is reflected in the fact that the South Coast District's plan contains 22 transport measures and one land use measure. The Sacramento air quality attainment plan emphasizes:

> Cities and counties regulate land-uses; air districts regulate the emissions associated with those land-uses ... air districts simply exercise concurrent jurisdiction with local government, and cannot infringe upon the existing authority of cities and counties to regulate land-uses (Sacramento Air Quality Management District, 1991, p. I-5.19).

The Sacramento plan proposes the use of the California Environmental Quality Act and the National Environmental Policy Act to evaluate new projects for significant adverse air quality impacts. The South Coast District has already commented on one major development project considered to have adverse air quality impacts.

In the South Coast plan, the one land use measure (Measure 17) is intended to obtain reductions in vehicle miles travelled. A number of possible steps are identified, such as encouraging housing development in job-rich subregions and reducing housing construction limitations in job-rich areas, while locating new public facilities in job-poor subregions. While local governments are to be encouraged to amend general plans, adopt ordinances and perform conformity review for regionally significant projects during Tier 1, much of the work is scheduled for Tier 2 or the next century with full implementation by 2010. This includes the definition of the strategies for the reduction of vehicle miles travelled and the development of enforceable commitments by local governments.

In practice, the main action to be taken in Tier 1 is the formation of an Advisory Working Group co-staffed by the South Coast District, SCAG and the Air Resources Board, and with representation from local governments, county transportation commissions, environmental organizations and industry. This Advisory Working Group, which comes close to being a general assembly of the policy community, will be expected to, 'identify quantifiable control strategies and an enforceable mechanism to accomplish the targeted emission reductions, recommend enforceable local implementation commitments, and identify potential legislation' (Air Quality Plan appendix, 1991, p. I-257).

If there are difficulties in the horizontal relationship between the South Coast District and SCAG, there are at least as great tensions in the relationship between SCAG and the six counties and considerable number of cities (88 in Los Angeles County alone) within its jurisdiction:

> ... regional bodies lack legal authority to impose upon local governments, land owners, employers and real estate developers the requirement that they redirect the location of new development or mandate transit and carpool use by their citizens and tenants ... If past experience is indicative of public attitudes, the absence of clear authority to impose such programs on local governments will make it extremely difficult to implement them (Wachs, 1990, p. 244).

Although SCAG is responsible as a regional planning agency for a number of state and federally mandated planning functions, it remains a voluntary association of governments with a small staff in relation to the range of its tasks. It also has to cope with the dual and potentially conflictual role of leader and coordinator. 'In its leadership role, SCAG, in cooperation with local jurisdictions, develops transportation and land use control strategies for these jurisdictions to implement; as a coordinator, SCAG facilitates the implementation of these strategies' (Air Quality Plan, 1991, p. 1-1).

Although the plans for air quality management place considerable emphasis on a variety of joint working groups between the South Coast District and SCAG as a means of resolving implementation problems: 'The focus for successful implementation of most land use and transportation strategies is on local government' (Air Quality Plan appendix, 1991, p. I-4). One strategy that has been pursued by the South Coast District is to develop direct links with local government bodies. The Interagency Air Quality Management Plan Implementation Committee provides a mechanism for coordination between key local government entities and the South Coast District. It is made up of 24 members representing local government, transport agencies, water districts and sanitation districts. The South Coast District also offers support to local governments by commenting on the adequacy of the air quality analysis offered as part of the environmental impact document required under the California Environmental Quality Act. 'Through commenting and the suggestion of mitigation measures the District has the opportunity to apply some of the control strategies in the AQMP earlier than anticipated, on a project-by-project basis' (Air Quality Plan, 1991, p. 7–50).

The Problem of Limited Resources: The Example of Airports

There are many areas of potential activity, however, where even the resources available to the South Coast District are insufficient to allow much progress in the development and monitoring of policy. Airports in the Los Angeles area are a significant source of pollution, both in terms of ground movements at the airport itself, and the attraction of the airport as a magnet for vehicular traffic for travellers, greeters and airport and airline staff. The implementation of earlier aviation-related control measures, 'has met with little success' (Air Quality Plan appendix, 1991, p. I-160). It is planned to implement by 1995 a rule which would require permits for airport facilities. To receive a permit, an airport operator would have to prepare a plan for reducing emissions from aircraft and ground support vehicles at the airport. The greater part of emissions originate, however, from passengers travelling to and from the airport. A permit system would again be put in place, and airport operators would be responsible for developing a ground access plan. However, airports have budgets which are constrained by federal legislation and contractual arrangements, limiting their ability to participate in ground access projects. Hence: 'The cooperation of surrounding local jurisdictions in the preparation and implementation of each airport's ground access plan will be essential to the ultimate acceptability and viability of these plans' (Air Quality Plan appendix, 1991, p. I-181).

The timetable envisaged adoption of the relevant rules by 1992 for implementation in 1995, but adoption of the rules has been postponed until 1995. When the issue of airports was raised in interviews at the South Coast District, the researcher was told:

> We've got one fellow who basically is just working specifically on airports. The concept that we're looking at now at airports is to take all the activities of an airport, take a look at all the emissions, and then figure out what we can address mostly (interview, Diamond Bar, 1 April 1993).

In other words, the South Coast District has to priortize its tasks in the light of the resources available to it, and the likelihood of accomplishing real progress in a given area of activity. It then has to assess the priority steps that appear to be most effective in reducing emissions from a particular type of source. Although the plan itself provides a timetable of activities, these have to be modified in the light of what is attainable, given available resources and political constraints. A comprehensive plan is thus implemented in a way that is more incremental in practice.

REGULATION XV: TRIP REDUCTION

Downs notes (1992, p. 64): 'The most effective means of reducing peak-hour congestion would be to persuade solo drivers to share vehicles'. Under Regulation XV and Rule 1501 of the South Coast District employers with more than 100 employees at any place of work must develop and implement trip reduction programmes to reduce emissions from vehicles driven for work-related trips. A similar rule, but with a number of distinctive innovative features of its own, is being developed by the Sacramento Air Quality Management District.

In Los Angeles, an average vehicle ridership (AVR) is calculated by dividing the number of employees reporting for work in working hours (6 a.m. to 10 a.m. Monday to Friday) by the number of vehicles driven by these employees over the working week. If there are 300 employees reporting for work each day, and they drive 1 327 commute vehicles over the week, the AVR is 1 500 divided by 1 327 which equals 1.13, a not untypical figure for the region. AVR targets are set which are 1.75 in the downtown area, 1.5 in intermediate areas and 1.3 in outer areas. This compares with an average peak load factor of cars in London of 1.2 (Transport Committee, 1994, p. x).

While the implementation of Regulation XV began in 1988, Sacramento's regulation was still at the proposal stage in 1993, but this later start allowed the Sacramento District to learn from experience elsewhere, and to propose some modifications of its own. Instead of the AVR, Sacramento uses the VER (vehicle-employee ratio) standard adopted by the Bay Area AQMD. 'The use of VER represents certain mathematical advantages over AVR. To improve VER it must be decreased which presents an important, and perhaps easier to understand, connection to the reduction of vehicle trips; reduction of congestion; and the reduction of emissions' (Sacramento Air Quality Management District, 1993, p. 4). The proposed Sacramento target is a VER of 0.71 which is equivalent to an AVR of 1.40 and represents 71 vehicles per hundred employees. These requirements can be met in part by credits accumulated elsewhere, for example, by voluntarily implementing emissions reduction programmes that are not required by another District rule.

Trip reduction plans in Los Angeles have to include a list of specific incentives to be provided by the employer to the employee, and a schedule for their implementation which can reasonably be expected to lead to achievement and maintenance of the target AVR level within 12 months of plan approval. Examples of ways to increase AVR suggested by the South Coast District include direct financial incentives for ridesharing; full or partial subsidization of carpools or use of public transport; preferential parking for ridesharing vehicles; facilities to encourage the use of bicycles; compressed work week programmes; and telecommuting. Each employer has to designate one staff member to be the programme coordinator who then has to take part in a training programme.

When the South Coast District asked if it was pleased with the results being achieved, the answer was:

> In terms of the accomplishment – I'm going to say a qualified yes ... over the four year period of time we've moved from a 1.14 AVR baseline for those who've submitted their baseline data to 1.3 something. While it hasn't achieved the goal, it's got about 35 per cent of the goal achieved in a relatively short period of time (interview, South Coast Air Quality Management District, 1 April 1993).

It was thought that progress had been hindered by original goals that were unrealistic:

> I think that we made a very bad strategic mistake at the District when politically we said these plans had to achieve 1.5 AVR in the first year. You're not going to change a significant number of people's behaviour in the first year and that was an unrealistic goal. If we would have said 1.2, 1.3, 1.4 each year, you would have had people saying this is achievable, this is worth purusing. By setting such an unattainable goal in the first year, setting expectations so high, many people say 'well see, it didn't work' (interview, South Coast Air Quality Management District, 1 April 1993).

The measure is a process rather than a performance-based measure. Plans are submitted for approval every two years, with survey data on progress being submitted in the intervening year. If the plan is not approved, it has to be re-submitted, with a re-submission fee being paid. It should be noted that there has been a high level of compliance enforcement activity by the South Coast District. Hundreds of firms have been fined for failing to submit a plan, $150,000 in the case of a large retailing firm, with total fines amounting to $2 million by June

1992. Some 260 work sites have been audited to see whether they were complying with Regulation XV (figures from Guiliano, Hwang and Wachs, 1992, p. 4). A performance-based rule might have been more effective, but would have been politically difficult to achieve:

> I always wonder what would have happened if the District had decided to embark on a performance-based rule. It would have said you must achieve this performance this year, this performance next year, this performance that year and then assess penalties for failure to achieve that. Whether politically we could have sold that, I doubt, but maybe the achievement would have been more significant (interview, South Coast Air Quality Management District, 1 April 1993).

Trip reduction schemes have traditionally focused on the commuting trip. This is understandable because it is concentrated in peak hours when higher congestion may lead to higher levels of pollution, and it can also be addressed through measures which operate through employer compliance. However, in Sacramento, the commute segment is estimated to be less than 15 per cent of all trips on the transport system (Sacramento Air Quality Management District, 1993, p. V-3.2) In Los Angeles: 'Commuters are about 25 per cent of the traffic, and this programme covers about one-third of the commuters' (interview information, South Coast Air Quality Management District, 1 April 1993). Only employers with more than 100 employees at any one work site are required to file a plan, a work site being defined as a site under the control of an employer that is not separated by more than one public thoroughfare. Although employers are allowed to aggregate sites located within half a mile of each other to produce a composite plan: 'Some employers would prefer not to do that because they don't have to comply with the rule' (interview information, South Coast Air Quality Management District, 1 April 1993). Practical problems have arisen over the treatment of construction sites, and over the treatment of temporary agency employees at all types of site.

The long-term trend is for work trips to decline as a proportion of all trips. The freeways in Los Angeles are congested throughout the day, and, 'non-work trips are the most rapidly increasing component of peak hour traffic' (Guiliano and Wachs, 1992, p. 13). The Sacramento plan uses the acronym 'GRACIE' to distinguish six travel markets – goods movement; recreation; activity centre (for example, hotels); commercial (for example, retail centres); institutional (schools, hospitals); and employment. In Los Angeles:

> The state requires the air basin to achieve a 1.5 average vehicle ridership
> and that's for all traffic, not just commute traffic, so we're going to have to
> be looking at what we do with shopping centres, with courts, with hospi-
> tals, with airports, to achieve that traffic goal ... There are many compo-
> nents to it and we're not going to be able to achieve clean air with just
> focusing on Regulation XV. But I think that working with employers, and
> particularly with larger employers, was the best first step to take (interview,
> South Coast Air Quality Management District, 1 April 1993).

While an incremental approach may be more feasible, a truly effective
trip reduction programme would ultimately have to address all types of
vehicular travel for whatever purpose. However, any marginal reduction in congestion that is achieved may be offset by other motorists
joining the traffic stream to replace those who have been induced to
leave, causing congestion and air pollution levels to rise again.

Research on Regulation XV's first year results concluded that the
regulation had made ridesharing incentives more widely available to
commuters in Los Angeles, and that the ridesharing market for long-
distance commuters with moderate incomes and/or limited vehicle access could be exploited relatively easily (Guiliano, Hwang and Wachs,
1992). There was considerable variation in the extent to which employment sites were meeting the requirements of the regulation, and it is
encouraging that the greatest improvement was found among employers whose initial AVRs were the lowest. There is evidence of a certain
amount of token or minimal compliance by companies: 'Most companies want to comply with the least amount of corporate effort and
without deep commitments to achieving the goals of the program'
(Wachs, 1990, p. 254). Wachs and Guiliano (1992, p. 427) conclude:

> Regulation XV is a new program imposed on an unenthusiastic clientele by
> a centralized regulatory organization. The regulated community, not sur-
> prisingly, appears to be devoting as few financial and personnel resources
> to program implementation as possible, while retaining a healthy skepticism
> of the regulating body.

The way in which Regulation XV has been operated has been relatively
demanding of administrative resources, reflecting a centralized regulatory style:

> What we found we needed was a lot of data collection capability to cover
> 5 500 work sites in the air basin, at one time it was 6 200 before the
> economy had a recession. That's an awful lot of file space, an awful lot of

people opening envelopes and trying to track dates (interview, South Coast Air Quality Management District, 1 April 1993).

The Sacramento District has decided not to require employers to submit programme documentation to the District, but to have documentation available about the strategies being followed. Site visits will take place to ensure that the strategies are in place, and there will be a random sample-based audit procedure. Larger employers will be allowed to conduct random sample surveys of their employees rather than mandatory comprehensive surveys, thus helping to reduce implementation costs.

The relative failure of the South Coast trip reduction scheme was acknowledged in November 1994 when the District's board voted to ease the regulatory burden imposed on employers by cutting back on the programme. The programme had achieved only 1.31 riders per vehicle, compared with the goal of 1.5, while emissions had been reduced by less than half the level sought. One member of the board commented, 'We tried to push the state of art with this strategy and we failed. Now we need a new approach.' (*Sacramento Bee*, 20 November 1994). Alternative measures being favoured included exhaust monitoring devices in company car parks and the encouragement of company programmes to buy and scrap high polluting cars owned by employees.

The Relative Effectiveness of Different Trip Reduction Methods

There is a wide range of trip reduction methods available. Downs observes (1992, p. 70).

> Many people drive to work alone because they are able to park free. The amount they save from free parking is often much greater than the gasoline costs of commuting ... Raising parking costs would be most effective in reducing peak-hour solo commuting where public transit services were readily available. But even if no nearby public transit existed, higher parking costs would surely encourage more ride sharing.

Unfortunately, the most effective methods are often those that encounter the greatest resistance. 'The single most effective measure that an employer can do is to charge for parking. That's politically untenable' (interview, South Coast Air Quality Management, 1 April 1993). 'Charging for parking leads to an "over my dead body" reaction' (interview, Sacramento Air Quality Management District, 7 September 1993).

Employer-paid parking offers a hidden subsidy to employees which encourages solo driving. United States tax rules classify an employer's payment for parking as a tax-free fringe benefit, but if the employee pays for parking, it cannot be deducted from the individual's tax liability. Analysis of a large-scale survey of commuters in Los Angeles has shown that the average variable cost of driving to work (vehicle operating cost plus parking cost) was $6.22 a day if the driver paid for parking, and only $2.35 if the employer paid for parking:

> Employer-paid parking thus reduced the average variable cost of driving to work from $6.22 to $2.35 a day, or by 62 per cent. Everyone would call it an environmental outrage if an employer offered all employees free gasoline as a subsidy for driving to work, but employer-paid parking provided these commuters an even bigger subsidy for driving to work (Shoup, 1994, p. 2).

Advocates of cashing out employer-paid parking argue that employers who subsidize employee parking should be required to offer employees the option to take a taxable cash travel allowance equal to the value of the parking subsidy. Evidence from case studies and a statistical model suggests that this would reduce solo driving to work by 20 per cent and lead to substantial reductions in carbon dioxide emissions (Shoup, 1992). In the Bay Area, a survey of 3 200 commuters in 1994 found that of the 79 per cent who said they had free parking at work, 72.7 per cent drove alone, but that figure dropped to 39.7 per cent for the 21 per cent without free parking at work.

State legislation in the form of AB 2109 (Katz) which was based on research carried out by Shoup required that employers of more than 50 persons in air basins designated as 'nonattainment' areas who provide a parking subsidy to employees must offer a parking cashout programme. There are some practical problems with implementing this legislation when employers have some parking spaces which they own and lease others from a variety of private operators at a wide range of prices which could in turn mean that employees would receive variable cash payments.

In any case, the legislation is not being implemented:

> It is not being implemented because the state Air Resources Board has failed to use implementing guidance ... It has to do with the Wilson administration's view that any sort of pricing is a bad thing, so we have legislation, but we don't have guidance to implement it, basically nothing will happen to put it into effect (interview, air quality official, 12 August 1994).

One innovative measure, telecommuting has attracted particular attention. Telecommuting involves either working from home or from a satellite 'telecommuting' office centre, typically for one working day a week. Within the Los Angeles area, there are a dozen satellite telecommuting centres on the periphery of the metropolis, usually supported by a mixture of government grants and private investment.

Although telecommuting was given a big boost in Los Angeles by the disruption to the freeway system resulting from the 1994 Northridge earthquake, it is still the exception rather than the rule. The South Coast District database shows that less than 10 per cent of the employers covered are using telecommuting as a form of trip reduction incentive, and in terms of participation they are covering less than 1 per cent of the employees. The District database may, however, underestimate the extent of telecommuting, as most of those who do telecommute work for smaller businesses which are not subject to Regulation XV. Across the United States, 95 per cent of regular employees who telecommute work for small or medium-sized businesses (*Independent on Sunday*, 20 February 1994). It might have been thought that it would be large employers who would be more likely to experiment with new working practices. Their concepts of supervision rely, however, on the amount of time employees can be seen working, rather than what they actually accomplish:

> Unfortunately in a lot of the bigger organizations the bureaucratic mind set is if I see John in the office, I know he's productive, but if I don't see John I know he's screwing around. Therefore I need to see John to know he's working … Smaller employers tend to be a little less bureaucratic (interview, Diamond Bar, 1 April 1993).

MARKET-BASED INITIATIVES

As noted earlier, Regulation XV has been applied in the manner of traditional, 'top down' regulation with carefully specified rules focused on process rather than outcome, with penalties for a failure to meet filing requirements. The Air Quality Management Districts have, however, been influenced by the increased emphasis on the use of market-based incentives, or market mimicking mechanisms, as a means of achieving environmental policy goals. As the South Coast District has noted:

Adoption and implementation of source-specific rules is often a laborious struggle between the regulatory agency, the regulated industry, and the public ... Although air quality goals can be met through traditional rules and regulations, market-based approaches can reduce compliance costs, allow greater compliance flexibility, and stimulate technological innovation (South Coast Air Quality Management District, 1992a, pp. 1–2).

Stationary Sources of Pollution and the RECLAIM Programme

Although the emphasis in this book is on vehicular sources of pollution, some discussion of stationary sources is desirable, both to set the context for the policy measures being taken in the mobile sources area, and to draw attention to the policy innovations occurring in relation to stationary sources. Although there is a modest national secondary market in sulphur dioxide allowances run by the Chicago Board of Trade, the South Coast District has created in Los Angeles the first 'smog market' in the United States, allowing companies to buy and sell pollution credits.

RECLAIM is an acronym for the Regional Clean Air Incentives Market. After three years of discussion, RECLAIM was adopted by the South Coast District board in October 1993 for introduction in January 1994. Originally envisaged as covering 2 000 emitters of reactive organic gases and 700 emitters of nitrogen oxides (South Coast Air Quality Management District (Technology Advancement Office), 1992b, p. 3), the scheme adopted covers 387 businesses that are considered major sources of air pollution. Each of them emits more than four tons of nitrogen oxides or sulphur dioxide each year. They include oil refineries, power stations and aerospace companies.

Under RECLAIM, each firm's allocation is based on its past emissions, and the permissible limits decline by 5 per cent to 8 per cent each year. By 2003 the goal is to have 75 per cent fewer nitrogen oxides and 60 per cent less sulphur from these major stationary sources. For example: 'Chevron, the biggest polluter of all, spews roughly 2,800 tons of nitrous oxides into the Los Angeles basin each year; now it will have to reduce that figure to a little over 1,000 tons by 2000, and no more than 750 tons by 2003' (*The Economist*, 30 October 1993).

Each firm taking part in RECLAIM will receive RECLAIM trading credits equal to its annual emissions limit. Credits are assigned each year and can be bought or sold for use within that year. Plants must hold credits equal to their actual emissions. They can sell excess credits to firms that cannot meet their limits. Large firms will also be able to earn credits by scrapping old vehicles and making contributions to public transport in Los Angeles.

The scheme relieves regulators of the task of trying to create workable rules for different types of specialized industrial plant. From the point of view of industrialists: 'Allowing sources to "bubble" facility emissions to meet annual reduction targets increases compliance flexibility at each facility' (South Coast Air Quality Management District, 1992a, p. 2–1). The emissions at larger companies are monitored by computer networks that link remote sensors directly to monitors at South Coast District headquarters, although environmentalists have complained that the computer system has not been field tested.

The programme has won the support of the region's largest industries, but has encountered some resistance from smaller businesses who have argued that, 'it is unworkable and financially risky for all but the biggest polluters' (*Sacramento Bee*, 16 October 1993). The most vocal criticism has, however, come from environmentalists:

> The whole point of RECLAIM is that companies with high control costs will choose to buy permits instead of reducing their emissions. It is incorrect to say that RECLAIM provides a disincentive to emissions increases. RECLAIM provides a financial incentive to find the least cost means of compliance with the declining balance. For companies with high control costs, this will mean purchasing emissions credits rather than reducing them. As a result, people living near facilities who elect not to reduce their emissions will be subject to greater air toxics exposure than they would have under the AQMP (Schwartz, 1992, not paginated).

The advantages and disadvantages of operating polluting credit markets can only be properly tested by an experiment of the kind being undertaken in Los Angeles. After it has operated for a few years, it will be possible to determine whether it manages to combine greater flexibility and lower administrative costs with effective achievement of air quality goals.

Mobile Source Emission Reduction Credits

Mobile source emission credits have attracted considerable attention in California, being the subject of papers in 1992 by both the Sacramento and South Coast Districts, followed by the issue of guidelines by the Air Resources Board in 1993 for the generation and use of mobile source emission reduction credits. As was noted in relation to the

RECLAIM programme, mobile source credits can complement pollution credit trading programmes related to stationary sources.

Such a programme does not necessarily benefit air quality, but does provide flexibility to industry in meeting requirements for emission reductions. 'Mobile source emission reduction credits are created when reductions in emissions from cars, buses, or other mobile sources exceed the reductions required by federal, state, and local laws' (California Air Resources Board, 1993, p. 2). They could be earned by applying control technology earlier than the regulations require or by the use of emission control equipment not otherwise required. For example, they could be obtained by the purchase of low-emission transit buses or by the elimination of old, gross emitting cars through an accelerated retirement programme. They might also be obtained through the purchase of zero-emission vehicles in excess of regulatory requirements, although the Air Resources Board regards this as a more complicated route because manufacturers are already required to produce a minimum number of zero-emission vehicles. 'Consequently, for another party to obtain mobile source emission credits by purchasing ZEVs, vehicle manufacturers must first be willing to sell or transfer their rights to use those ZEVs to meet the ARB's low emission vehicle regulations, something they may be reluctant to do' (California Air Resources Board, 1993, p. 3).

The Sacramento Air Quality Management District regards the Rule 1005 it is developing on emissions reduction credit/banking as an innovative policy contribution. 'We're trying to create a programme where all the different mobile source regulations that are developing have a common tradeable credit' (interview, Sacramento Air Quality Management District, 7 September 1993). The scheme would cover commute alternative rules, fleet rules and, if they are ever obtained, land use entitlement regulations which would require a developer to provide some offset against the additional traffic created by his development. As well as purchasing gross emitter vehicles, or using alternative fuels, credits could be earned by elimination of vehicular trips through telecommuting. Credits would be good for three years and may be sold to any buyer. In response to a suggestion by Air Resources Board staff for light- and medium-duty low-emission vehicles, credits earned would be held in an 'escrow' account until real emissions benefits can be demonstrated. A trading ratio of 1.3:1 is proposed, yielding 1 pound credit, 0.2 pounds as a windfall air quality benefit, and 0.1 pounds for the escrow account.

The Air Resources Board has been concerned about the creation of 'false credits' in relation to low-emission vehicles. Historically, credits have been granted only for emission reduction activities which exceed the requirements of law, but under the Sacramento District proposals, credit may be granted in certain cases whether or not the sale of the vehicle is in excess of the Air Resources Board rule. This problem has led to prolonged negotiations between the District and the Board. The District is concerned that deleting the low-emission vehicle proposal would result in a loss of public support, but pushing ahead might lead to the rejection of the proposal by the Board. State bodies thus constrain innovation at the District level.

In the meantime, the Sacramento District has entered into a public–private partnership with the Pacific Management Dynamics Corporation called 'Breathe Easy Sacramento' to scrap gross emitting cars. Also involved are the Sacramento Municipal Utility District, Ford, a metal recycling firm and the Northern California Auto Dismantlers Association. The objective is to remove 25,000 polluting vehicles from the roads of Sacramento County over a three year period. Pacific Management's plan is to offer a reasonable price for any pre-1982 model car – the definition of a gross emitter – and then sell the emission reduction credits it earns to businesses needing them for expansion or relocation purposes. Around 9 per cent of the emissions eliminated will go towards helping the District to meet federal air quality requirements. The intention is that overall air quality improves since the amount of pollutants reduced through the scrap programme exceeds the allotment of emission credits sold.

The programme got off the ground slowly, with Aerojet being the first company to sign a contract to eliminate some of its vehicle fleet. Within the first few months of the programme, about 500 members of the public had expressed an interest in giving up their cars. In order for the scheme to be a success, more companies are needed to make a commitment to buy credits.

Congestion Pricing Schemes

There has been an increasing interest in road pricing as a market-based approach to air pollution problems. It is evident that, 'the charges levied on road users relate very little to the costs of providing and maintaining the infrastructure provided let alone to wider notions of optimising its use either from a purely traffic perspective or from a much wider social perspective' (Button, 1993, p. 99). The actual relationship between congestion and environmental costs is a complex one but, in general, stop-and-start driving is likely to lead to higher levels of air pollution. There is considerable interest in California in work being done on congestion pricing. 'In terms of California, I think the academic community, economists, air quality people throughout the state realize that until we restructure the transportation pricing system we now have it will be hard to ... clean up parts of the state that are now dirty' (interview, Bay Area Air Quality Management District, 12 August 1994).

The Bay Area Air Quality Management District has successfully applied for federal funds under the provisions of the Intermodal Surface Transportation Efficiency Act to a plan a congestion pricing demonstration project on the San Francisco–Oakland Bay Bridge. It should be noted that this Act gives legal authority for charging fees for using parts of the federal interstate system for the first time. The Bay Bridge is one of the most congested facilities in the United States and is seen as a good site to test peak period tolls:

> The interests of my agency in doing that are, one, that would reduce emissions of vehicles travelling in that corridor, but, two, that would, if successful, give credence to the idea that road fees, peak period pricing, are a good thing. You see that corridor's a good place to begin, both because there are already tolls being collected in that corridor so that helps tremendously with public acceptance, and there are very good alternatives to driving alone in that corridor [such as BART and an extensive bus service] ... Many people could, without much effort, shift their mode (interview, Bay Area Air Quality Management District, 12 August 1994).

It is estimated that to clear congestion on the bridge the toll would have to be raised from one dollar to five dollars. It is thought that the state legislature would not accept such an increase, but might accept an increase to three dollars which would cut the average morning peak period delay from 20 minutes to ten minutes. Approval from the state legislature would release another 23 million dollars of federal funds.

The more general point that this example raises is the question of public acceptability of road pricing. Whatever the technological possibilities of electronic road pricing, 'the public resents being charged for a service they believe they have already paid for' (Chu and Fielding, 1994, p. 1). From an economist's perspective, charging for roads might appear to be the most efficient solution to urban congestion which in turn contributes to air pollution. A political scientist would caution that such proposals would have to pass sceptical legislatures influenced by hostile publics.

FEDERALISM AND THE POLITICS OF CHAOS

To the British observer of American politics, used to a centralized system of government in which the executive usually controls the legislature, and there are limits to the extent of judicial review, the questions that recur are: how is anything ever decided and, more important, how is anything ever implemented? Checks and balances are, after all, the essence of the system of government, erected by the founding fathers to prevent too great a concentration of power. In this and the preceding chapter, it has been noted that the actors in the politics of air quality management include: the federal government (which is itself a mass of conflicts and overlapping jurisdictions); inter-state bodies such as the Ozone Transportation Commission; the state government, again divided within itself; and, most chaotic of all, the various forms of local government with weak coordinating mechanisms between them, and Air Quality Management Districts seeking to carve out their slice of the territory. 'If there is one lesson from the existing councils of governments, it is that voluntary federations are too weak to do the job of supporting metropolitan development. And special-purpose agencies inevitably are distorted by their single functional nature' (Teitz, 1990, p. 74). Even when decisions are arrived at, they may well be overturned by the courts.

Government continues to function through a process of bargaining and compromise. In that process, some bargainers carry a stronger hand than others. Nevertheless, progress towards cleaner air has been made:

> I think we're doing a hell of a job considering, but it's a little like Professor Lindblom's and the art of muddling through ... in some ways we have lost the vision but at the same time we've held a lot of ground compared to other countries ... The one benefit we've had that I think makes all this easier is the role of the federal government which under the federal Clean Air Act is a quite strong authority that insulates the state from drifting too far from the shore and provides some back stop (interview, environmental lobbyist, Sacramento, 9 September 1993).

One of the great benefits of a federal system is that it permits policy innovations to be experimented with at the state and local level. These innovations, if they are successful, can then be adopted elsewhere. California has clearly played a key role both in pioneering and diffusing innovations which have been adopted by the eastern seaboard states.

The way in which policy development is managed in a federal system becomes of increasing relevance to the European Union as it develops as a political entity. In the next chapter, there is an examination of a federal–state conflict in air quality management; of the policy innovations in alternatively fuelled vehicles developed in California; and of the difficulties faced in attempting to develop more environmentally friendly land use policies in the face of the desire of existing local governments to defend their prerogatives.

5.   Policy solutions at the state level

In Chapter 4, after reviewing the federal framework within which air quality management policy is conducted, a number of policy initiatives taken by the Air Quality Management Districts were examined, such as trip reduction programmes and emission reduction credits. In this chapter, three types of statewide policy solution are reviewed. The first policy solution discussed is the improvement of the state's inspection and maintenance programme for motor vehicles, popularly known as 'smog check', as a means of dealing with the gross emitters who are thought to be responsible for at least half of mobile source pollution. The second policy solution discussed is the state's efforts to mandate and encourage the development of alternatively fuelled vehicles, notably electric vehicles, an innovative programme that has attracted worldwide attention. Although each of these first two programmes is beset by considerable difficulties, the third potential solution is a clear example of policy failure: the absence of any effective land use policy at the state level which seeks to reduce air pollution as one of its goals. In discussing each of these areas, it is necessary to pay attention to the political context in which policy has developed, or failed to develop.

THE SMOG CHECK PROGRAMME

Decisions about the development of the state's smog check programme in 1993 and 1994 were taken in the context of a complex conflict between the federal and state authorities. Apart from the fact that different levels of authority were involved, the complexity of the problem was enhanced by the number of dimensions involved: 'We have a political problem, we have a technical problem, and we have an economic problem all wrapped into one' (interview, environmental lobbyist, 9 September 1993). The eventual outcome was a compromise in which both sides got something of what they wanted, and the state was able to balance its goals of improving air quality, maintaining motorist convenience, and protecting the economic interests of independent garages.

Since 1984 a motor vehicle inspection and maintenance programme has been used to identify and repair vehicles with excessive emissions in California. Cars and trucks have to be inspected every two years at one of 9000 smog check stations run by garages throughout the state which have been licensed by the Bureau of Automotive Repair (BAR). Inspections also take place when ownership changes, or if a vehicle is registered in the state for the first time. Inspections involve the measurement of exhaust emissions and the visual and functional inspection of emission control devices. Vehicles that fail the inspection have to be repaired and retested, although there is a limit to the amount that vehicle owners are required to spend to correct defects not related to tampering (ranging from 50 dollars for pre-1971 cars to 300 hundred dollars for 1990 and later model years). These arrangements are supposed to protect lower income persons from the costs of compliance, but it has been suggested that it leads motorists to, 'seek out repair shops that will help them exceed the repair limit and thereby achieve a waiver' (Zane and Schwartz, 1993, p. 6). Federal legislation which came into effect in 1995 increases the level of expenditure required before a waiver is issued from $300 to $450.

Supporters of the programme claim that it has made a significant impact on air quality, reducing smog-forming hydrocarbon emissions by 19 per cent (*Sacramento Bee*, 28 November 1993). In the South Coast basin, for example, the programme has secured twice the level of emission reductions achieved by the use of reformulated gasoline (California I/M Review Committee, 1993a, p. 26). However, as Table 5.1 shows, the programme falls short of achieving both federal and state

Table 5.1   California smog check programme emission reductions

	Hydrocarbons (%)	CO (%)	NO$_x$ (%)
1986 results	12.3	9.8	3.9
1992 results	18.2	15.3	6.1
State legislative target	25	25	n/a
New federal requirements	28	31	9

Source: California I/M Review Committee, 1993a.

requirements. In the spring of 1993, the federal EPA made it clear that the California smog check system violated the Clean Air Act and must be radically changed. The EPA preference was for what came to be known as a centralized system of some 200 state operated smog check stations in place of the existing decentralized system of 9000 privately owned garages. Testing and repair would be separated, with vehicle owners going to private garages for any necessary repairs, and then returning to the testing station. This set the scene for the federal–state conflict that ensued.

The Limitations of the Smog Check Programme

The state government was well aware of defects in the smog check programme. The programme was regularly reviewed by a California Inspections and Maintenance Review Committee made up of members drawn from the Air Resources Board and a number of the more significant air pollution control districts including the South Coast, the Bay Area, Sacramento and San Diego. In February 1993, the committee submitted its fourth report to the legislature, a lengthy and carefully researched evaluation of the programme. The report identified a number of ways in which programme failure could occur: the equipment used in the garages was inadequate for the task; the inspections were often inadequate; the mechanics who used it were poorly trained; repairs were often insufficient (in some cases because the repair cost ceilings were too low); and in any case, some motorists tampered with adjustments once they had been carried out. Although there was evidence in testimony to the committee of a fraud problem, this was not much emphasized in the report, although it was clearly an issue of central concern to the EPA. A number of garages operate 'pass or don't pay' schemes under which the garage only earns the inspection fee if it issues a certificate.

The report found that the test procedures in use, which measured emissions with the vehicle at idle and 2 500 rpm, were not capable of identifying many vehicles that have excessive emissions during stop-and-go driving which is characteristic of driving conditions in smog afflicted areas in California. These procedures were becoming less effective because more vehicles being inspected were equipped with computer controlled engines and mechanics seemed less able to identify and diagnose faults in these vehicles. The committee argued that the test procedures in use needed to be replaced with new procedures involving a treadmill-like device called a dynanometer which can measure emissions with a load on the engine. The dynanometer test procedure which was recommended by the EPA would involve equipment costing $400,000 for a system – ten times higher than the cost of the equipment in use under the programme and prohibitively expensive for most repair facilities (although the cost was projected to fall to $145,000 once mass production started). However, an alternative high load, steady-state procedure developed by BAR would add only $25,000 to the cost of existing equipment.

Defects missed during the tailpipe test can be detected through visual and functional inspections, but the record of smog check mechanics in underhood inspections was found to be poor. 'Data collected during the 1,100-vehicle testing program indicate that only 24% of all vehicles are receiving thorough and accurate underhood inspections' (California I/M Review Committee, 1993a, p. 2). It was suggested that most mechanics would benefit from additional training and that: 'Some mechanics lack the fundamental skills necessary to inspect and repair vehicles with relatively simple defects, and should not be participating in the program' (California I/M Review Committee, 1993a, p. 4). As one interview respondent put it more bluntly: 'I think that we've got a lot of people out there who fundamentally simply don't know what they're doing' (9 September 1993).

A number of garage owners who gave evidence to the committee argued that, 'fraud and abuse were out of control' (California I/M Review Committee, 1993b, p. 239). Of course, garage owners have an interest in claiming that the review committee was, 'murdering honest people to make it easier to get at the dishonest people' and that, 'the current problem is that BAR doesn't go after the crooks in the business' (California I/M Review Committee, 1993b, p. 240). Rather more credence may be given to the representative of the LA District Attorney's office who argued that the review committee's draft report minimized the problem with tampering and fraud and claimed that, 'because the fraud problem is not accounted for, the benefits of the current program are overstated' (California I/M Review Committee, 1993b, p. 242). Certainly, a number of interview respondents thought that the fraud problem was widespread:

> The corruption and the fraud aspect, which I think is real, it's another part of our underground economy. In every city of the state I can probably arrange within 24 hours through making connections to get a smog check

through friends of mine or family members of theirs (interview, environmental lobbyist, Sacramento, 9 September 1993).

The Political Stakeholders

Before discussing the series of events in the smog check controversy, an understanding of what happened will be enhanced by an examination of the political stakeholders in the dispute. At the state level, some of the strongest opponents of the scheme were the garage owners. A principal exception was ARCO, the operator of the SMOGPROS smog check stations, which was most supportive of revisions to the current programme. ARCO argued that there should be more effective dynanometer test procedures at smog check stations. However, a large corporation like ARCO would be better able to meet the additional capital costs. Greater problems were faced by all 'these little neighbourhood garages that bought the equipment and invested $40,000 or $50,000 of machine, they are saying, what are we going to do? What are we going to do to this equipment that you promised that would be technologically applicable for the next ...?' (interview, Senate aide, Sacramento, 26 March 1993).

The garage owners were represented by a number of bodies such as the Southern California Service Station Association, the California Service Station and Automotive Repair Association and the Automotive Service Councils of California. The latter body made a number of training and service information recommendations which were incorporated in the report of the review committee. There was also an organization, Clean Air Performance Professionals, which a garage owner had set up in an attempt to mobilize his fellow traders to oppose centralized testing, which shows how much concern the issue provoked in the auto service sector. His statement that centralized testing would be akin to emulating the way things were done in Russia seems to have made little impact on the committee. Some of the statements made by individual garage owners to the review committee were also somewhat lacking in political sophistication. Larry Armstrong of Quality Tune-Up Shops gave, 'testimony that was basically a 20-minute statement in opposition to changing from a decentralized program. He said that EPA should be told to "go to hell"' (California I/M Review Committee, 1993b, p. 247). While some California legislators may have shared this sentiment in private, such advice to the EPA was not really an option open to them. In general, however, the motor trade lobby was very effective. Dan Walters, a leading California political columist, noted that: 'Many legislators fear backlash from service station operators' (*Sacramento Bee*, 13 September 1993). At a time of recession in the Californian economy, lobbyists for smog check stations emphasized the employment losses that would result from abandoning the present system which they claimed amounted to 20,000 jobs.

Legislators were also concerned about how their constituents would react to having to drive longer for their smog check, and perhaps wait in line longer, although this particular concern does not seem to have been well founded. Nevertheless, legislators always have to pay attention to the concerns of motorists. As a Senate aide commented:

> There is an issue of public convenience, right now it's very convenient to get the check done because you drive down to your local mechanic and for the most part you get it done and you don't have to go somewhere else. Under this other system you go get tested, if it didn't pass then you've got to go to another facility somewhere else, and then you have to come back and get it retested at the place you started, they call it the ping-pong effect, you're going back and forth and back and forth until you get it right (interview, Senate aide, Sacramento, 26 March 1993).

One interest that was not mobilized, but could have been if the conflict had been prolonged, was stationary source polluters. The sanctions to be taken by the central government would have reduced their permitted emissions:

> I think it's going to be tough when the result of sanctions for stationary sources become clear. Right now it's not in their interests to press for a strong smog check programme, but once sanctions come into play, it will be in the interests of large stationary sources to press Clinton not to impose the programme (interview, American Lung Association, Sacramento, 10 September 1993).

There were, however, interests that were supportive of reforming the programme. Firms that would install equipment in any centralized system saw opportunities for new business. Firms involved in centralized testing were also very active, especially Envirotest Systems of Arizona which held virtually all of the existing centralized system contracts in the United States. An additional dimension to their lobbying was provided by the fact that Envirotest is one of the largest African American owned companies in the United States. The American Lung Association commissioned a study from SRI International which sought to refute the job loss argument by contending that a centralized testing system would provide a net increase in employment of 8 378 jobs, including multiplier effects (SRI International, 1994).

In examining the stance of the federal government, it is necessary to distinguish between the position of the EPA and that of the White House and the president. The EPA started from the position that it was obligated by the Clean Air Act to take action against the state 18 months after it failed to upgrade efforts to identify and police polluting vehicles. The agency's bureaucratic mission is to enhance environmental standards. It is worth noting that a high-ranking official of the EPA who was closely involved in the smog check dispute is Mary Nicholls, a former chair of the California Air Resources Board. She was head of the Board when, against her objections, the legislature decided to support a statewide decentralized smog check system, rather than expand the centralized system which had operated in metropolitan Los Angeles from 1979 to 1984.

The president has a rather different set of concerns. President Clinton was the first Democrat to win California since President Johnson's landslide victory in 1964, and the state's 54 electoral college votes are crucial to his re-election in 1996. During the first year of his presidency, Clinton visited California an average of once every six weeks, and even appointed a special Cabinet-level team to monitor California and accelerate federal aid in such areas as defence conversion. He was anxious not to give Governor Wilson any more opportunities to blame the federal government for problems in California. Throughout the smog check dispute, the White House was always looking for feasible ways out of the problem. Divisions in the federal government made it difficult for state-level actors to anticipate the likely outcome: 'We're stuck here in this conundrum of what the feds might accept and might not accept' (interview, Senate aide, Sacramento, 26 March 1993).

The Course of the Dispute

Although the EPA had made its dissatisfaction with the smog check programme in California known in the spring of 1993, matters really came to a head in the last frantic few days of the legislative year in September. The legislature had to decide what, if any, legislation to pass to reform the smog check programme. A number of bills had been brought forward, but the one that found most favour was SB 629, introduced by Senator Newton Russell (R-Glendale). It had support from the Wilson administration, the Air Resources Board and the then chair of the Assembly Transportation Committee, Richard Katz. The bill basically offered an enhancement of the existing system with more sophisticated testing equipment in the garages, monitoring of cars on the road through the use of remote sensors, increased penalties for fraud (including jail sentences for repair shop owners who issued fraudulent certificates), and improvements in the training requirements for mechanics. It also contained a trigger mechanism so that if sufficient progress was not made in cleaning up the air, California would switch to an EPA-approved centralized system in the smog afflicted areas.

The EPA supported a bill introduced by Senator Robert Presley (D-Riverside) that would have replaced the decentralized system by a network of centralized testing stations. This bill was shot down in committee. What ensued was a game of chicken between the state and federal governments, although Assembly speaker Willie Brown thought that the federal threat to impose sanctions was a bluff as the Clinton administration would never withhold highway money in the run up to the 1996 presidential campaign. Governor Wilson, speaker Brown and Senate Transportation Committee chairman, Quentin Kopp, wanted the legislature to pass SB 629 and negotiate with the EPA subsequently.

From the Clinton administration's point of view, forcing the state into a centralized system, or cutting off its highway funding, would be politically damaging, but backing down would lead to a loss of face. 'The phone lines between Sacramento and Washington were busy during the final week as the political options were weighed' (*Sacramento Bee*, 13 September 1993). The writer was present in an environmental lobbyist's office while a call was placed to a high-level EPA official in Washington. Across the street in the Capitol: 'Top state Democrats pleaded with the Clinton White House' (*Sacramento Bee*, 12 January 1994).

Their pleas were evidently heard, as on the last day of the legislative year, the EPA backed down. The EPA's administrator, Carol Browner, wrote a letter to legislative leaders saying that she would rather have no bill than SB 629. She offered to hold off imposing sanctions until 15 November, a deadline set by the Clean Air Act to have a plan in place. She promised to delay the imposition of sanctions long enough, 'for my staff and the legislative leadership to craft an acceptable bill which can be enacted soon after the Legislature reconvenes in January 1994' (*California Journal Weekly*, 20 September 1993). 'US yields in smog face-off' was the *Sacramento Bee* headline, while Richard Katz said that, 'Browner's letter represented a drastic switch on the part of the EPA' (*California Journal Weekly*, 20 September 1993). The bill needed a rule waiver to be heard on the Senate floor on the last day of session, and the then Senate leader, David Roberti, persuaded the Rules Committee not to grant one on a 3–2 vote.

A wild card was played in September when Senator Tom Hayden (D-Santa Monica), who often upsets the political applecart in California, announced that he would bring a court action to force the federal government to begin bringing California into compliance with the federal smog check law. This he did in the US District Court in Sacramento after the 15 November deadline had passed without any EPA action. There had been accusations in Sacramento that EPA officials had solicited, 'legal action to take them off the political hook. If the courts ordered Browning to impose sanctions, so went the theory, Clinton would not suffer from as much political backlash' (*Sacramento Bee*, 8 October 1993). Hayden insisted, however, that he was acting on his own initiative, and that his concern was with childrens' health and the lungs of all Californians.

On 7 January 1994, the EPA announced that California had six months to pass a tougher smog check law or the government would impose sanctions that would severely restrict the expansion of highways and industry. The EPA sanctions would cost California $250 million in highway funds in 1994, and more than $1.4 billion in subsequent years. Industries would be required to make further cuts in air emissions in order to expand. The EPA announcement was greeted with surprise and consternation in Sacramento, although the EPA had said in November that it, 'was prepared to seek sanctions sometime after January 1' (*Sacramento Bee*, 26 November 1994). Legislators and executive officials in Sacramento could not understand, however, why the sanctions had been imposed while negotiations were in progress. The EPA claimed that the Clean Air Act required them to impose sanctions, but the California EPA pointed out the sanctions were discretionary rather than mandatory. 'Exactly why EPA decided to impose the sanctions is unknown' (*California Journal Weekly*, 24 January 1994). There had been some pressure from other states such as Louisiana which said that they would not proceed with their own enhanced programmes unless the EPA showed that they would be tough with California. Perhaps the EPA had decided the time had come to force the pace.

The EPA action attracted a robust response in Sacramento. Richard Katz wrote to the EPA complaining that, 'for whatever reason the US

EPA derailed the negotiations, questioning the veracity of the legislators and representatives of the governor' (*California Journal Weekly*,
17 January 1994). Within a few days of the EPA announcement, the
Senate Transportation Committee passed SB 629 which the EPA had
made clear was not acceptable to it. 'It was an in-your-face gesture by
an obviously angered pack of politicians' (*Sacramento Bee*, 12 January
1994). On 20 January the Senate passed SB 629 on a 21–5 vote. The
thinking was that, 'the courts could settle the legal question of whether
California could have a test-and-repair smog-check system' (*California
Journal Weekly*, 31 January 1994).

The EPA decision placed the Clinton administration in an embarrass-
ing and politically difficult position, but a way out was offered by the
Northridge earthquake in Southern California. On 24 January, Carol
Browner wrote to Governor Wilson stating:

> As a result of the earthquake, including the damage to the highway system
> and the economy, EPA will cancel the recently announced accelerated
> deadline for imposing sanctions for the state's failure to adopt an accept-
> able smog check program (*California Journal Weekly*, 31 January 1994).

In March the federal and state authorities came up with a compromise
which subsequently became state law. Most motorists would continue
to receive their smog checks at the existing independent stations. However, 15 per cent of cars in smog afflicted areas would go to new test-
only stations, including high polluting vehicles, fleet vehicles and ran-
domly chosen cars. In addition, a pilot programme would be conducted
in the Sacramento area to assess the impact of the state's enhancements
of the smog check programme, such as better enforcement, more testing of technicians and alternative testing with remote sensors. If smog
isn't reduced in Sacramento and other urban areas by 1996, all cars
over six years old will have to go to test-only stations.

In the summer of 1994 remote sensing devices placed on freeway
ramps and at other busy locations tracked the smog output and license
plates of almost all the approximately 800,000 vehicles registered in
Sacramento County. In addition, six thousand motorists were selected
at random and required to submit their vehicles to an exhaust test. The
data gathered from these exercises will be used to build a profile of the
fifteen per cent of vehicles responsible for the most pollution. From the
middle of 1995, owners of vehicles in smoggy areas that match the
profile will have to go to special test only stations to obtain their smog
check certificate. These procedures face technological and political

problems which are discussed in a subsequent section on remote sensing.

Senator Presley commented: 'The question remains as to whether we could have improved the air more ... but I think we worked out a pretty reasonable compromise' (*Sacramento Bee*, 10 March 1994). On the whole, the compromise was more favourable to the Californian than the EPA position, as the existing smog check system was largely retained with the modifications proposed by the state. This outcome was not a surprise to some experienced observers of California politics. An environmental lobbyist interviewed at the beginning of the dispute commented: 'I believe that in the end it is possible that EPA will be unsuccessful in forcing the centralizing of the smog check by the state'. The strongest card held by the state was that President Clinton did not want to offend California voters, or play into the hands of the state's Republican Governor and his 'blame the feds' strategy. At the end of the day, the White House has more political clout than the EPA. The achievement of a really effective smog check programme remains uncertain, 'but everyone agrees that if it were really good, really effective, and we really did get the clunkers off the road, we would vastly improve the air pollution problem' (interview, American Lung Association, Sacramento, 10 September 1993).

Inspection and maintenance plays an important role in the EPA's FIP for California. The EPA's view is that a programme 'which combines the functions of testing and repair in a single facility [is] only roughly half as effective as programs which separate the two functions' (Federal Register, Vol. 59, No. 86, 23338). Although it is disappointed with state legislation, the EPA is 'continuing to work with the California legislative leadership in the hopes of achieving consensus on a program design that would meet both the Clean Air Act requirements and California's unique needs.' (Federal Register, Vol. 59, No. 86, 23338). Quite what California's unique needs are apart from its political clout is not clear, although part of the EPA's concern is that it wants, 'to design a program which will divert as few as possible resources from the national environmental effort to the day to day operation of what would ordinarily be a state-run emission control program' (Federal Register, Vol. 59, No. 86, 23339). One possibility is a state-run programme that would protect the position of the politically influential repair station owners by giving as much business as possible to the current inspection stations, but would have compensating increases in stringency elsewhere.

Remote Sensing

The use of remote sensing was part of the enhancement package for the smog check programme approved by the California legislature. It won support among the decentralists who saw it as one way of defending the existing programme. The EPA is interested in the possibility of requiring the diagnostic systems of new vehicles to be capable of communicating to roadside sensors the operational condition of the emissions system.

Current methods of remote sensing involve a computer controlled device that transmits an infrared beam across a single lane of traffic. As a vehicle crosses this beam, emissions are measured from the exhaust plume and recorded, while a video camera records the vehicle's licence plate. Remote sensing is not without its technical problems. The remote sensing device cannot recognize whether the vehicle is in cold-start mode, when carbon monoxide emissions in particular tend to be higher. Not all exhaust plumes pass through the beam at a uniform height, and vehicles with high tailpipes may escape detection. In rainy conditions, water splashed up by the tyres can interfere with the beam. The Air Resources Board carried out tests on the reliability of remote sensing measurements in 1992 by driving 431 vehicles across the remote sensing beam at a uniform 20 miles per hour on a level road:

> ARB's analysis of the data showed that the remote sensing system's readings of several of the vehicles varied widely, even under these tightly controlled conditions. Such uncertainty as to whether the vehicle is truly high-emitting points out the limitations that must be considered before using the results of remote sensing measurements to impose penalties ... although ... remote sensing is correct approximately 90 per cent of the time, the remaining errors of commission would result in thousands of motor vehicles being falsely failed (California I/M Review Committee, 1993b, p. 128).

One can just imagine the angry letters that California legislators would receive from constituents falsely accused of having cars with emission failures. In any case, it may take several weeks to trace the vehicle owner, by which time the fault may have been rectified, especially if it was the result of deliberate tampering. Voters would also not be particularly pleased about the channelling of multi-lane highways down to one lane so that the remote sensing device could be used. Ramps have been used in Sacramento, but this may be less practical in larger cities.

It might be difficult to use remote sensing in peak traffic conditions on freeways. Remote sensing can play a supplementary role in identifying vehicles that have become high emitters between biennial smog inspections. 'Its most beneficial use would be to provide a deterrence to the operation of tampered vehicles, and to identify especially high emitting vehicles so their timely repair could be required' (California I/M Review Committee, 1993b, p. 134).

Vehicle Scrapping Programmes

One way to reduce the impact of the gross emitter problem is to scrap the older vehicles which have less sophisticated emission control systems. In Chapter 4, there was a discussion of the hesitant start made by a market-based scrapping programme in Sacramento. A more draconian approach that has been aired would be to ban the registration of all vehicles built before a certain date, but that is unlikely to be adopted:

> One of the proposals that the EPA was kicking around for imposing on our Air District was the prohibition of registering vehicles that were pre-1980. Theoretically you'd be eliminating a lot of gross polluting vehicles if you wouldn't let them operate. The will to do that, and the political strength to be able to make it happen, is just not there. I don't know how you can regulate people's lifestyle by forcing tighter and tighter restrictions, sooner or later you end up with a revolt (interview, Sacramento Air Quality Management District, 7 September 1993).

> Non-registration of pre-'80 vehicles is a pretty big meat axe to use, it's going to have a lot of hardships, I don't know anyone who accepts the socio-economic impacts of something like that (interview, American Lung Association, Sacramento, 10 September 1993).

A more feasible approach is to provide cash incentives for the scrapping of cars earlier than would otherwise occur. Unocal, an oil refinery, conducted a scrapping programme in the South Coast basin in 1990, largely as a public relations exercise, and disposed of 8000 vehicles.

One problem with such a programme is that owners may offer vehicles which are on the point of being scrapped anyway because of their poor condition. Although the average remaining life of a 15 year old vehicle is estimated to be six years, it is accepted that the vehicles offered for scrapping are likely to be in poorer condition. An average remaining life of three years has thus been used in California in calculating the benefits of scrapping programmes, although this may be a little too generous. Any large-scale programme might attract old cars into the state to collect the scrapping bounty. The administrative costs of such a programme can be quite high, although Unocal estimated them to be $100 a vehicle in their programme (California I/M Review Committee, 1993b, p. 139). One question that can be difficult is whether to offer a set price for vehicles of a given age, or whether to offer a price for each vehicle based on the retail 'Blue Book' price.

Funding would have to be found for any large-scale programme, but this could be found from a number of sources such as increased smog check fees, penalty fees on automobile manufacturers for warranty recalls, increased vehicle registration fees, or an increase in fuel tax. For example: 'A $0.001 to $0.004 tax per gallon would provide $13 million to $52 million per year for a scrappage program' (California I/M Review Committee, 1993b, p. 140). The California I/M Review Committee (1993b, p. 142) concluded that 'a vehicle retirement program appears to have significant potential for achieving cost-effective emission reductions in the near term'. For example, retiring just 1 900 vehicles pre-1972 in the South Coast basin would, after allowing for the emissions from replacement vehicles, yield an annual emissions reduction of 160 tons of hydrocarbons and 545 tons of carbon monoxide.

Scrapping programmes do, however, raise distributional issues which are rarely raised in the discussion of air quality management in California. If you are a poor African American or Hispanic living in South-Central Los Angeles, the decline in the number of jobs in the immediate area can mean that owning a car significantly increases your chances of obtaining work. Such poorer individuals are more likely to own older cars. If they scrap their vehicle, they may find it difficult to afford a replacement, while transit services may be an inadequate substitute. Respondents were not always very willing directly to address the distributional issue in questions, giving replies on the lines that not all older cars were gross polluters. One respondent who did reply directly when asked whether there was a distributional issue behind the question of older cars on the road, so that the less well off section of the population could be hit very hard by their removal, replied:

> Yes, that's one of the major concerns, that's what raises the red flag when that particular proposal is brought forth, what about people that need the car, and if they don't have the car, they won't be able to get the job, and to force them on to the Los Angeles county bus system is just almost inhu-

mane, it could be up to two hours to get to another destination which would take 25 minutes in a car (interview, Sacramento, 30 March 1993).

A fair and effective car scrapping programme would need to be accompanied by improvements in public transport so that the less well off sections of the population were not unduly disadvantaged.

ALTERNATIVELY FUELLED VEHICLES

A central feature of air quality management programmes in California has been efforts to require the development of alternatively fuelled vehicles ranging from electrically powered vehicles to those powered primarily by methanol. A fundamental constraint faced by such policies is that:

> There's no transportation fuel that's better than gasoline or diesel in terms of just power. They've got more energy per unit of weight and volume than any alternative fuel does. So you're never going to beat them in that sense (interview, Sacramento Air Quality Management District, 7 September 1993).

This means that the success of alternatively fuelled vehicle policies in California must rely on a mixture of requirements and penalties, imposed on vehicle manufacturers and large-scale purchasers, combined with incentives to consumers to purchase vehicles that might not otherwise be attractive to them. California legislation requires increasing proportions of manufacturers' sales to be of low-emission, ultra-low-

Table 5.2   Cleaner cars in California

Model–Year	Low-emission	Ultra-low-emission	Zero-emission
1997	25	2	0
1998	48	2	2
1999	73	2	2
2000	96	2	2
2001	90	5	5
2002	85	10	5
2003	75	15	10

emission and zero-emission vehicles, with all vehicles being in one of these three categories by the 2000 model year (See Table 5.2). Given current technology, zero-emission vehicles means, in practice, electric vehicles. Two per cent of all cars, light vans and trucks sold in the state in 1998 will have to be electric vehicles (some 30,000 sales a year), rising to 10 per cent by 2003 (some 150,000 sales a year).

Under section 43150 of the Clean Air Act only those motor vehicles which meet California's stringent emission standards can be used or registered in the state. Manufacturers, distributors and dealers are prohibited from importing into the state vehicles which do not meet state standards. Any manufacturer which attempts to sell a vehicle that does not meet the applicable emission standards is made subject to a civil penalty of $5 000 for each such action.

The Electric Vehicles Programme

The electric vehicles programme is the most ambitious and innovative aspect of the state's drive to achieve cleaner air. If it succeeds, it will give a considerable impetus to the adoption of electric vehicles elsewhere in the world. The programme faces, however, a number of technological, social and political obstacles which will have to be overcome before it can succeed. Above all, electric vehicles still suffer from the shortcomings of greater weight, high cost, long recharging times, short range and the need to replace batteries.

Technological constraints

Lead acid batteries are the principal available technology for powering electric vehicles, and are likely to remain so for the next decade (See Table 5.3). Lead acid batteries have a number of disadvantages. In particular they are heavy, which has the effect of limiting the range and size of electrically powered vehicles. Lead acid battery packs in an electric vehicle would weigh between 600 and 800 pounds, with most of the weight accounted for by the lead content. 'Pound for pound they hold about 1 per cent as much energy as gasoline' (*Sacramento Bee*, 7 September 1993). Lead is also hardly an environmentally friendly material.

Some progress has already been made in lead acid battery technology, and some experts consider that further technological progress could be achieved. An Advanced Lead Acid Battery Consortium has been formed in the United States, and is giving particular attention to

Table 5.3   The problem of battery technology

Battery	Energy (watt-hours per kg)	Power (watts per kg)	Cost ($ per kw hour)
Lead-acid	33–50	65–300	$70–$200
Comment:	Cheap but limited energy; heavy; lead is toxic		
Nickel metal hydride	55–70	150–200	$230–$1000
Comment:	Good performance, but costly materials and manufacturing		
Lithium polymer	150	100	$50–$500
Comment:	Manufacturing may be costly. Lingering safety fears		
Sodium-sulphur	80–140	90–175	$200–$1200
Comment:	Costly; possibly dangerous materials; high temperature		
Zinc-air	185–200	60–225	$100
Comment:	Excellent performance, but need to replace part of battery to refuel		
Zinc bromine	75–80	35–60	$150–$300
Comment:	Requires pumps and hazardous bromine; performance is good		

Source: *Business Week*, 30 May 1994.

improving energy density. GM's purpose-built Impact electric car, which was a fresh design rather than a conversion of a petrol driven model, 'is powered by conventional lead-acid batteries, but it minimizes the traditional handicap of short range by employing lightweight materials and a highly aerodynamic shape' (Hughes, 1993, p. 90).

There are a number of new battery technologies being developed which hold some promise for the future. Ford is developing the sodium-sulphur battery which it invented in 1965 for use in its Ecostar truck. The sodium-sulphur battery has twice the energy storage capacity of leading lead acid batteries, giving more vehicle range, and is able to accept a greater number of, and more frequent, recharges before battery replacement. Unfortunately: 'Sodium-sulphur batteries tend to explode and have to be kept red hot when not in use' (*The Economist*,

23 October 1993). Thus apart from needing, 'to be kept at a temperature of 300–350° centigrade ... the contents must be heavily protected from accidents, since sodium is a highly reactive metal' (Hughes, 1993, p. 91). If that was not enough, another major drawback is cost. 'According to Ford the battery pack alone costs them one hundred thousand dollars. That's certainly a pre-commercial price' (interview, CEC, 25 March 1993). In 1994, the director of Ford's electric vehicle programme announced that the company may cancel its programme to develop a purpose-built electric vehicle as the effort was financially wasteful until advanced battery and related technology is developed (*Sacramento Bee*, 14 January 1994).

Experiments with nickel-iron batteries have shown that the current generation of such batteries cannot be effectively used in vehicles. Among the problems encountered have been, 'the need to overcharge, causing excessive hydrogen gassing, which lowers efficiency, requires a cumbersome watering regime, and can lead to occasional battery pack ignitions' (Lloyd, Wuebben and Leonard, 1991, p. 4). A subsidiary of Chrysler built three prototype vans with nickel-iron battery packs, but considerable delays were experienced in development. The vehicle sent to the South Coast Air Quality Management District had to be returned after a few days for additional work. The District's Technology Advancement Office (1992b, p. 21) gives the following laconic assessment of, 'projections and prospects: none at this time.'

GM and the Ovonic Battery Company are engaged in a joint venture to develop nickel metal hydride batteries. It is hoped that the batteries will offer an electric car range of 300 miles and a one hour recharge, compared with a six to eight hour recharge for lead acid batteries. Such a battery would undoubtedly make electric cars more attractive, but GM made no forecasts about when such a battery might be commercially available, and repeated its view that the current state of technology does not permit a practical electrical vehicle (*Sacramento Bee*, 11 March 1994).

In 1993 it was announced that a consortium made up of 3M, Hydro Quebec and Argonne National Laboratories, a federally funded research laboratory, had won a contract from the United States Advanced Battery Consortium to develop a lithium-polymer battery. Such batteries are thought to offer significant breakthroughs in the area of low cost manufacturing, but more work is needed to develop cost-effective, high quality manufacturing systems. The base cell of the battery is a thin film. 'Such batteries represent a significant manufacturing challenge because the films must meet rigorous thickness and uniformity standards' (*Sacramento Bee*, 17 December 1993). They are unlikely to be commercially available until early in the next century. Fuel cells have attracted increasing attention as a possible future technology for electrically powered vehicles. In essence, a fuel cell is a mini power plant that produces power without combustion. Like batteries, fuel cells produce electricity through a chemical reaction based on hydrogen and oxygen, but unlike batteries they carry out the reaction through continuous replenishment of chemicals, so they can run almost indefinitely as long as the chemical fuel is present. They have the potential of offering a lighter weight, higher power, longer lasting alternative to batteries. If fuel cells can be developed so that they offer the power to weight ratio of an internal combustion engine, fuel cells rather than batteries are likely to power vehicles in the future. 'The commercial viability of fuel cell technology is currently limited by problems of low power density and high capital cost' (Wuebben, Lloyd and Leonard, 1991, p. 110). An array of fuel cells used in a 'Green Car' devised by Energy Partners Inc. of Florida cost $180,000, which might fall to between $15,000 and $20,000 over time. Further technological developments are needed if fuel cells are to be used in vehicles, including proton exchange membranes, which, because they eliminate a liquid transfer medium, allow the fuel cell to be much smaller. In the summer of 1994 the federal Energy Department awarded nearly $29 million of contracts to Ford and Chrysler to work on proton exchange membrane cells fuelled directly by hydrogen.

Daimler-Benz, operating in conjunction with Ballard Power Systems of Vancouver, claims to be a world leader in its field and already has a test van in operation. Before it becomes a viable option, Daimler-Benz's research and technology director considers that the current cost of DM10,000 for each kW of electricity needs to be reduced by a factor of at least 50, which could take ten to 20 years (although the company's Canadian partner thinks that California's regulations could force faster progress) (*Financial Times*, 15 April 1994). The South Coast District is contributing to the development of a prototype transit bus by Ballard.

Further progress also needs to be made in the standardization of technology in what is still an infant industry. Discussions between utilities and auto companies about recharging characteristics have taken place only recently. There are significant differences between inductive and conductive recharging systems, and without agreement on standards it will be difficult for many electric vehicles to get on the road.

Coupling device manufacturers are also interested in the standardization of their product.

Considerable technological progress has been made in recent years, and credible electric vehicles are available, particularly if it is borne in mind that it has generally been assumed in California that the electrically powered car will be the second or third car in a household. Under a programme which started in 1994 electricity customers in Los Angeles, Sacramento, the Bay Area and San Diego will have the opportunity to test drive GM Impacts for two to four weeks at a time. These two seater cars are powered by sealed lead-acid batteries made up of 32 ten volt batteries. A regenerative braking system is used so that when the driver's foot is lifted off the accelerator, the motor drive electronic system temporarily operates the motors as generators. Acceleration problems have largely been solved, with the vehicle offering 0 to 60 miles per hour in eight seconds, and 30–60 miles per hour in 4.6 seconds. The programme also includes a small number of Honda Civics and converted Geo Prizm sedans.

However, technological progress is a necessary rather than a sufficient condition of the success of the electric vehicles programme. In order for the programme to be a success, manufacturers have to produce the vehicles in commercial numbers, and consumers have to be prepared to purchase them.

The attitude of the motor vehicle manufacturers

When the Energy and Public Utilities Committee of the California Senate held hearings on electric vehicles in March 1993, Senator Tom Hayden commented that with investment in conventional automobile technology, the auto industry found the new technology of electric vehicles almost impossible to contemplate. He saw a shared reluctance by, 'the friendly behemoths of the gas age', although there was a difference of outlook between the American and the Japanese companies. To say that the Americans were committed was too strong a word, but they were more resigned than their Japanese counterparts (author's notes on meeting). Senator Hayden is one of the more left leaning members of the California Senate, and is unlikely to take a sympathetic view of the auto industry. A similar view was, however, expressed in interview by a representative of the electric utilities:

> I think it's very clear that the auto makers are opposed to the entire Air Resources Board low-emission vehicle programme, not just the zero-emis-

sion vehicle requirement but the whole thing, including all four tiers of increasingly stringent standards, and they would just as soon not to have to do any of that (interview, Sacramento, utilities lobbyist, 26 March 1993).

From the point of view of the manufacturers, they see themselves faced by high costs involved in small production volumes for an uncertain market, quite apart from the need to set up new dealer services. GM is the company which has had the greatest commitment to developing an electrically powered car for commercial sale. In 1993 it postponed its production plans because of business conditions and uncertainty about consumer acceptability. Such developments do produce some scepticism among informed observers:

> GM committed in 1970 to build an electric vehicle, ten years later they established a concepts centre, that didn't pan out. Again in 1990 GM committed to bring this vehicle to market by the mid-1990s. Unfortunately, it didn't happen in 1970, it didn't happen in 1980, and it didn't happen in 1990 and now General Motors has once again pulled the plug and gone back on what some people believed was a realistic promise. Getting these vehicles to market is a very non-trivial commercial exercise (interview, South Coast Air Quality Management District, 1 September 1993).

Even in those companies which are committed to some form of electric vehicle production, the proponents of electric vehicles are relatively weak in terms of internal company politics. Ford formed an Electric Vehicle Segment in 1992, and this was portrayed by the Ford representative at the California Senate hearings as conveying an important message in terms of Ford's commitment to the development of electric vehicles. What it perhaps says more about is the internal organizational politics of Ford rather than its level of commitment to electric vehicles. After Alexander Trotman was named chairman and chief executive of Ford in late 1993, the company began to reassess its spending on electric vehicles. Trotman is considered to be more pessimistic about electric vehicles than his predecessor and stated at the Detroit auto show that he hoped to persuade the Air Resources Board to drop its mandate in favour of proposals that would rely on other fuels and measures (*Sacramento Bee*, 14 January 1994). The Ford representative commented at the California Senate: 'One of the fundamental problems of bringing new technology into the market is the cheap price of gasoline. It is very difficult to compete with gasoline' (author's notes). This difficult competitive environment for electric vehicles is in part the result of the political influence of the auto companies which have succeeded in keeping petrol prices in the United States at a low level by international standards.

One way of making progress would be to encourage the auto companies to share development costs, and they have expressed a willingness to cooperate more closely on the development of an electric car. The US Council for Automotive Research announced in December 1992 that its members (the 'Big Three' auto manufacturers) have signed an agreement to investigate cooperation in the design, development, testing and possible manufacturing of electric vehicle components. The group will explore opportunities for common designs and specifications of electric vehicle systems and subsystems that would ultimately be used in each company's own vehicle. It is possible that the consortium would pool resources for design, development, testing and possible manufacture of electric vehicles (communication from Wayne Henegar, GM Electric Vehicles, 2 April 1993).

The auto companies were put under more pressure by President Clinton's personal statement of support for the state's stringent clean air strategy delivered in Los Angeles in December 1993, and the decision by the northeastern states early in 1994 to adopt California's programme. Taken together, California and the northeastern states represent more than half of the national auto market. A Calstart official predicted that, 'the auto industry, having lost a round in the North-east, will step up its efforts to weaken California's air quality standards' (*Sacramento Bee*, 1 February 1994).

In a clever ploy, the 'Big Three' auto makers were reported in February 1994 to have entered into negotiations with Governor Wilson to ease the electric vehicle requirements in return for a commitment to build auto assembly plants in California (which has only one auto plant) (*California Journal Weekly*, 21 February and 14 March, 1994). In May 1994 the Air Resources Board held hearings on its electric vehicle mandates with Ford, GM and Chrysler forming a united front of opposition. The Board decided that the car manufacturers could provide a commercially viable car by 1998 and that its mandates need not be revised. The car makers counter argued that the result could be to bring electric vehicles on the market before they were ready, producing a negative consumer response. Chrysler said that it would move ahead with production of its electric minivan, but was not sure that it was a marketable car. Republican parity in the state Assembly after November 1994 might give the manufacturers some hope of a stay of execution, although the elections also produced a more polarized legislature by unseating moderate Democrats while liberal Democrats in safe urban seats were re-elected.

Given the reluctance of the major auto manufacturers to make electric cars, some supporters of electric vehicle technology consider that more could be achieved by the non-profit consortium, Calstart, which draws on aerospace or engineering expertise with the aim of making California the world leader in electric vehicle technology. Calstart is a public–private partnership involving businesses, state and local government agencies, electric utilities, educational and research institutions and a federal laboratory. Rent-free space has been provided by the Lockheed Corporation. Of the total programme budget of $19.8 million, $6 million comes from federal and state grants. The programmes include one to develop electric vehicle components and subassemblies, an electric transport infrastructure programme, and an electric bus programme.

Another approach is to rely on smaller companies which could make electric vehicles either on their own behalf or by badging by the larger companies to meet their commitments under the California regulations. Sacramento is seen as a potential centre for this fledgling industry. In October 1993, the first venture in the country to be devoted exclusively to developing and manufacturing electric vehicles was announced as a public–private partnership located at McClellan Air Force Base, in part as a response to lobbying by Vic Fazio, the member of the House of Representatives for West Sacramento, to obtain federal defence funding for such projects. The plan involves the Synergy Electric Vehicle Group and the Sacramento Municipal Utility District, strong backers of electric power, as well as McClellan. An initial $5 million in federal funds will be used to set up a research and development centre to produce prototypes, followed by all-electric utility vehicles for the military, which would later be sold to the private sector.

Smaller companies have complained that federal research money is concentrated on the 'Big Three' auto manufacturers. There is, however, some scepticism about the ability of smaller companies to make a significant contribution to the manufacture of electric vehicles for the general consumer:

> Our emphasis is exclusively on working with the major manufacturers because when you work with them you have a sort of commitment that you're going to end up with an engineered finished product, but you also have parts availability, you have service network, warranty on product and

all those kinds of consumer protections that you don't normally think about any more in the automotive area (interview, Sacramento Air Quality Management District, 7 September 1993).

An initiative to promote the production of electric vehicles has been undertaken by Los Angeles City Council, which sponsored an international competition for the development and sale of at least 5000 electric vans and 5000 electric passenger vehicles in Southern California by 1995. From the 18 proposals that were received, Vehma International was selected to provide one-ton vans, Unique Mobility will market a hybrid minivan and full-size pickup, and Clean Air Transport (CAT) will market a four passenger car, together with a microvan. CAT is a new Gothenburg company that undertakes its technical development at Worthing, England. CAT's LA 301 has a small petrol engine which drives an electricity generator which increases the range of the car's operation to around 250 kilometres. The petrol engine is started automatically when the car is driven at a high and even speed. Like all electric or hybrid models, the purchase price will be high, at around $25,000, which makes it more expensive than 86 per cent of current US new car sales. Even if electric vehicles are produced in significant numbers, their price and performance characteristics may make them unattractive to individual consumers.

Consumer resistance

A representative of Nissan commented at the California Senate hearings that drivers of electric vehicles had to accept reduced range, high price, reduced carrying capacity and lower performance. It was like driving a modest sub-compact with the fuel warning light always on. People were unlikely to be willing to pay more than $20,000 for such a car which was 1.5 times the cost of a similar competitive vehicle, while the production cost was actually times three.

One of the central drawbacks for potential purchasers of electric cars is that of range. 'Vehicle owners in survey after survey state that they want a vehicle with a driving range similar to that of their current gasoline vehicle – about 300–400 miles' (Sperling and Turrentine, 1991, p. 3). This preference represents a misperception of what their actual requirements generally are, but it is a powerful and persistent misperception none the less. It is fundamentally an issue about lifestyle. As one clean fuels expert commented: 'You look at how people have become dependent on the lifestyle that vehicles afford them and try to factor in' (interview, Sacramento Air Quality Management District, 7 September 1993).

In focus-group discussions among residents of the Pasadena area of Los Angeles who had test driven electric vehicles, 'many participants discussed flexibility as a basic want: their need for unlimited range was a "lifestyle" issue; they wanted that freedom' (Turrentine, Lee-Gosselin, Kurani and Sperling, 1993, p. 5). Younger drivers, 'considered unlimited range a need in the evening and suggested they could not always count on recharging' (Turrentine, Lee-Gosselin, Kurani and Sperling, 1993, p. 5). Participants in the 45–55 age group seemed most likely to consider purchasing electric vehicles. Favourable attitudes towards electric vehicles also correlated positively with the number of vehicles in a household, providing evidence in support of the policy assumption that electric vehicles are most likely to be purchased as a second or subsequent car. Commuting distance, which very rarely exceeded electric vehicle range, was not such an important influence on attitudes as, 'the perceived and actual-degree of routine in the travel patterns of participants and their households' (Turrentine, Lee-Gosselin, Kurani and Sperling, 1993, p. 6).

Preliminary findings published in 1994 from the first 175 returned surveys of an ongoing survey of 600 Californian households suggested that, 'range is much less important and home recharging more important than previous, less intensive studies, indicate. Accordingly, we find a larger EV market than many previous surveys' (Kurani, Turrentine and Sperling, 1994, pp. 11–12). This study suggests that enough cars could be bought to satisfy the 2 per cent mandated share in 1998. Its findings, however, do depend on keeping the average price of each vehicle below $20,000 which could be argued to be unrealistic.

Some households may therefore be prepared to consider having one electric vehicle among their cars, filling a niche as a second or third car, but the fundamental problem remains that electric vehicles are likely to cost more while offering inferior performance characteristics. It is therefore likely to be necessary to offer a range of financial incentives to potential purchasers. A mail survey of 1 164 respondents, principally living in Los Angeles, that was conducted for GM found that a package of incentives did appear likely to have a considerable impact on the willingness of consumers to purchase an electric vehicle. A package of incentives raised the proportion of those contacted who would definitely or probably consider the purchase of an electric vehicle from 17 per cent to 68 per cent. The most popular incentive was the provision of a free replacement battery after 30,000 miles, followed by a federal income tax credit of $2 200 and a state sales tax waiver worth $1 320.

One cost that consumers would encounter is the installation of wiring upgrades, special metering equipment and connectors in their garages. The average cost of such work would be around $800 and its subsidization might encourage consumers to consider electric vehicles. Preferential rates for off peak recharging, which are not currently available in California, might also be desirable. These matters have been considered by the electric utilities in California, which have also considered providing a $1 000–$1 500 rebate against the initial purchase of an electric vehicle, although such rebates have been challenged on the grounds of equity by the PUC. The GM evidence that the most powerful incentive for purchase would be a free replacement battery, which would normally have to be replaced by the motorist at a cost of $2 000 after three years, has had some influence on the thinking of electric utility representatives:

> The news in the hearing was quite interesting to the utilities that maybe consumers would prefer to have or see more value in some kind of guaranteed battery replacement and so it has started us thinking whether or not it would be better, rather than just offering a flat $1 500 or $2 000 against the initial vehicle purchase, maybe some kind of a guaranteed battery or a second battery is a better way to go (interview, California Electric Transportation Commission, Sacramento, 26 March 1993).

The provision of generous incentives has been emphasized by the auto companies in their statements on electric vehicles. For example, the Nissan representative told the California Senate hearing that it was not prepared to cross-subsidize the production of electric vehicles, and requested support in the form of price incentives, user incentives and production incentives. The National Energy Policy Act passed in 1992 does provide for a 10 per cent tax credit for electric vehicles up to a ceiling of $4 000. GM is reported as estimating that it needs a $5 000 purchase incentive from all sources, together with a $5 000 reduction in operating costs over the life of the vehicle (interview, California Electric Transportation Commission, Sacramento, 26 March 1993). If such incentives could be provided, the cost of the vehicle could be near the $20,000 level, below which approximately two-thirds of all new cars in the United States are sold. GM calculates that it would be impossible to meet the mandated target of 10 per cent zero-emission vehicles by 2003 if electric vehicles were priced above $25,000 at current prices.

A variety of incentives could thus help to offset the purchase cost disadvantages of the electric car. The range issue remains a psychological barrier, although one that it may be possible to overcome, along with the negative image of the electric vehicle as 'a glorified golf cart' (Sperling and Turrentine, 1991, p. 3). 'The EV market clearly grows larger as the range capability of vehicles increases, but a high enough percentage of respondents chose EVs of even short range to satisfy the ZEV mandates for 1998' (Kurani, Turrentine and Sperling, 1994, p. 10). Vehicles like GM's Impact, 'may deliver about 100 miles of motoring before they need recharging in the ideal conditions of a test run, but be a bit heavy-footed, use the lights, air conditioning, heater or windscreen wipers and the range is halved' (*The Economist*, 23 October 1991), In really cold conditions the vehicles can be difficult to operate, although this is not generally a problem in California. As one respondent commented: 'I think a hundred miles for California driving habits, there's enough headroom there' (interview, California Energy Commission, 25 March 1993). The problem is to a large extent one of perception, as an interview respondent driving an electric vehicle pointed out:

> I do think range is a problem and that although I think most Californians don't really need a 100 mile range, there's something about 100 miles that captures people's imagination, they think they need 100 mile range, they really don't. The electric vehicle that I drive back and forth to work every day has got about a 40 or 50 mile range between charges and whenever I mention that range to people they kind of grimace, and you can tell that they really think that they need about a 100 mile range. Whereas if you look at their actual driving patterns that wouldn't be the case ... they don't really need to have a very big range for normal day-to-day driving (interview, California Electric Transportation Commission, Sacramento, 26 March 1993).

An underlying problem is that, 'consumer purchase behavior is fundamentally conservative' among other reasons, 'because drivers have become accustomed over the past century to the attributes of gasoline vehicles' (Sperling and Turrentine, 1991, p. 4). Sperling and Turrentine argue that consumer behaviour can be changed, just as behaviour over smoking or seat belts has been changed. This overlooks the problem that a car is a high cost consumer purchase, and consumers may be reluctant to invest in a new technology where supporting infrastructure such as recharging stations may not be fully developed.

Generating electric power

One concern is that the benefits of electric cars displacing conventional vehicles may be offset by additional emissions from power stations generating the necessary electricity. A senior official at the California Energy Commission commented in interview:

> I guess the overarching question is that when you shift from an internal combustion engine to an electric motor you haven't done away with emissions, you've moved them. We have the ability to estimate whether or not that's going to result in a net reduction in emissions and in many cases it's a close call. A lot of the marginal electricity comes to California from thermal power plants, natural gas in California or coal in the southwest United States. To me it's going to be important to think through whether or not electricity actually is the best strategy (interview, California Energy Commission, 30 March 1993).

Hughes (1993, p. 93) argues that: 'Electric vehicles can ... offer reduced greenhouse emissions, but only if the electricity is provided primarily by non-fossil sources or natural gas'. Supporters of the electric car strategy would argue that California electricity generation is particularly clean and diversified in its sources. In the early 1990s, 37 per cent of California's electricity came from natural gas plants; 17 per cent from hydroelectric plants; 10 per cent from nuclear plants; 8 per cent from cogeneration; 7 per cent from out of state coal plants; and the balance largely from 'environmentally friendly' sources such as geothermal power, biomass, solar and wind. These overall balance figures do not, of course, tell us where additional marginal power would be generated. However, the electric utilities consider that, given a preponderance of off peak recharging, one or two million electric vehicles could be absorbed without requiring any new generating capacity.

If additional electricity generation at coal fired plants in Arizona or Utah did create significant pollution problems, it would not, of course, necessarily be reflected in evaluations of the problem in California, where the clear preoccupation is with local air pollution which threatens health rather than, say, with issues of global warming. However, even if the targets of the zero-emission vehicles programme are attained, most of the additional electricity could be provided at night through generation from relatively environmentally friendly sources. Stationary sources are also easier to monitor and control than millions of vehicles.

The likely response to programme failure

The 2 per cent zero-emission vehicles target is unlikely to be met, and the 10 per cent target for 2003 appears to be even more unattainable. The electric vehicles are unlikely to be available in sufficient numbers to consumers. Even if they are available, a relatively small number of individual consumers are likely to want to purchase a vehicle that is more highly priced, can seat fewer passengers, and has a more limited range than their existing vehicles. What will the state of California do when its targets are not achieved?

The state of California could apply a $5 000 fine to manufacturers for each electric vehicle they have failed to provide (the initial obligation is limited to the leading seven manufacturers), or it could prohibit the sale within the state of all vehicles manufactured by a firm that had failed to comply. State officials argue that, 'the California market is extremely important to all the major auto manufacturers and if it's mandated that they have to have a certain percentage of ZEVs in California it's not likely they're going to walk away from the market' (interview, California Energy Commission, 25 March 1993). The market exclusion penalty is such a drastic penalty, however, that many of those interviewed thought that it was unlikely to be used.

As far as the financial penalty is concerned, it was suggested by some auto companies that as they would lose more than $5 000 on each electric vehicle, they would be better off paying the financial penalty. The response of the Air Resource Board was that if that was the case they would seek legislation to increase the fine. Directors of companies might also place themselves in legal jeopardy by intentionally breaching the law.

What seems to be the most likely outcome is that those vehicles that are available in the late 1990s will be purchased largely by state and local government agencies and the utilities, and run as fleets. Indeed, GM did press for a guaranteed sale of 5 000 vehicles that could only be met by public agencies. A clean fuels expert commented:

> Electric vehicles to us don't represent something that's commercially available to a general consumer in the next year or two. When it comes to purchase decisions, people are going to say, 'this doesn't work for me' (interview, Sacramento Air Quality Management District, 7 September 1993).

This respondent thought there would be niches for electric vehicles in centrally parked fleets with a limited range, such as parking enforcement vehicles and airport shuttle buses. Another respondent agreed that fleet sales offered the best prospects for electric vehicles:

> We actually think that one of the biggest opportunities towards meeting the goals is to look at the mandatory fleet conversions that are required at the federal and state level. California has large government fleets at federal, state, local [levels], utilities have fleets. Thus we are working with a number of very large private companies, UPS, the Post Office because it has a lot of urban, short-range vehicles. So while I don't think we're going to see large penetration in your traditional commuter [market], in the early years we think we can get the large institutional buyers that are subject to federal and state requirements to become a substantial part of the EV market (interview, aide to Senate Energy and Public Utilities Committee, Sacramento, 8 September 1993).

A few environmentally conscious individual consumers may also purchase the vehicles. A package of financial incentives would increase purchases by individual consumers. The early years of the programme, when innovative consumers ('the first guy on the block') purchase the vehicles may well be the most difficult in terms of winning consumer acceptance. Research on consumer attitudes suggests that, 'as EV technology becomes more familiar and is improved and modest incentives are provided, much higher levels of penetration are likely' (Sperling and Turrentine, 1991, p. 1).

A major constraint in meeting the targets in the 1998–2003 period seems likely to be that insufficient electric vehicles will be available for purchase. In part, this is dependent on further technological progress. Inadequate battery technology remains, 'the Achilles heel of electric vehicles' (Lloyd, Wuebben and Leonard, 1991, p. 4). 'Until the current limitations of battery-only EVs are resolved, hybrid EVs may play an important role in California ... This kind of technology will enable motorists to operate their vehicles solely on battery power most of the time, especially when driving in urban areas, where ambient air quality is the worst' (Lloyd, Wuebben and Leonard, 1991, p. 6). A director of the Sacramento Municipal Utility District has argued that, 'hybrid electric vehicles had largely been ignored by policy makers responsible for air quality' (*Sacramento Bee*, 7 September 1993).

The fundamental problem is how to overcome the reluctance of the automobile companies to invest heavily in new production facilities for small volume production of what they see as an insufficiently developed technology serving an uncertain market. The response of the state of California might in part depend on how much priority the Governor in office in the late 1990s gives to the electric vehicle programme. A Democratic Governor would have wished to associate herself closely with the programme and give it additional political impetus. Governor Wilson, on the other hand, vetoed AB 564 to create a consortium supporting the clean fuels industry.

Informed observers think that it is likely that there would be a relaxation or renegotiation of the targets, but not until very close to the deadline in order to maximize pressure on the auto manufacturers:

> I think they're really going to try and hold the auto makers feet close to the fire and it won't be until very close to 1998 that they would even consider any kind of relaxation or something like that. I think it's very likely between now and then that the Air Resources Board and others will try to soften the blow on auto makers and to try to make a more receptive market place for these vehicles through legislation (interview, California Electric Transportation Commission, 26 March 1993).

One of the greatest obstacles to reaching a political deal with the auto manufacturers has been a lack of political sympathy with their position, particularly as they are perceived as 'Detroit', that is, firms headquartered outside California which have undertaken relatively little manufacturing in the state. That is why the offer to manufacture in the state is such a smart move which could be taken up by a re-elected Governor Wilson. However, any attempt to deviate from the legislation could also be challenged in the courts by environmental groups. The political outcome is therefore uncertain, but the general predisposition in California is to settle controversies by compromise whenever possible.

The electric vehicles programme in California is unlikely to succeed in the sense that it will meet the targets that have been set for it on schedule. That does not mean, however, that it should be regarded as a potential failure. Some electric vehicles will appear on the public roads eventually, and the programme provides incentives for pushing forward the technological frontiers of electric vehicle design and engineering.

Methanol Fuelled Vehicles

Vehicles fuelled by a mixture of 85 per cent methanol and 15 per cent gasoline (M-85) are running on the roads in California, largely cars in fleets such as that operated by the South Coast Air Quality Management District, while buses are operating on 100 per cent methanol. A small percentage of gasoline is added to methanol for safety reasons.

Pure methanol in sunlight does not burn with a visible flame, making it difficult to detect fires, but adding gasoline makes the flame visible. It also makes the liquid unpalatable for substance abusers to drink, which is important as methanol if drunk causes blindness.

In the early 1980s, the state of California reviewed the possibilities of ethanol as a fuel. Ethanol is grain alcohol made from organic matter. Its main drawback is, 'there is not enough farmland available to produce the corn needed to make significant quantities of automotive fuels' (Nadis and MacKenzie, 1993, p. 67). In California:

> It all came to a head in 1983 when we realized that ethanol, although it could be a very, very good engine fuel simply did not make a lot of sense in terms of economics and supply ... California agricultural products have a far higher value in the market place as a food and not as a resource for energy production ... So we really began to focus on methanol as a major transportation alternative (interview, California Energy Commission, 25 March 1993).

'CEC proved to be the most influential advocate of methanol through the 1980s', developing an, 'organizational commitment to methanol fuel' (Sperling, DeLuchi and Wang, 1991, p. 19). California had a demonstration programme with 500 methanol fuelled cars in the early 1980s, but although this was a technical success, it was a failure for consumers. The main reason was the absence of an adequate network of filling stations providing M-85. Some progress has been made in that area since then, with 26 filling stations in Southern California, a number that is planned to expand to 200. Methanol has only about half the energy density of gasoline, so twice the storage volume is needed. On bulky vehicles, there is plenty of room for additional storage tanks, so there have been substantial programmes to use methanol fuelled vehicles for school buses and transit vehicles. The Metropolitan Transport Authority in Los Angeles has spent about $102 million on methanol buses since 1989, but nearly a third of these have had engine failures. 'Records show they break down about once every 4 000 miles, about twice as much as conventional diesel buses. Experts blame the corrosiveness of methanol' (*Sacramento Bee*, 20 December 1993).

Of the available alternative fuel technologies, the auto industry has preferred the methanol–gasoline blend (M-85). Methanol is more attractive to the auto manufacturers than other alternative fuels because, 'it is a liquid and therefore more similar to gasoline and diesel fuel than other leading candidates, thus requiring less costly changes in motor vehicles and the fuel distribution system' (Sperling, DeLuchi and Wang, 1991, p. 17).

Support has not been confined to the auto manufacturers, however. The CEC developed a strong commitment to methanol, although by 1993 they felt that, 'in a year or two our activity at least with methanol and light-duty vehicles will come to a close, that we have really provided sufficient incentive to introduce that technology on a commercial basis and therefore there's no longer a need for government assistance' (interview, CEC, 25 March 1993). Other clean fuel experts expressed a preference for methanol in interview: 'Methanol is by far the cheapest way to displace one billion barrels of oil a day' (interview, South Coast Air Quality Management District, 1 April 1993). Environmentalists were more sceptical: 'The problem is that methanol isn't clean enough relative to reformulated gasoline to build a whole programme on it' (interview, environmental lobbyist, Sacramento, 9 September 1993).

'Most scientists agree that methanol vehicles produce somewhat lower quantities of certain key pollutants, but few experts agree on how much lower' (Nadis and MacKenzie, 1993, pp. 64–5). Its extensive use would certainly bring about no reductions in greenhouse gases. One of its major drawbacks is that methanol vehicles produce, 'more formaldehyde – a toxic pollutant, a potent smog-forming chemical, and a proven carcinogen – than gasoline-powered cars do' (Nadis and MacKenzie, 1993, p. 65). Given that it may produce less carbon monoxide or nitrogen oxides than conventional vehicles, the, 'promise of reduced ozone is the primary attraction of methanol vehicles; they are likely to have few other environmental benefits' (Sperling, DeLuchi and Wang, 1991, p. 29). These reductions are, however, likely to be modest, of the order of 'a maximum reduction in peak ozone levels of 0 to 15 per cent in multiday smog episodes.' (Sperling, DeLuchi and Wang, 1991, p. 30).

Methanol offers modest gains over gasoline, but it has some value as a transitional technology. With electrically heated catalysts, M-85 may have the potential to meet ultra-low-emission vehicle standards. It is likely to meet less consumer resistance, because it offers the same handling characteristics as gasoline, its cost-per-mile is equal to premium unleaded, and it does not require the changes in patterns of vehicle use which result from the need to recharge an electric vehicle. 'The auto industry, with a short-term focus, prefers methanol because it is physically and chemically more similar to gasoline than electricity and natural gas and is more compatible with gasoline in multifuel engines' (Sperling, DeLuchi and Wang, 1991, p. 51). In developing short-term strategies, it is politically necessary to take account of the interests of the motor industry, but longer-term strategies require a different balance of considerations and are likely to lead to less emphasis on methanol in the future.

Compressed Natural Gas

Compressed natural gas (CNG) vehicles have been attracting increasing attention as they are seen to offer 'a more cost-effective strategy for reducing ozone than methanol' (Sperling, DeLuchi and Wang, 1991, p. 40). By using CNG it is possible to cut carbon monoxide emissions by 90 per cent and hydrocarbons by 50 per cent compared to gasoline, although greenhouse gas emissions are only slightly lower (Nadis and MacKenzie, 1993, pp. 69–70). It is possible to retrofit gasoline powered vehicles with CNG, but the retrofits can be of a variable standard, and dedicated vehicles are thought to have a greater potential for reducing emissions.

CNG is more suitable for buses and trucks than for cars. 'Because the fuel holds only about one fourth as much energy on a volume basis as gasoline, a CNG vehicle needs bulky storage tanks to achieve a decent range' (Nadis and MacKenzie, 1993, p. 70). Because of the need to compress the gas at the pump, the infrastructure cost of a retail station can be five times higher than for a conventional one selling only gasoline:

> Natural gas just by itself at the well head is cheap, by the time you get it to a compressor unit it's still pretty cheap, but when you run it through that compressor unit, it takes a heck of a lot of energy to take natural gas at half a pound per square inch and turn it into natural gas at 3 000 pounds per square inch (interview, Sacramento Air Quality Management District, 7 September 1993).

Chrysler was the first auto manufacturer to have a CNG vehicle certified for sale in California as an ultra-low-emission vehicle. Its minivan emits one-tenth of the hydrocarbons and one-third the nitrogen oxides of a gasoline powered vehicle. The retail price of the minivan is around $22,000, but incentives to purchase include $2 600 from Pacific Gas and Electric, $1 500 from the California Energy Commission, a state income tax credit of $1 000, and a $2 000 federal income tax deduction. The range of the vehicle is 100–150 miles in town and 150–200 miles on long-distance routes. By the end of 1994, there were expected to be nearly 100 CNG refuelling stations in Northern California. At the stations, drivers of the vans could expect to pay 80 cents a gallon for CNG against $1.10 for unleaded regular gasoline in 1994. It is anticipated that the main purchasers of the van, which is expected to have sales of around 2 000 a year, will be fleets of utility and service companies.

In the summer of 1994, Chrysler, Ford and GM announced that they were forming a Natural Gas Vehicles Technologies Partnership. The main research objective is to cut the cost of storage tanks used in natural gas powered vehicles. This could mean using different materials to the aluminium, steel or composite currently used in making tanks, and a shape other than the usual cylinder. The tank is estimated to account for around 70 per cent of the extra cost of a natural gas vehicle.

For transit fleet operators, a mixture of subsidies and bargaining power may make natural gas an attractive operation. In Sacramento, the Regional Transit buses burning natural gas can be identified by a 'hump' in their roofs. The transit district in Sacramento used public funds to build a three million dollar compressor, and negotiated a price with the utility district of around 30 cents per gallon for their natural gas. In the Bay Area, the Air Quality Management District has helped to fund a scheme to have a mother station with a big industrial compressor which is then compressed into a tube trainer (a set of cylindrical tubes) for use at a fleet yard. These experiments all assist the wider adoption of natural gas vehicles, but it does not represent a 'silver bullet' fuel that is going to replace gasoline any more than any of the other alternatives.

Hydrogen

In the long run, hydrogen powered vehicles offer the best potential for emission reductions, but inexpensive, feasible technology is not likely to be available until well into the 21st century. Hydrogen powered vehicles would generate hardly any emissions, the one exception being nitrogen oxide, but even that would probably be at a level that could meet current emission standards. One major problem is that liquid hydrogen storage systems are about six times bulkier than those for gasoline. Range would be limited by the fact that, 'all hydrogen storage systems are bulky and costly and will remain so, even with the major advances that are likely to occur with expanded R & D efforts' (Sperling, DeLuchi and Wang, 1991, p. 42). Another major obstacle is the cost of hydrogen fuel. It is forecast that, 'hydrogen vehicles will be cost competitive in the middle term only if the most optimistic cost projections are realized *and* the price of gasoline at least triples' (Sperling, DeLuchi and Wang, 1991, p. 44). There is concern that, 'the technical difficulties of handling a liquid that must be kept at –423° F (and is dangerous to contact) may make it impractical for the general public' (Nadis and MacKenzie, 1993, p. 88).

Interview respondents saw hydrogen as, 'pretty far in the future … there are all kinds of problems, it's the cost of producing the hydrogen, the energy required to produce the hydrogen, the storage of the hydrogen, and the dispensing of the hydrogen' (interview, CEC, 25 March 1993). Nevertheless, 'none of the problems are necessarily insurmountable' (Sperling, DeLuchi and Wang, 1991, p. 45). A 30 year time horizon is, however, too long for the problem that California faces and the deadlines that it has to meet. In the medium term, electric vehicles remain one of the more attractive options, but much development work remains to be done on battery technology before individual consumers become extensive purchasers of such vehicles.

LAND USE PLANNING

Critics of Californian policy argue that an emphasis on alternatively fuelled vehicles allows attention to be focused on a problem that has to be solved by other actors such as the auto manufacturers, whereas the underlying problem is a pattern of low density land use that leads to a reliance on the auto as a means of transport for work, shopping and recreation:

> Once certain land use policies are established, you almost automatically have certain roads or highways being established. Once these transportation infrastructures are put in place, you perpetuate the need for single occupancy vehicles (interview, CEC, 25 March 1993).

The available evidence suggests that the achievement of higher densities is best worked for at a statewide level (Downs, 1992, p. 95). Apart from the California Coastal Commission, which was established by the voters in an initiative in an effort to protect the coastline, there are no statewide land use bodies and: 'its subsequent history has shown the difficulty of such an effort at a statewide level' (Teitz, 1990, p. 63). There has been an attempt within the Governor's office to develop a statewide growth management plan, but in general the state government has little effective control over land use planning decisions:

> It's a very difficult problem to really control because there are so many intermediate bodies that have some jurisdiction in how communities develop. No one state entity has real overall control of authority in this particular area. You do get differing kinds of policies being established by different entities. Basically, it has led to a very low density pattern of cities (interview, CEC, 25 March 1993).

The traditional division of responsibilities for growth planning between the different levels of government was as follows:

> The role of state government was to plan, finance and build capital infrastructure, such as highways ... and to oversee the management and protection of the state's natural and environmental resources. The role of county government was to provide basic urban services to unincorporated areas and to manage the broad process of urbanization by discouraging the development of those areas. The role of city governments was to provide a higher level of services than was available in unincorporated county areas (thus discouraging urban sprawl) and to plan for, and manage, service growth within their own borders (Landis, 1993, p. 7).

Landis argues that this, 'loose but workable approach' was broken up by four forces: the rate of growth in California; the way in which Proposition 13 undermined the revenues of cities and counties and encouraged them to compete in a form of 'cashbox zoning'; the national trend towards suburban job growth and the emergence of 'edge cities'; and the gradual withdrawal of state government from the business of planning for growth. The expansive 'new deal' politics of Governor Pat Brown gave way to the conservatism of Ronald Reagan, the 'era of limits' and fiscal conservatism of Governor Jerry Brown, and the extreme caution of Governor Deukmejian. Governor Wilson was credited by one interview respondent with making, 'the most sustained effort in this area but has been plagued by the recession and so the economy and the budget problems have overshadowed his efforts' (interview, Air Resources Board, 30 March 1993).

The Limits of Local Planning

At the local level, 'many local planning documents are so general as to make it very difficult to say how much development, and what kind, would be allowed, at a level of specificity appropriate to a transportation analysis. The same is true of some zoning, where the range of permitted uses is extremely broad' (Deakin, 1988, p. 11). Although Air Quality Management Districts are specifically prohibited by law from intervening in land use planning matters that are the prerogative of other authorities, there are some signs of an increasing sensitivity to the importance of taking account of the impact of transport demand on air quality in the formulation of long-range land use plans. In the Sacramento region, where population is forecast to grow from 1.6 million people in 1992 to 2.9 million in 2015, the General Plan, which took six years to formulate, includes the concept of high density development along transport corridors. Although environmentalists thought that the new general plan was a considerable advance on its predecessors, they also pushed for mitigation measures such as financial incentives for builders constructing projects within a quarter mile of existing or proposed light rail stations.

There is also a serious imbalance between jobs and housing growth within the plan, with job growth in the downtown area, South Natomas (to the north of downtown) and Rancho Cordova (along the American River). Much of the population growth will, however, occur well to the south of these areas. For example, it is anticipated that 100,000 people will be added to the population of the already fast-growing Franklin-Laguna area between Interstate 5 and Highway 99, with two houses expected to be built for every job. This area is well beyond any foreseeable light rail extension in the next two decades.

The Sacramento area has been identified by analysts as facing particularly serious threats to long-term air quality. Los Angeles and San Francisco do have local governments which have had some impact on the pattern of development. In the Central Valley, there is a mix of local governments serving concentrations of population arranged in a linear fashion along major highways. Long commutes result from the need to access lower priced housing, but also for lifestyle reasons. Commuters may travel 50 to 75 miles into Sacramento so that they can live on a five to ten acre property in the foothills (interview, Sacramento Air Quality Management District, 7 September 1993). The general pattern of development in the Central Valley has been characterized as a, 'recipe for disaster in several respects'. Compared with the patterns of development on a dense freeway grid in Los Angeles: 'The traffic and air pollution problems to be anticipated in a linear city are even worse' (Teitz, 1990, p. 68).

One of the fundamental problems that planners face is the preference of house purchasers (who are also voters) for a particular kind of lifestyle:

> We don't want to be living in high density housing with people sharing walls in common houses like you do in Europe. Everyone wants to have their own half acre with their own little plot of land and their own little garden and their own little lawn and that means low density, and it goes back to the very fabric of our life in California (interview, CEC, 25 March 1993).

Quite apart from cultural preferences for a particular lifestyle, there are financial incentives to relocate in lower density areas. Land prices mean that properties on the desert fringe, a considerable commuting distance from metropolitan Los Angeles, cost considerably less than those nearer the main employment centres. Travel costs the average household less than land, so the household, 'can greatly reduce its housing costs by increasing its transportation costs somewhat' (Downs, 1992, p. 101). 'Suburbs within Los Angeles County have much higher densities than the suburbs of Chicago ... or those of New York City' (Downs, 1992, p. 89). These densities are sufficient to support mass transit systems in certain parts of the metropolitan area. 'However, the fastest population growth is occurring in the outlying areas which have much lower population densities' (Downs, 1992, p. 91).

The old pro-growth consensus in California has collapsed, but it has not been replaced by a new consensus: 'There is no broad consensus about appropriate policies for the state or its regions to address growth and environment in the twenty-first century' (Teitz, 1990, p. 55). Moreover, new office, retail and housing developments continue to be built in a way that is unfriendly to pedestrians and cyclists and friendly to motorists. Outside of downtown and historic areas, sidewalks are often non-existent. 'Few people want another Los Angeles, but the system of development that we have will almost certainly produce one' (Teitz, 1990, p. 70).

The Prospects for Reform

A widely held view in California is that, 'the current system of cities and counties has failed to adequately or comprehensively manage land use during California's intensive population growth' (Hamley and Block, 1990, p. 530). This has led to a number of proposals being brought before the legislature to establish effective regional governments with primary responsibility for land use planning. These measures have ground to a halt in the Assembly Local Government Committee because, 'it is clear that local entities wish to forfeit as little land-use authority as possible, no matter what new governmental structure the Legislature might create' (Hamley and Block, 1990, p. 534).

As a number of our interview respondents made clear, local governments are unlikely to be willing to surrender their land use prerogatives:

> Because politicians basically revolve around their land use decisions, their continued existence is largely dependent on their land use decisions, they're very reluctant for us to get involved (interview, Sacramento Air Quality Management District, 7 September 1993).

One approach to these problems is to try and work within the existing institutional structures by providing information:

> I think our approach is to try to influence local land use planning decisions by providing them with information so that they can do a better job of integrating energy issues into their local land use planning. You've got to do it through the grass roots level, rather than trying to impose something at the top because it won't work (interview, CEC, 25 March 1993).

It is difficult to avoid the conclusion that some structural reforms are necessary, both in the division of responsibilities between different levels of government, and in the overlapping of territorial and functional responsibilities at regional level. An underlying problem is that the state's budgetary problems have been to some extent solved by cutting back funds to local governments while giving them new responsibilities. As a consequence, 'the local governments need money and so they'll let an incompatible development come in just so they can get the tax money off that development and it's become that desperate in terms of their budgets' (interview, South Coast Air Quality Management District, 1 April 1993). Achieving a balanced and agreed distribution of resources and responsibilities between state and local governments is, however, probably asking for the impossible.

Even if effective measures could be taken to increase land use densities, or at least to increase them in transport corridors, it would be decades before the full effects of the policies would be felt. Moreover, 'because land development is overwhelmingly a private sector initiative, communities have relatively little ability to assure that their plans will be realized' (Deakin, 1988, p. 11). Land use planning does, however, set the context within which other strategies, such as the encouragement of alternatively fuelled vehicles, have to operate. As far as possible, barriers between the land use and air quality management policy communities, such as that erected by the California Clean Air Act, should be removed.

A normative lesson that is rarely drawn from the policy communities debate is that, while such policy communities may foster the development of an expert and informed debate, they may also narrow the focus of that debate and screen out links with other, relevant policy debates. This outcome is, of course, not accidental and is partly the result of the efforts of established institutions (such as counties and cities) to protect their territories against emerging institutions (such as Air Quality Management Districts). Although, as has been apparent from this chapter, the technical component of debates in policy areas such as air quality management is very important, more traditional political science concerns about institutional design, management and reform are also very relevant.

6. Commuter rail services in California

One way of reducing air pollution is to persuade motorists to leave their cars at home when they travel to work and use public transport. The principal means of doing this in California has been by bus. 'Los Angeles has the country's largest bus system, transporting 1.5 million riders a day and coming closer to achieving full capacity than in any other system in the United States' (Nadis and MacKenzie, 1993, p. 126). However, buses suffer from an image problem and are seen as more attractive to lower income users. A public transport activist commented in interview:

> Especially in California buses are seen as the very last resort of transportation and the only people who ride that are the people who don't have cars and don't have enough money to afford cars and are pretty much on the welfare system. You really don't want to even go on there, it's just dirty and the graffiti is all over the place, it's seen as a trashy way to go ... The only time you hear about transit in the state is when there is a shooting on a bus or a bus was carjacked or something like that, so the perception is a very negative one (interview, Sacramento, 18 August 1994).

Train services are seen as a way of attracting upscale commuters out of their cars. The availability of federal funds for various rail projects has increased their attractiveness, as has the voting of state funds by California electors in referenda. Politicians find the ceremonial associated with opening a new rail service or system far more attractive than the designation of a new bus route. The companies that build the lines and construct the cars are a powerful lobby for expenditure on rail services, accounting for many of the 1 500 lobbyists registered with the MTA in Los Angeles (several hundred more than cover the state legislature). Whether committing substantial funds to rail expansion is the most cost-effective way of developing public transport is a question which will be addressed in this chapter.

Three types of rail system have been expanded throughout the state:

Table 6.1   Rail commuter services in the state of California in 1994

Operator	Type of service/ opening date	Mileage/ stations	Route characteristics
BART (Bay Area Rapid Transit District)	Subway (1972)	71.5/35	Four lines converging to provide transbay service between San Francisco & Oakland; 34.5 miles of extensions building
Los Angeles County MTA	Light rail (Blue Line) (1990)	20/21	Runs from Los Angeles central business district to Long Beach
Los Angeles County MTA	Subway (Red Line) (1993)	4.4/5	Runs in Los Angeles central business district; extensions being built
Municipal Railway of San Francisco (MUNI)	Light rail (1912)	24/9 in subway	Runs in subway under Market Street downtown; five lines fan out over city
Peninsula Corridor Joint Powers Board	Heavy rail (state rescue, 1981)	76.8/34	San Francisco south to Palo Alto, San Jose, Gilroy
Sacramento Regional Transit District	Light rail (1987)	18.8/27	U-shaped route linking central business district with suburbs, extension being built
Santa Clara County Transit District	Light rail (1987)	19.33/30	Single long line with short branch
San Diego Trolley	Light rail (1981)	34.5/35	Two branches, one running to border with Mexico
Southern California Regional Rail Authority	Heavy rail (1992)	347/35	To expand to 400 route miles, fanning out from Union Station

1. 'Heavy rail' systems which use existing freight trackage to provide commuter services, often with a very limited number of trains.
2. 'Light rail' systems which operate both on reserved tracks and through the streets in city centre areas.
3. New subway systems such as that being constructed in Los Angeles.

The different types of service provided in the state are summarized in Table 6.1.

All this has been achieved only with considerable political effort, and continues to suffer from a number of setbacks, mostly associated with funding. Historically, the principal role of the California Department of Transportation (Caltrans) has been to build and maintain roads and bridges. 'The State's view of rail transportation can be characterized as one of reluctance compared to the historic public mandate for the State's responsibility for the State highway system' (Caltrans, 1991, p. 15). The Office of Rail Services within Caltrans has encountered a number of difficulties. Governor Deukmejian was highly sceptical of what he termed, 'exotic forms of transportation' in his first State of the State address. However, Deukmejian's Undersecretary of the Business, Transportation and Housing Agency, Dana Reed, was more sympathetic to rail transport. The rail officials within Caltrans themselves developed a strong *esprit de corps* during these years. The rail division within Caltrans has now grown to nearly 100 employees, but critics of the agency argue that: 'In just four years of bad management, the Caltrans rail program has gone from national leadership to a backwater of ignorance and inaction' (*Moving People*, September/October 1993). A public transportation activist complained in interview:

> The Office of Rail Services is small and it's staffed with highway folks so basically what you have is a whole bunch of highway people who are disgruntled because they lost their highway jobs and are now forced to work with the choo-choo. That's where a lot of our organization's frustration comes because we're not dealing with people who understand trains, let alone the possibility of trains. They just see it as, 'well, I have to do this' (interview, Sacramento, 18 August 1994).

In considering rail transport one is dealing with a rather different policy community from that concerned with air quality management. In many respects, it has not developed as a policy community in the way that air quality management has. At the state level, instead of having its own institutionalized policy focus in the form of the Air Resources Board, rail transport is a subordinate function within a department which historically has had different and conflicting priorities. Within the legislature, Jim Costa from the San Joaquin Valley has acted as an advocate of new legislation in the way that Byron Sher has in relation to air quality, with some support from Richard Katz and Quentin Kopp. Kopp is, however, very pro-BART (which is good politics in the Bay Area) and has attacked the CalTrain peninsula service. There is not the same insistent external pressure from citizen organizations that there is in relation to more general environmental issues. The Train Riders Association of California (TRAC) and the Modern Transit Society have some 10,000–12,000 members throughout the state, but are substantially dependent on the support of the Planning and Conservation League.

A significant contrast with the air quality management policy community is the absence of a group of committed professionals who are able to advance policy solutions based on an assessment of technical data and couched in scientific language. Apart from high speed services, which are often talked about in the United States but never seem to come to anything, railways are not a technological frontier in the sense that electric vehicles are. They therefore have less appeal in the context of the Clinton administration's emphasis on enviro-technology. The 'advocacy coalition' approach seems less relevant in the case of rail transport than it is in relation to air quality issues.

As the current president of TRAC acknowledges: 'There are a lot of institutional problems in improving the state's rail services' (*California Rail News*, May 1994). What one has in the rail area is a policy network rather than a fully developed policy community. Much depends on initiatives by individual legislators (there were eight rail-related bills before the two houses in the spring of 1994) and on the use of the state's system of direct democracy. However, as discussed later in this chapter, public opinion can be unreliable and fickle. From a British perspective, heavy reliance on the direct democracy route looks like the tactic of an 'outsider' group whose priorities are not embedded in policy assumptions and state law in the way that air quality management and cleaner fuelled vehicles are. In so far as there is institutionalization of the rail transport policy community, it occurs at the local level, which means that different areas of the state are often competing with each other for funds.

Most of the action on commuter services is thus at the local rather than the state level, although the state government is a significant provider of funds. The state government helps to provide intercity rail passenger services by funding Amtrak, the national rail service, to provide them. Commuter and urban rail services are planned and administered by local and regional transportation agencies. A commuter rail service is defined in state law using a 1971 decision by the Interstate Commerce Commission using such criteria as use by regular patrons, morning and evening peaks, frequency of stops and upper distance limit of 100 miles. In practice, however: 'The distinction between intercity and commuter service is less clear as our metropolitan areas expand' (Caltrans, 1991, p. 16). For example, the Amtrak services between the Bay Area and Sacramento (the 'Capitol' corridor) and between San Diego and Los Angeles carry some commuters, although the former service was threatened with complete withdrawal in 1995 following the announcement of nationwide cutbacks in Amtrak services. 'Data for ridership on current rail lines are limited, but indicate that interregional ridership is a mixture of regular commuters, business travellers on one-day trips, and recreational travellers' (Bernick and Hall, 1991, p. 4). As with the earlier analysis of air quality policies, the experience of Los Angeles and Sacramento in terms of the development of rail services will be examined in some depth.

THE POLITICS OF FUNDING

The federal government provides funds under a variety of schemes for commuter rail projects, although, in general, these funds are for capital outlays rather than system maintenance. The Federal Transit Administration's Section 3 Discretionary and Formula Capital Program provides funds for the establishment of new rail projects and the improvement of existing rail systems, as well as for the rehabilitation of bus systems. In California, Section 3 grants have provided significant funding for certain systems such as Metrorail in Los Angeles. In federal fiscal year 1993, transit agencies in California are estimated to have received $200.3 million in Section 3 funds. The Section 9 Urbanized Area Formula Grant is a formula-apportioned grant for capital and operating assistance for transit agencies in urban areas which may be used to fund both rail and bus services. In federal fiscal year 1993, transit agencies in California were estimated to have received $237.3 million in Section 9 funds.

The Intermodal Surface Transportation Efficiency Act of 1991, discussed in Chapter 4, will make it possible for rail programmes to access a higher percentage of federal transportation funds than was previously possible. The Act also includes the Congestion Management and Air Quality programme which funds primarily capital projects in federal air quality nonattainment areas. Given the number of nonattainment areas in California, the state expects to, 'receive a high percentage of funds under this program' (Caltrans, 1993, p. 29). Poor air quality can thus be used as a means of leveraging federal funds.

Acts such as the Intermodal Surface Transportation Efficiency Act are a classic way for members of the House of Representatives and the Senate to 'bring home the bacon' to their districts. The Act is full of specific arrangements affecting particular districts such as the $8 million set aside for the purchase of track to extend commuter rail service from San Jose to Gilroy. The availability of federal money, while no doubt welcome to hard pressed state and local governments can, however, lead to distortions in policy which undermine its effectiveness:

> The decision of planners in Los Angeles to build a 22-mile subway system in one of the world's least densely settled urban centers may seem bizarre, but federal funds will pay for half the subway's costs, while alternatives, like restoring street trolley lines, must be built solely with local money (Hamilton 1993, quoted in Nivola and Crandall, 1993, p. 42).

At the state level, the 1989 'Blueprint Legislation' was a five bill package that established a ten year plan for providing an additional $18.5 billion in revenues for transportation projects. The legislation called for $3 billion in rail bonds to be used on rail projects, together with $500 million for bus operations and capital improvements from the regular transport budget. The legislation placed three $1 billion rail bond measures before the electorate in 1990, 1992 and 1994. In 1990 voters approved the first $1 billion dollar rail bond measure, the Passenger Rail and Clean Air Bond Act of 1990 (Proposition 108), although nearly half ($491 million) of the bonding authority authorized in 1990 had not been spent by July 1992. In the same year, Proposition 116, backed by interest groups supporting public transport, provided a $1.99 billion one-off source of funding with $1 373 million for urban and commuter rail projects, $382 million for intercity rail, and $235 million for bus and bus-related projects (note the greater emphasis on rail as opposed to bus transport).

The results of these bond votes seemed to indicate substantial public support for increased spending on rail transport. It was therefore a great disappointment to rail transport advocates when the next $1 billion dollar bond measure in 1992 was not approved by the voters. This means that there will be $1 billion less in total 'Blueprint Legislation' rail bond funds than was originally envisaged. This will clearly have a negative impact on a number of programmes. Because of the significance of the 1992 decision by the voters, it is worth considering why there had been an apparent shift in public opinion since 1990.

In the intervening period the state had moved into recession, and this less expansive climate led voters to be more generally sceptical of bond measures, although voters did pass a school bonds measure by a margin almost as narrow as that by which they defeated the rail bonds measure (51 per cent to 49 per cent). In terms of the geography of support, 'precipitous declines in support in urban Southern California and the southern San Joaquin Valley were what tipped the balance against rail' (*California Rail News*, December 1992). The loss of support in Southern California seems to have been related to months of negative publicity over a plan to buy Japanese cars for the Los Angeles subway, and over a collapse in ridership on the new Metrorail system. Public hearings by Caltrans in the Central Valley seem to have created an impression that popular train services might be moved, leading to a very sharp collapse of support in Kings County which contains towns with the biggest per capita use of train service statewide. It is also striking that support for rail funding increased in three counties (Imperial, San Benito and Highlands) whose main population centres were all just beyond recently implemented or proposed rail service.

Looking at the overall pattern of support statewide, the highest levels of support for the measure were in the Bay Area (San Francisco County, 74.2 per cent; Marin County, 66.1 per cent; and San Mateo County, 62.8 per cent). The lowest level of support (20.5 per cent) was in Modoc County, a remote area in the far northeastern corner of the state which had nothing to gain from the measure. While California's system of direct democracy offers a means of translating diffuse public support for rail transport into concrete funded measures, it also has its drawbacks. It is susceptible to voters' perceptions of their immediate interests and of events which either have little direct connection with the measure or cannot be readily managed by those involved. Even those matters which can be managed by state agencies have to be handled with sophistication and care:

Establishing new rail services a week before a vote for rail bonds looks like it is definitely counterproductive. With today's cynical and suspicious body politic, voters may be prone to view the timing as manipulative. Also, any pratfalls or service shortcomings will be trumpeted by the press (*California Rail News*, December 1992).

The third rail bond voted on in 1994 appeared to be so doomed in advance, given the conservative mood of voters, that Democratic leaders in the legislature attempted without success to have it removed from the ballot. Reflecting the shift in public opinion, the bond was defeated by 65 per cent to 35 per cent. A measure to increase the gasoline tax to fund mass transit backed by the Planning and Conservation League was defeated by the massive margin of 81 per cent to 19 per cent. This measure was attacked by Assemblyman Katz and Senator Kopp as a huge public bailout of the Southern Pacific Rail Corporation. If the measure had been passed, it would have provided funds to buy a coastal route owned by Southern Pacific which had donated $449,000 in cash and services to the 'yes' campaign by the end of June (*Sacramento Bee*, 22 September 1994).

Local funding for rail projects includes the state's Local Transportation Fund, local sales taxes raised specifically for transportation purposes, and other sources such as property taxes and local general funds. The Local Transportation Fund has become a principal means of funding local bus services. The revenues in the fund are generated by a local 0.25 per cent sales tax for transportation purposes. Each county receives the amount of sales tax that was collected in their county. In 1991–92 allocations totalled $760 million statewide. These funds can be used for intercity or commuter rail services, but this has only happened to a very limited extent.

Four transit districts, including the Bay Area, directly impose a sales tax on their district. Eighteen counties have also enacted sales taxes for transportation purposes. Other local funds are also used for rail purposes. For example, 47 per cent of the San Francisco Municipal Railway's operating revenues came from the City General Fund in 1990–91 (Caltrans, 1993, p. 28).

In a litigious society local governments have to take care that any actions they take are not open to legal challenge by fiscal conservatives. In 1992 voters in San Jose approved a half cent sales tax increase for rail and highway improvements that would raise $3.5 billion over 20 years and that would have funded the Mountain View extension of the light rail system. Anti-tax activists sued, arguing that because the tax was approved with less than a two-thirds vote, it violated Proposition 13. The Sixth District Court of Appeals ruled that a two-thirds vote was necessary, so the future of San Jose's light rail expansion programme will, in effect, have to be decided by the State Supreme Court.

COMMUTER RAIL SERVICES IN LOS ANGELES

The development of heavy rail, light rail and subway services in Los Angeles symbolizes the shift towards more rail friendly policies in California. As part of the change, a new Los Angeles MTA was created by state legislation, merging the Southern California Rapid Transit District set up in 1964 (which ran the buses and built the subway) and the Los Angeles County Transportation Commission founded in 1976 (which built the light rail lines). 'The two agencies have had a long-simmering rivalry, often duplicating each other's functions with overlapping responsibilities' (*Passenger Train Journal*, July 1992, p. 11). The MTA is responsible for the light rail and subway services and has a budget of $3.3 million and more than 9 000 employees. The heavy rail commuter service to outlying parts of the metropolitan area is run by an organization which shares offices with the MTA, the Southern California Regional Rail Authority (SCRRA) which brings together Los Angeles, Ventura, Orange, San Bernadino and Riverside Counties. Some commentators have argued that, 'so much authority and tasks are vested in one agency that MTA will become, like the Bay Area's MTC, an agency with its hands frozen to the wheel, constructing transportation decisions for the region, but unable to comprehend opportunities or lead decisively' (*Moving People*, February 1993, p. 1).

The three principal elements of the new rail services in Los Angeles will be reviewed in turn in order of their establishment: light rail, subway and heavy rail. The Blue Line from Los Angeles to Long Beach was opened in 1990 and has been the most successful of the new systems in attracting riders – 42,000 a day in 1993 – although the area it serves has been hit by recession and unemployment. The Blue Line begins at the Metro Center subway station at Seventh and Flower streets, where it connects with the Red Line subway. The line follows an underground and surface route to reach the right-of-way once used by Pacific Electric's Long Beach line, which it follows for some 18 miles through South-Central Los Angeles, reaching downtown Long Beach via a line in the median of Long Beach Boulevard. Trains run on

15 minute headways through the day and every six to ten minutes in peak periods.

The line was not cheap to build, costing $877 million, in excess of $40 million a mile. Although it is the best used of the Los Angeles rail services, it only, 'recoups about 10 per cent of its operating cost through fares' (*Passenger Train Journal*, October 1991, p. 11). Operating subsidies cost $37.6 million in the 1992–93 fiscal year. The average subsidy per trip works out at $11.34 (*Sacramento Bee*, 18 February 1994). The line's overheads are boosted by a substantial security budget, reflecting the fact that it passes through some of the most gang infested areas of Los Angeles. Some $13.7 million dollars a year is spent on 124 LA county deputies who police the line (*Pacific Rail News*, February 1993, p. 9). Vandalism has been a problem on the Metrolink services, with refrigerators, shopping carts, twisted metal, furniture and old cars being placed on the tracks, while one driver was shot at. The MTA spends about $1.29 on security per passenger on Metrolink, in contrast to 0.03 cents per passenger on the most crime-ridden bus line, Line 204 (*Sacramento Bee*, 29 May 1994).

It is hoped that Blue Line ridership will be boosted by the opening of the Green Line in 1995. The Green Line is a 20 mile route constructed along the median of the recently completed Century Freeway, probably the last freeway to be built in Los Angeles. It runs from Norwalk to El Segundo, intersecting with the Blue Line at the Imperial Highway station. The cost of the Green Line has escalated from $254.5 million to $725.5 million, with a long-running political row about whether the line should be automated, an option backed by former mayor Tom Bradley but dropped after he left office. There are no reliable forecasts on the potential ridership of the line, although defence industry cutbacks at the western end of the line have depleted its market. Moreover, 'passengers will be treated to what may well be the most boring LRV ride in North America. They will have close-up views of sound walls, whizzing freeway traffic, and occasionally the top of a building' (*Pacific Rail News*, January 1994).

In 1994 work started belatedly on the third MTA light rail line that will connect Pasadena to downtown Los Angeles, estimated to cost $841 million, or over $60 million a mile. The 14 station, 13.6 mile line is scheduled to open in 1998, and is expected to carry 55,000 passengers a day between Union Station and Pasadena. It will rather confusingly also be called the Blue Line, although it is physically separate from it (plans for a subway connector between the two lines are way in the future). The Pasadena line will start from a location at Union Station near the Red Line subway entrance, and will largely use ex-Santa Fe right-of-way.

The initial seven minute ride on the Red Line subway has attracted humorous comment. Daily ridership was at 15,300 at the end of 1993, although somewhat higher at weekends because of tourists and curiosity riders. 'A lunchtime "rush hour" has developed with many downtown office workers heading for a popular rib restaurant at MacArthur Park/Westlake terminal' (*Pacific Rail News*, June 1993, p. 42). The subsidy per passenger in 1994 worked out at $21, an expensive ride for the taxpayer, the most expensive per mile in American history. Admittedly, the line has been expensive to construct because of the need to provide earthquake protection, particularly where the line crosses active faults, and the difficulty of dealing with methane gas and hydrocarbon deposits encountered during construction in abandoned oil and gas fields. Reflecting California's political clout, not least with the Clinton administration, the line has been heavily subsidized by the federal government, with more than half of the $2.45 billion cost of the third phase being met by federal money (the light rail schemes are far more dependent on local funding).

A series of construction difficulties, including Hollywood Boulevard sinking by several inches, led the federal government to take the drastic step in October 1994 of cutting all funding from the subway until local officials demonstrated that they could competently manage the construction. The work was resumed but not before mutual recriminations had occurred between the head of the MTA, Frank White, and members of the MTA board. Assemblyman Katz complained that he thought White had expected to find a place, 'where professionals were allowed to do their work without political interference or micro-managing from the board' (*Sacramento Bee*, 8 October 1994). If the work is completed, the system should eventually run for 22.7 miles with terminals at East Los Angeles, at Pico and San Vincente Boulevards and, having burrowed under the Hollywood hills, at North Hollywood in the San Fernando valley. It is hoped to extend subway services to Wilshire and Western by 1996 and to Hollywood and Vine in downtown Hollywood by 1998. Daily ridership for the completed system is expected to be over 300,000.

The Metrolink service uses existing trackage acquired from the Southern Pacific and Santa Fe to provide a commuter service to Union Station in Los Angeles, principally in the morning and evening peaks, although some trains have been added in the middle of the day. The service was started on three lines in 1992. It was expanded on lines to the western part of the metropolitan area after the Northridge earthquake shut down part of the Golden State and Antelope Valley freeways, causing serious problems for Santa Clarita and Antelope Valley commuters. By the spring of 1994 the following services were in place:

1. Santa Clarita/Antelope Valley line. A 78 mile route from Lancaster. The former route length was 35 miles before an emergency extension after the earthquake from Santa Clarita to Lancaster. Daily trains were increased from 14 to 28, and average daily ridership increased from 1 000 to 9 000. Following the reopening of the Golden State freeway in May, daily ridership fell back to 3 700 by early June.

2. Ventura County line. A 58 mile route from Camarillo to Los Angeles, extended from the former route of 47 miles to Moorpark. Twelve trains a day operate on this line. Average daily ridership increased from 2 200 to 3 000 after the quake.

3. Riverside line. Eight trains operate daily on the 58 mile route from Riverside (to the east of the central business district) and Union Station. Average daily ridership has been steady at 2 200.

4. San Bernadino line. Twenty-two trains a day operate on this 57 mile route with an average daily ridership of 4 050, up slightly from a pre-quake ridership of 3 900.

5. Orange County line. Services started in March 1994 on this 87 mile route between Oceanside in northern San Diego County and Union Station, with three rush hour trains in each direction. Ridership initially averaged 2 100 a day. Metrolink services replaced a single train in each direction that had been operated for the previous four years by the Orange County Transportation Authority. There will be a connection at Oceanside with San Diego County's 'Coaster' rail line scheduled to open in October 1994 between Oceanside and downtown San Diego.

The route map has been criticized on the grounds that it, 'has been designed to please rich interest groups rather than customers ... On present plans, a Metrorail customer will miss, among other things, Los Angeles Airport, Beverly Hills, Dodger Stadium, the Forum, the Hollywood Bowl, Santa Monica and the County Museum' (*The Economist*, 6

February 1993). Rail advocates in California have been critical of the lack of integration of the service with bus lines:

> One of the real mistakes they've made is that they haven't restructured their bus systems when they implemented new rail systems so they have, say, a dozen peak hour buses and then three or four peak hour trains competing in the same market, and they haven't managed to figure out that they could have the buses and have them feed the trains from intermediate points instead of having them run parallel all the way in ... so there is a lack of feeder bus service, the fares are set too high, and, third, the additional handicap of an ex-urban station [Union Station] with an additional transfer to a metro system (interview, rail transport advocate, Sacramento, 28 March 1993).

Before the earthquake, Metrolink ridership was around 10,000 a day. It peaked at 31,276 on 25 January 1994, fell back to around 19,000 and subsequently to under 15,000, even taking account of the new Orange County line. The experience of BART after the 1989 Loma Prieta earthquake suggests that a permanent boost of around 20 per cent in ridership might be expected. One disincentive for using Metrolink is that Union Station is a long way from some offices, so that some users in the post-earthquake period found their commute time doubling. For example, one environmental services firm where ten employees wanted to use Metrolink after the quake, had to park a car at Union Station to shuttle employees to the office which is five miles and four bus rides away from Union Station. The trains themselves are not very fast, with the 87 mile run on the new Orange County line taking around two hours.

The MTA has been beset by financial problems throughout its existence. Its 30 year Integrated Transportation Plan, developed at a time when the local economy was booming, envisaged spending $183 billion from 1990 to 2010 on light and heavy rail, subway services, electric trolley lines and new technology buses. Sales tax revenues have, however, been hit by the recession and subsidies from the federal and state governments have been smaller than expected. An anonymous Department of Transportation official is quoted as stating: 'The costs are completely off the map. We could spend the entire federal allocation for mass transit in the U.S. in L.A. for the next ten years and still not finish the rail system' (*Sacramento Bee*, 29 May 1994).

A review completed in May 1993 indicated that the MTA would have to restructure its spending programme. The 1993–94 budget planned $3.7 billion of spending, including $1.5 billion for all urban rail projects and $200 million for Metrolink. The budget anticipated a $140 million deficit, blamed on lower than anticipated tax revenues, reduced federal funding and ridership hit by the recession. The MTA has already used up a $350 million emergency cash reserve supposed to last three decades. Increasing rail fares could well depress ridership levels and initiate a vicious cycle of decline.

For a time the fate of the Pasadena line was in the balance, but the MTA managed to find enough money to complete final design and for the first construction contract, a new crossing of the Los Angeles river near the downtown area. With a $300 million deficit forecast for 1995, the plans for the Pasadena line were again affected, with the 1997 completion date likely to be extended. The MTA plans to eliminate 300 jobs and scale back some major expansion plans. Its head commented: 'We have no alternative but to make hard painful decisions' (*Pacific Rail News*, June 1994).

The MTA cannot simply sit down and make decisions on the basis of which lines are likely to attract the largest ridership, or make the greatest contribution to relieving road congestion. Delicate political considerations involving various local constituencies and the federal government have to be balanced. For example:

It was expected that L.A.'s new mayor, Richard Riordan would push hard for a start on construction of a rail line crossing the San Fernando Valley, because much of Riordan's political strength comes from this bastion of conservatism. However, the MTA decided to postpone action on the Valley line until it can attract federal funding. Valleyites are divided over whether a rail line is needed and, if so, where it should be built (*Pacific Rail News*, November 1993).

For all the effort made to expand rail services in Los Angeles, 95 per cent of the population still travel to work by car, and most of the remaining 5 per cent travel by bus. Some 75,000 passengers a day were using the various rail systems in Los Angeles in the first half of 1994, compared with 1.3 million riders a day on the buses. Supporters of Metrolink hope that it will eventually remove 40,000 cars a day from the road which, even if achieved, is of little significance in terms of the total volume of traffic in the Los Angeles metropolitan area.

SACRAMENTO

If legislators want to be reminded of the development of light rail services in California, they only have to walk a short distance from the Capitol to K street to observe the smart two or three car trains of the Sacramento system. The Sacramento system was developed with economy in mind. Siemens-Duewag U2a cars were bought off the shelf. Much of the line was single tracked, although most of it has since been doubled. When a lumber yard wanted too much money to relocate, the track was wrapped around three sides of it in a reverse curve. A review of the system noted that: 'It does not penetrate the suburban areas that should bring it substantial ridership, nor does it come close to Old Sacramento, the California Railroad Museum [these are major tourist attractions] or the Amtrak station' [used by Capitol corridor trains] (*Passenger Train Journal*, October 1988).

For all its shortcomings, weekday riders reached 23,000 by 1993, an increase of 57 per cent since the opening of the line. To a considerable extent, however, this has been at the expense of transfers from the bus service. The bus fleet carried 90.5 million passenger miles in 1983. Ten years later the trolleys carried 31.5 million passenger miles and the bus fleet 57.5 million, for an overall passenger mile total of 89 million. A senior planner with Caltrans writing in a personal capacity commented:

> In other words, we have spent more than $200 million on a light rail system and lost more than a million passenger miles a year ... The district's reports on passenger mileage suggest that virtually all of the ridership on light rail has been drawn from the pre-existing bus system. A recent State Travel Study by Caltrans reveals that public transit now accounts for only 1.5 percent of all the trips taken in the Sacramento area, an all-time low. Meanwhile, travel on Route 80 has increased by 55,000 vehicles daily and by 40,000 on Route 50. There's no evidence that the trolleys have taken any vehicles off those highways. To make matters worse, the district is now cutting its bus service – the one component of its system that has the best chance of serving a community such as ours – in order to keep the trolleys running (*Sacramento Bee*, 1 March 1994).

Plans were approved in 1995 for an early start on work on a 2.3 mile extension of the Folsom Corridor end of the route from the present Butterfield terminus to Mather Road using local money. The budget passed by the Regional Transit board in June 1994 included an allocation of $9.6 million to complete this work. This would eventually run 8.3 miles to Hazel Avenue. A proposed seven mile branch from the northeast end of the line to Antelope Road would be operated by a shuttle service. The biggest expansion would be the addition of a 12 mile line to the south side of Sacramento, but this depends on federal money and is unlikely to be completed before the early years of the 21st century. Even more speculative are plans for lines to the airport and to the university town of Davis.

The real problem with expanding the system is, however, operational rather than capital funding, although there is a view that the Clinton administration was distracted from transit issues by the health care battle. More than half of the $84 million raised for transportation projects from a local sales tax has been siphoned off for operational purposes. In 1993–94, more than 75 per cent of the tax revenue was used for daily operations, most of it for salaries for drivers, mechanics and administrators (an experienced driver was paid $17 an hour). Moreover, in order to qualify for federal aid, the Rapid Transit District has to meet the requirements of the Americans with Disabilities Act, which means that a special service for the disabled must be provided which is comparable to the service provided on regular fixed routes and with no pattern of trip denials. This service is currently provided for the Regional Transit District by Paratransit Inc. with 800 trips a day being made by April 1995. In 1994–95, provision of this service cost the Regional Transit District $2.3 million out of an operating budget of $57.5 million, a figure expected to double by January 1997 when full compliance with the federal law is required.

In 1993–94, 45 per cent of the Regional Transit District's money came from the state government, 25 per cent from the fare box, 21 per cent from local tax, 7 per cent from the federal government, and 2 per cent from other sources. Interview respondents suggested that the District needed another 50 million dollars a year to be able to provide an effective service. That would require a half cent sales tax or ten dollars a month on electricity bills. There were many competitors for the sales tax, but repeated effort might lead to a breakthrough on the sales tax front. However, cheap gas and free highways were deeply embedded, and transit services were not significant for most people. An expansion of transit services might have to be combined with road projects to make it politically attractive (round-table discussion with transit officials and environmental activists, Sacramento, 10 September 1993). A general lack of trust in government's ability to use money wisely has led voters to turn down proposals for additional taxes, with even a plan to fund additional police officers and other measures to fight crime being turned down by Sacramento voters in the June 1994 ballot.

One scheme that has been mooted is for the Sacramento Municipal Utility District (SMUD) to take over the Regional Transit District. 'By promoting and helping fund an expansion of light rail and the projected electric trolley bus network, SMUD could acquire clean air credits to use in securing state approval to build power plants that contribute to pollution' (*Pacific Rail News*, July 1993). Some respondents argued that the institutional separation of SMUD, air quality and transit authorities did not help the development of effective policy. It would be possible to make a charge on utility bills in return for one or two free transit passes per household. There might be a case for a joint powers agreement between SMUD and the Transit District, but as one interview respondent commented, it would, 'not be politically viable like many potentially effective solutions in this country' (round-table discussion, Sacramento, 10 September 1993).

Meanwhile, the Transit District is squeezed between raising fares (which invariably depresses ridership) and following the risky path of asking voters for another sales tax increase, although it managed to approve a 1994–95 budget which increased services for disabled users without raising fares on regular routes. One former District board member (who resigned to join the Clinton administration) complained: 'Most communities with transit systems have support. People here want the system on the cheap' (*Sacramento Bee*, 8 February 1994). Sacramento has, however, got relatively good value for money in its transit system. The subsidy level of $5.53 per journey was the lowest in a Department of Transportation study of ten systems built with federal money. The underlying problem is a more general one of building political support for public transport in a society centred around the motor car.

HOW COST-EFFECTIVE IS SPENDING MONEY ON PASSENGER RAIL SERVICES?

Are the billions of dollars being spent on creating a new passenger railway system for Los Angeles money well spent? Is this really a cost-effective way of bringing about significant improvements in air quality? The short answer is no. In the official California ballot pamphlet for the November 1992 election, Martin Wachs, professor of transportation planning at UCLA, and Ryan Snyder, a transportation specialist, succinctly put the case against the passenger rail bond which was defeated:

> Rail transit is so expensive to build that the measure will be able to finance very few new facilities ... there are other transportation programmes which provide far more benefit at lower cost ... Based upon average costs of rail projects in California, the total of $1 billion will build only four miles of urban subway, or 25 miles of light rail lines. How much will projects of this magnitude really do to clean up the air? ... Rail transportation works well in cities having dense residential corridors, like New York ... but not in California, where we have one car per adult and very low population densities (Secretary of State, 1992, p. 15).

In expressing such views, Wachs and Snyder are reflecting the consensus among experts. Charles Lave, an economics professor at UC Irvine, has claimed: 'There isn't a single university-level professor familiar with transportation issues in this country who would say that a rail system should be built in Los Angeles' (*Sacramento Bee*, 29 May 1994).

The Los Angeles rail service, even when completed, will meet the needs of only a limited number of commuters, so that even those who would like to use the service may not find it practical to do so:

> Everybody wants [rail service], very few find it serving their personal commute needs. The commutes here in Southern California are so diverse, less than 15 per cent of the commute trips go into the central business district. Most of the rail corridors serve the CBD, so that means that 85 per cent of the employees find it difficult to use fixed rail transit. When I say that most people support it, it's because if you take rail, you're not in my way when I come to work (interview, South Coast Air Quality Management District, 1 April 1993).

Many of the transfers to rail that take place occur from bus services rather than private cars. In the case of the Blue Line, which has been the most successful service in Los Angeles, survey evidence shows that, 'only one in four have forsaken private cars to ride the train' (*Passenger Train Journal*, November 1991, p. 12). As far as Metrolink is concerned: 'Some studies show that roughly half of Metrolink's riders used to travel by bus' (*The Economist*, 31 October 1992). However, supporting bus travel is less politically attractive because, as one interview respondent put it, 'the public bus is thought to be second rate transportation for only the poor folks'.

In 1994 the National Association for the Advancement of Colored People held up a bus fare increase in Los Angeles through an action brought in the federal district court. The lawsuit accused the MTA of spending money to improve commuter rail services largely serving white suburbanites, while bus services serving the poor and minorities are allowed to deteriorate. Some transportation researchers made the counter argument that running a rail service to the outer suburbs and making it comfortable enough to encourage affluent commuters to transfer out of their cars was bound to be expensive. This distributional problem is likely to be a recurring one for advocates of rail transport.

Los Angeles is a particularly unfavourable environment for the train, but the picture isn't much better in the Bay Area, which has much longer established rail and streetcar services. The BART system carried, 'only 3.04 percent of all the persons employed in the San Francisco and Oakland areas combined in 1990' (Downs, 1992, p. 94) At one set of office buildings adjacent to a BART station, less than 4 per cent used the subway service, the vast majority travelling to work by car (Downs, 1992, p. 42). Because BART was built in many ways as an experimental standard, it was thought it would set a standard for other lines which didn't happen. It is thus incompatible with other systems and expensive to upgrade and expand. 'Here in the Bay Area we're unfortunately saddled with the most expensive rail line to be built short of the Channel Tunnel and that's BART' (interview, Bay Area Air Quality Management District, 12 August 1994).

Spending money on rail systems does not compare well with other alternatives such as encouraging ridesharing (which would be much easier if free parking at work was taxed as a fringe benefit) and removing gross emitters from the roads:

> For example, removing one vehicle from commuter traffic in 1992 using Southern California's rideshare program (Regulation XV) was estimated to cost nearly $3,000. Investing the same amount of money in remote sensing and related programs for identifying and fixing, or retiring, gross polluting vehicles ... would result in emission reductions that were ... at least 14 times greater and probably much more than that. Similarly, air quality gains from light rail transit compare very unfavorably on an abatement cost basis with clean car programs, and offer little justification by themselves for the enormous subsidies involved in transit ridership – up to $8,000 per roundtrip passenger per year in Southern California (Hempel, 1994, p. 2).

Advocates of parking cashouts note that, 'the no-cost policy of offering downtown employees the option to cash in their employer-subsidy would remove more than twice as many, and perhaps three times as many, cars from the road' as the expensive Blue Line (Shoup, 1992,

p. 63). Even concentrating housing and workplaces around rail stations brings about a reduction in car use only in particular circumstances. It is important that clustering around rail facilities occurs at both the work and housing end of the commute trip if high rates of rail commuting are to be produced. In any case, a number of intervening factors influence the choice of travel mode. 'The most important is parking at the workplace. If people living and working near rail stations receive free parking where they work, the odds of commuting by rail drops sharply.' Moreover, 'transit-focused development, in and of itself, is unlikely to yield substantial secondary benefits like ... lower levels of air pollution' (Cervero, 1993, p. 128).

So how does one explain the political popularity of new rail systems? The rail advocate organizations are relatively weak and even the environmental movement is divided on the issue: 'Many people, including some who call themselves environmentalists, oppose transit improvements because they fear "growth" in areas that are already urbanized' (Schneider and Capo, 1991, p. 170). The starting point for analysis has to be the realization that in a state where many voters do not even bother to register, the minority who turn out to vote (35 per cent in the June 1994 elections, representing 26 per cent of those eligible to vote) are predominantly high income whites. For example, in the November 1990 elections, 81 per cent of those who were voting were white, although they made up only 57 per cent of the population (*California Political Almanac*, 1993–94, p. 10). 'The most likely political scenario for the early years of the 21st century is for dominance by an affluent, politically active overclass using its position to protect its privileges against the larger but weaker underclass' (Walters, 1992, p. 20).

Rail services like Metrolink in California tend to serve relatively wealthy, distant bedroom communities. The average income of the suburban commuters who use Metrolink is $63,000 a year; 90 per cent of them are white. Bus services serve poorer districts: according to the MTA, over 60 per cent live in households with total incomes under $15,000 and the non-white population accounts for 80 per cent of passengers. Funds used to subsidize the bus lines were transferred to the rail programme in 1986, leading fares to rise from 85 cents to $1.10 and services to be cut back (*Sacramento Bee*, 29 May 1994). Every time a passenger gets on a Metrolink train, the taxpayer provides a subsidy of $8.34, although the average commuter trip is 32 miles and the MTA claims that the per mile subsidy is equivalent to that of the average Los Angeles bus trip (*Passenger Train Journal*, September 1994).

High income whites in California tend to be relatively well disposed to environmental measures, particularly rail services which they can use if they want to and which might in any case get the other person out of their car and make the freeway less congested. Voting for rail transit is a relatively costless way of demonstrating one's environmental credentials. In Los Angeles, downtown business interests have tended to favour rail services as a means of bolstering their competitive position in relation to the 'edge cities'. Rail equipment manufacturers are very effective lobbyists and can make the politically attractive argument that a transportation-based regional economy could replace the declining defence–aerospace axis. Last but not least, the availability of substantial sums of federal money is a considerable incentive. This was particularly important in the case of the Red Line, where the initial 4.4 miles cost $1.45 billion dollars, making it, 'the nation's most expensive rail transit project' (Lange, 1993, p. 69).

The comparison between rail and road is in some ways an unfair one because motorists do not pay for the full cost of their journeys:

> User fees cover only 65 per cent of direct expenditures on highways, not even counting collateral expenditures on other government services related to highways (such as police and medical) or the costs of environmental impacts ... Just requiring the average motorist to pay for external air pollution and congestion costs caused by automobile operation would require a 50 per cent increase in the cost of driving above the current cost of thirty to forty cents per mile (Lange, 1993, p. 68).

However, even charging for parking at work raises a strong reaction so motorists are unlikely to have to pay anything approaching the real costs of their journeys. Building rail lines is an expensive and not very cost-effective way of being seen to 'do something' about air quality problems. As is often the case, political attractiveness and policy effectiveness pull in opposite directions, although rail advocates claim that the real benefits of the policy will be seen in the next century.

7.   Conclusions

This chapter sets out to achieve two objectives. It examines air pollution problems from mobile sources in Britain and the measures proposed to tackle them at the national and European Union (EU) level. It also reviews the theoretical perspectives set out in this book and suggests directions for future research, both in the area of air quality and in relation to the study of other policy areas by political scientists.

In assessing the relevance of Californian experience for Britain and other European countries, three problems of comparability arise. First, one has to consider the physical characteristics of the air pollution problem in California and whether the differences limit the applicability of any policy lessons for Britain and Europe. It has been argued that the development of standards based on Los Angeles's experience is inappropriate because, 'Los Angeles is not typical of many other parts of the world where ozone is perceived to be a problem' (Department of the Environment, 1994, p. 89). The United Kingdom Petrochemical Oxidants Review Group has warned:

> ... the Los Angeles Basin has markedly different characteristics in terms of meterology, topography, emissions and potential impacts compared with Europe. Although the physical and chemical mechanisms of ozone formation are identical, the persistence, frequency and intensity of ozone prediction are remarkably different ... The atmospheric conditions and mix of sources in southern California is very different to that which prevails in Europe and the outcome of the same policy applied in Europe may differ substantially (Department of the Environment, 1993, pp. 110–11).

Despite this warning, the Review Group accepts that: 'There are many lessons to be learnt in Europe from this Californian experience' (Department of the Environment, 1993, p. 111). Europe is affected by transboundary pollution problems in a way that the United States generally is not: for example, polluted air is often blown by light easterly winds from mainland Europe into the UK, leading to more frequent air pollution episodes in southern England. The European Union does, however, provide a policy formulation and implementation mechanism for dealing with transboundary pollution. Indeed, that is one of the reasons why environmental pollution is properly a matter dealt with at the EU level.

Another set of problems in relation to the drawing of policy lessons arises from the different character of the institutional setting in the United States, arising from such factors as the different roles of the executive and legislature, greater judicial intervention in the policy-making process, greater openness and weaker political parties. These differences are exacerbated in the case of California by the existence of a system of direct democracy. There may be some convergence in some of these areas: the role of the European Court of Justice is an important one in relation to the development of EU policy, while Britain is edging towards greater openness in government. It will be suggested later in this chapter that some of the coalition- and network-building processes observed in California do have some relevance for Europe.

A third set of differences arises from the earlier adoption of catalytic converters in California. In Britain, it is estimated that only 11 per cent of vehicles were fitted with catalytic converters in 1994. As more vehicles become fitted, the level of emissions per vehicle mile should fall. 'It is certainly the view of the Department of Transport that, for this reason, the total level of vehicle-related pollution in London will fall over the next 15 years or so, before the graph resumes an upward path' (Transport Committee, 1994, p. xiii).

AIR POLLUTION EPISODES IN BRITAIN

For most people, the London smogs of the 1950s in which fog in the Thames Valley became mixed with smoke from domestic coal fires and stationary industrial sources are now as much a part of the historic past as ration books and trams. The smog problems of London and other big cities in the 1990s do not limit vision in the way that those of the 1950s did, but they still pose considerable risks to health.

In December 1991 cold, static air trapped air pollutants from traffic fumes in the London area. Nitrogen dioxide reached record levels of over 400 ppb, considerably higher than the level of 300 ppb at which it is considered desirable to issue health warnings to people with respiratory problems. The pattern of events in terms of, 'the correlation of concentrations of nitrogen oxides with concentrations of carbon monoxide, and the absence of correlation with sulphur dioxide, strongly suggests that vehicle emissions were the dominant source of pollution' (Royal Commission on Environmental Pollution, 1994, p. 28). Deaths in the London area increased by 10 per cent or about 160 during the period of the smog. The number of people dying from respiratory diseases was 22 per cent higher than expected during the week of the smog, while those who died of cardiovascular disease rose by 14 per cent.

Ozone pollution problems occurred in the hot summer of 1994. In late June, there were record breaking levels of admissions to hospitals for respiratory problems throughout southern England, although violent thunderstorms which whipped pollen and fungal spores into the air seem to have been a precipitating factor. In July, there were a number of smog episodes when air quality fell into the Government's 'poor' band.

In Britain the highest ozone concentrations are found in rural areas, particularly on higher ground. 'At night-time in hilly terrain cooled surface air continuously drains from the high ground into valleys, so that the hilltops are exposed to relatively high ozone concentrations throughout the night' (Department of the Environment, 1993, p. 71). The worst ozone records have been noted at two sites in rural southern Britain, Lullington Heath and Yarner Wood, which both recorded over 50 hours in excess of 90 ppb in 1989 and 1990. Whereas these two sites had 149 and 155 hours over 90 ppb between 1987 and 1991, Central London experienced only 12 such hours (data from Department of Environment, 1993, pp. 87 and 89). This is because in heavy traffic areas, nitric oxide from vehicles removes the ozone from the air, but polluted air drifts from urban into rural areas. However, Friends of the Earth have pointed out, 'that if the use of catalytic converters was successful in substantially reducing emissions of nitrogen dioxide, a consequence might be increased ozone levels in London and other urban areas' (Transport Committee, 1994, p. xxiv).

The available evidence suggests that ozone concentrations, 'have been increasing by 1–2% per year since the middle of the century ... the indication is that for the majority of the "rural sites" over the period of available data there has been a significant upward trend in ozone concentrations' (Department of the Environment, 1993, p. 2). However, the peak hourly concentrations can be as high in urban as rural areas. 'Concentrations of ground level ozone can be very localised. For example, in June 1993 monitoring points at Bromley and Bexley recorded levels of 100 parts per billion – within the official "poor" air quality range – when at the same time national sites were producing readings of "good"' (Transport Committee, 1994, p. xvi).

Much of the popular debate in Britain about air pollution has focused on the increased incidence of asthma. Newspaper reports with headlines such as 'Whitehall rigs car fumes data' and 'Plot to go soft on car fumes' have argued that: 'Car pollution in cities, linked to a rapidly-growing epidemic of asthma in children, is twice as high as the Government admits' (*Independent on Sunday*, 10 September 1993). An illness which causes distressing symptoms in children lends itself to an emotive campaign by the media and environmental pressure groups.

Asthma, 'is arguably the fastest growing disease in the United Kingdom, with recent estimates suggesting that up to 20% of the children born today, may suffer asthma at some stage before the age of 18 years' (Niven, 1994, not pagenated). At the very least, the incidence of asthma would appear to have doubled over the last 15 to 20 years, although in part this may be because doctors have been more willing to diagnose a condition as asthma. In looking for explanations of this growth in the disease, air pollution is not the only relevant factor. For example, the disease is more likely to occur in the children of mothers who smoke cigarettes. One of the most important factors appears to be changes in domestic living conditions, although this has less popular appeal as a cause than factors external to the home:

> In the United Kingdom, the major allergen associated with the disease is the domestic dust mite. The design of houses, with increased use of double glazing, central heating and wall to wall carpeting has left the internal environment perfect for the proliferation of mites, with warm, humid and controlled environments favouring mite reproduction (Niven, 1994, not pagenated).

As far as air pollution is concerned, one has to distinguish between it as a cause of asthma in genetically susceptible individuals (which is thought to be unlikely mechanistically, although it may trigger the condition in such individuals) and its impact on those who already have the condition, both as a direct initiating factor and as a co-factor. Controlled studies have indicated, 'that oxides of nitrogen, ozone and sulphur dioxide have a dose dependent effect on the lungs of individuals with pre-existing asthma' (Niven, 1994, not pagenated). The effects appear to be strongest for sulphur dioxide, while those for ozone are relatively complicated. 'Although the increasing prevalence of asthma has coincided with large increases in vehicle emissions, no causal relationship with levels of air pollution has been demonstrated' (Royal Commission on Environmental Pollution, 1994, p. 31). Further research is being carried out, and it seems likely that some kind of link between air pollution and attacks of asthma in those already suffering from the disease will be established.

It is clear that, 'emissions from road vehicles are the main influence on air quality over the large areas of the UK in which there are no significant industrial emissions' (Royal Commission on Environmental Pollution, 1994, p. 24). Road transport emissions of nitrogen oxides increased by 72 per cent between 1981 and 1991 and: 'In urban areas, motor vehicles provide more than 70% of the ambient ground level nitrogen oxides' (Department of the Environment, 1993, p. 29). For nitrogen dioxides, 'the more stringent of the two EU guide values has been exceeded in every year ... The World Health Organization (WHO) guidelines have been exceeded in most years except 1993' (Transport Committee, 1994, p. xxiv). As far as ozone is concerned, WHO and European Commission guidelines have been broken at every monitoring site in the UK at least once in the late 1980s and early 1990s. Although the episodic character of high ozone levels in the UK may mean that the health effects are limited, they may be serious for those members of the population who are particularly susceptible to ozone. There are certainly no grounds for complacency:

> We are concerned that the present use of road vehicles may be causing serious damage to human health ... Despite the many uncertainties about the effects of transport pollutants on human health and the environment, there is a clear case, on the basis of what is already known, for increasing the precautionary action taken to improve air quality (Royal Commission on Environmental Pollution, 1994, p. 36).

Greenhouse gases, notably carbon dioxide, have formed a more central focus of the debate about air pollution in Britain than in California. 'It is estimated that carbon dioxide emissions from road transport almost doubled between 1970 and 1990 ... carbon dioxide emissions from UK road transport will show further substantial increases over the next 25 years' (Royal Commission on Environmental Pollution, 1994, p. 40). The contribution of the United Kingdom to greenhouse gases is far smaller than that of the United States, but it still produces a level of carbon dioxide emissions three times as great as its share of world population (3 per cent compared with 1 per cent).

There are considerable scientific uncertainties in this area which complicate policy formation. Global warming in 2050 compared to

1990 could lie in the range 0.5°C to 2.5°C: outcomes which could have very different consequences for economic activity and human populations, and hence imply more or less radical policy solutions. 'Future global-mean temperature is largely dependent upon three unknowns: future global emissions of greenhouse gases ... the sensitivity of the climate system to greenhouse gas forcing (currently estimated to range from 1.5° to 4.5°C), and the timing of significance of non-greenhouse related climate forcing mechanisms (e.g. volcanic eruptions, solar variability)' (Hulme, 1994, not pagenated). This is not a very solid basis for long-run policy formation, but it does not mean that relevant policies should not be attempted:

> From a natural science perspective, such uncertainty may be so large as to render future climate change scenarios all but useless. From a policy science perspective, however, such uncertainty need not inhibit sensible policy formation since all policy is formulation under conditions of great uncertainty (Hulme, 1994, not pagenated).

Report of the Royal Commission on Environmental Pollution

In October 1994 the standing Royal Commission on Transport and the Environment published a major report on Transport and the Environment. The report argued that: 'The unrelenting growth of transport has become possibly the greatest environmental threat facing the UK' (Royal Commission on Environmental Pollution, 1994, p. 1). The report concluded that: 'At present pollutants from vehicles are the prime cause of poor air quality that damages human health, plants and the fabric of buildings' (Royal Commission on Environmental Pollution, 1994, p. 233). The transport system had become unsustainable to the extent that placing significant constraints on its future development was justified. Two key recommendations made in relation to air quality were the achievement of full compliance by 2005 with WHO health-based air quality guidelines for transport-related pollutants, and to limit emissions of carbon dioxide from surface transport in 2000 to the 1990 level.

The report was welcomed by environmental groups, which saw it as a major step forward in their campaign for greener transport policies. Business and motoring organizations were critical of the report, particularly of a proposal to increased fuel duty each year so as to double the price of fuel relative to other goods by 2005. Not surprisingly, the Government sat on the fence, with the transport secretary, Dr Brian

Mawhinney, calling for, 'a national debate about whether we are prepared for the costs and changes in our transport habits that will result' (*Financial Times*, 27 October 1994).

In terms of this analysis, it is interesting to examine to what extent the Royal Commission took account of Californian experience. The aspect of the Californian legislation that attracts most international attention is the electric cars programme, and this is referred to in the Commission's report. Given that most UK electricity is obtained from burning fossil fuels, the widespread use of electric vehicles could increase the amount of carbon dioxide emitted per vehicle-kilometre. 'We conclude that there is no overall benefit for the environment in the widespread use in the UK of electrically powered cars and heavy vehicles of the types at present available' (Royal Commission on Environmental Pollution, 1994, p. 143). The Commission did, however, favour the use of CNG as a substitute for diesel in vehicles making frequent stops in urban areas (such as buses and refuse collection vehicles), noting that some CNG vehicles have met the California ULEV standard.

The construction of new rail systems in California is mentioned by the Commission in relation to the work being undertaken in Los Angeles, 'the prime example of a car-based city' (Royal Commission on Environmental Pollution, 1994, p. 93). In Chapter 6 it was questioned whether the development of new rail systems was the most cost-effective response to the problem of air pollution from mobile sources. The Commission itself notes: 'Considered as a substitute for journeys hitherto made by car, public transport's fundamental limitation is that, however ingeniously it is managed and adapted, collective provision can never be completely reconciled with the individual's choice about what journeys to make and when to make them' (Royal Commission on Environmental Pollution, 1994, p. 93).

The gross emitter debate has attracted less attention outside California than the more glamorous aspects of the state's programmes. Nevertheless, it is an area in which progress can be made relatively rapidly. The Royal Automobile Club monitored the exhausts of 60,000 vehicles and found that, '12% of them produced more than half the total pollution' (*The Economist*, 17 September 1994). The Royal Commission notes that, 'a small group of cars (about 10%) produced more than half the carbon monoxide emitted' (Royal Commission on Environmental Pollution, 1994, p. 140). The Department of Transport takes a more cautious view, arguing that a lower proportion of pollution is accounted for by badly maintained vehicles (Transport Committee, 1994, p. xx).

Some London local authorities have campaigned to be allowed to enforce anti-pollution laws themselves. The Royal Commission is rather dismissive of this idea, arguing that, 'it is unlikely that resources would be available for enforcement campaigns that would have a noticeable impact on air quality outside the immediate area' (Royal Commission on Environmental Pollution, 1994, p. 142). The Transport Committee took a more positive view of suggestions put forward by the Association of London Authorities and the London Boroughs Association. They recommended that favourable consideration should be given to legislation, 'to give local authorities in the capital the power to carry out emissions checks on vehicles and to serve the driver, where necessary, with an enforcement notice requiring remedial action to be taken. Such a system could be financed through a fixed penalty charge' (Transport Committee, 1994, p. xl).

In January 1995 the Department of the Environment (1995) published a policy paper which stated that new legislation would be introduced giving district councils a new duty to review local air quality. Government funds would be provided to carry out the necessary assessments. Those councils covering areas where air quality targets have been breached would be required to set up 'Air Quality Management Areas' and to cooperate with neighbouring authorities in drawing up city-wide and regional plans. Both the title and the proposed structure reflect the Californian approach. As in California, however, more thought seems to have been given to structures and legal duties than to the actual measures which might improve air quality. For example, there was no commitment to restrain traffic during severe air pollution episodes.

The Transport Committee's idea of empowering local authorities to impose penalties on vehicles with defective exhausts might be a way of tackling particular forms of air pollution that have an adverse effect on health. For example, it has been suggested that, 'a 10% reduction in particulates would result in several hundred fewer early deaths a year in London' (Royal Commission on Environmental Pollution, 1994, p. 31). The Commission's main recommendation in this area is to have more stringent MoT tests for cars, and to apply them to cars one year after registration. However, the more stringent the test, the greater the incentive to evade it through fraud, particularly among those motorists most likely to be gross emitters. Making one year old cars take the test is not very useful, as most of the problems are with older cars. The Royal Commission questions the reliability of remote sensing technology, but there is a case for more research in this area, building on the work that has been undertaken in California.

POLICIES OF THE EUROPEAN UNION

The EU has issued a number of directives throughout the 1980s and 1990s concerned with air quality standards. In 1980 and 1985 it set limits for sulphur dioxide and suspended particulates and for nitrogen dioxide. A 1992 directive (92/72/EEC) dealt with ground-level ozone. The purpose of this directive was to establish a harmonized procedure for monitoring, for exchanging information, and for informing and warning the population. The intention was to obtain wider knowledge of this form of air pollution. A report on the subject has to be submitted to the European Commission within four years of the implementation of the directive.

In 1994 the Commission approved a draft directive on ambient air quality assessment and management as part of a review and simplification of EU environmental legislation for air and water standards. It was argued that:

> The existing Directives, particularly those on sulphur dioxide and suspended particulate matter and on lead, gave a major push to reduce the concentrations of the respective pollutants in ambient air and there are only a few 'hot spots' left in the Community where breaches of the limit values occur (European Commission, 1994, p. 1).

Nevertheless, a number of limitations in the effectiveness of the directives were apparent. The directives, 'differ in the times when they were adopted, and the philosophical basis on which they were agreed and do not provide an overall view of the situation regarding ambient air quality in the European Community' (European Commission, 1994, p. 11). Member states had not always acted with sufficient speed to meet the limit values. Large differences in monitoring strategies had been noted in comparable situations within and between member states. Most serious of all in terms of developing and delivering an effective policy, 'long term air quality objectives have not been considered to be very important by the majority of Member States' (European Commission, 1994, p. 2).

The five pollutants already covered by directives (sulphur and nitrogen dioxide, ground-level ozone, lead and hydrocarbon particles) would be extended so that up to 14 air pollutants would be the subject of regulations. Pollution limits for substances already covered by EU law would be set by the end of 1996, with a deadline of the end of 1999 for the other nine. A more standardized approach would be adopted with common reporting standards; setting pollution limits to be attained within ten to 15 years; and setting provisional ceilings. The Commission would eventually publish regular reports on air quality throughout the EU.

The Commission noted that there were large differences between member states, 'with regard to national air pollution strategy in general and ... the use of emission or product standards and/or ambient air quality standards' (European Commission, 1994, p. 11) As far as the UK is concerned, the Commission noted that: 'The major element of the UK's clean air policy is flexibility. This appears to be strongly effect-orientated but the fact that no national ambient air quality standards have been set as yet, other than those of the EC, contradicts this view' (European Commission, 1994, p. 8). The UK's reaction to the development of the Air Quality Framework Directive was qualified. 'Provided that the principles of subsidiarity and cost-benefit analysis are fully recognised, the UK will welcome the proposals as the basis for a rational approach to air quality management in Europe' (Department of the Environment, 1994, p. 89). In other words, the UK would not welcome proposals which interfered with its pragmatic and flexible national approach, or which imposed too great a burden on the economy. The Commission's efforts to drive forward air quality management policy may encounter resistance by member states and considerable implementation problems.

REVIEW OF THE THEORETICAL FRAMEWORKS

In Chapter 1, an account was presented of two analytical frameworks which could assist the study of the policy problem: policy communities and the advocacy coalition framework. The general position taken here is that these approaches are complementary rather than opposed alternatives. The policy community approach provides guidelines for drawing a general map of the actors active in a policy arena. Having made a preliminary map, it is possible to check its broad accuracy in the initial interviews with policy actors. The fieldwork suggested that the energy utilities were more significant actors in air pollution policy than had been realized at the design stage of the research.

The policy community approach is about more than political cartography, however. It draws our attention to the way in which interests are institutionalized both through continuing relationships between institutions with formal decision-making power and organized interests, and, in some cases, through the capture of institutions by interests (or of interests by institutions). What emerges is a fairly static policy-making picture in which there are broadly shared assumptions about who the key actors are and what policies are acceptable and feasible. If one relied on the advocacy coalition framework alone, one might miss the extent to which beliefs are constrained by interests, or, following Dowding's insight, captured and distorted by institutions or interests. The energy utilities are not advocating clean fuel vehicles because they have experienced a policy conversion, but because such vehicles can expand the market for their products.

Where the policy community framework is not very helpful is in explaining non-incremental change. Sabatier argues for the need to look at policy change over a decade or more because, 'a focus on short-term decision making will underestimate the influence of policy analysis because such research is used primarily to alter the perceptions and conceptual appartus of policy makers over time' (Sabatier, 1993a, p. 16). Sabatier also points out that we cannot evaluate programme success properly if we do not look at at least one time cycle of formulation, implementation and reformulation.

As this book focuses largely on the period since the passage of the California Clean Air Act in 1988, it does not provide a good test of Sabatier's approach. However, the development of air pollution policy in California since the Second World War has been reviewed. A crucial event in the development of air pollution policies in California and the United States more generally was Haagen-Smit's demonstration of the mechanism of photochemical smog formation. This finding was initially opposed by those whose interests were threatened, such as the oil and automobile industries which initially tried to discredit Haagen-Smit's argument. After some years, his views won scientific acceptance, and a well-qualified group of air quality professionals emerged who made a significant contribution to the policy debate. Research into air pollution became scientifically prestigous and, as the role of the motor vehicle in air pollution became apparent, local solutions were replaced by state and federal policy innovations.

Sabatier's framework distinguishes between a Clean Air Coalition of environmentalists and their allies and an Economic Feasibility Coalition which emphasized technologically feasible solutions and the use of economic incentives. The evidence reviewed in this book suggests that the Economic Feasibility Coalition was gaining ground in the early 1990s. Officials in the various air pollution agencies at state and local level operated within a framework which placed a high value on technological feasibility, and they were also influenced by the growing emphasis based on policy solutions which used the market mechanism rather than regulation. Vehicle manufacturers and the oil companies emphasized the limits of current clean fuel technology. The main business allies of the environmentalists, the energy utility companies, faced increasing challenges to the legality of their using income from charge payers to subsidize clean vehicles. The environmentalists found their membership base and political influence in decline.

Using Kingdon's policy stream approach, the passage of state and federal clean air legislation in 1988 and 1990 represented a coming together of the problem, policy and political streams. By 1994, the political stream had largely dried up. Under the impact of recession, voters' interest in environmental issues had waned, and they were no longer prepared to back bond issues to develop public transport. In her economic plan for California, Kathleen Brown emphasized such policies as making California the international hub of green technology, committing the state to purchasing clean fuel vehicles, and creating an incentive programme to stimulate the manufacture and purchase of cleaner and more fuel efficient cars. However, Kathleen Brown was decisively defeated by Pete Wilson. The way in which he used his veto as Governor suggested that he had little enthusiasm for programmes to develop cleaner vehicles or fuels. He was more than willing to listen to business concerns about more stringent air pollution enforcement campaigns. In doing this he was responding to a public mood which seemed to favour less government.

Looking at the overall structure of the policy community, it favoured a cautious, incremental approach to air pollution policy. The advocacy coalitions for cleaner air were weaker than those which placed a high value on economic feasibility. The overall political context weakened the clean air advocates even further. People who live outside California who are not air pollution experts have generally got hold of the idea that California is forcing the development of new technology in a way that demonstrates the ability of government effectively to advance new solutions to environmental problems. The reality is more murky, and it is quite likely that a political fudge will be devised to deal with the inability and unwillingness of the major motor manufacturers to meet the state's targets.

The debate on policy communities is showing signs of being played out, although there is more work to be done on the normative implications of a decision-making process in which relatively closed, inward looking policy networks play a large part. Doctoral students and other entrants to the profession need to know about the policy community debate; when they can use the policy community approach; and what its limits are. The advocacy coalition frameworks approach is more of an intellectual frontier on which more work remains to be done: for example, in relation to how coalitions form and maintain themselves over time, and the types of strategies coalitions are likely to adopt to pursue their policy goals (Schlager, 1994).

Sabatier, in a communication to the advocacy coalitions network (12 September 1994) has identified three voids in current versions of the framework: the absence of any serious attention to the problems in getting from shared beliefs to coordinated behaviour; the question of how major (policy core) policy change comes about; and the role of public opinion. He admits that viewing public opinion as an exogenous constraint is unsatisfactory because advocacy coalitions exert effort seeking to influence public opinion. What the findings in this book suggest is that public opinion has a number of influences on the policy process:

1. Through the outcomes of votes on initiatives and bond issues.
2. Through fluctuations in the income and support base for environmental pressure groups.
3. Through perceptions by candidates for public office of what constitutes a 'hot button' issue. Although environmental issues are rarely at the top of the electoral agenda, they were more prominent in 1990 than 1994.

Public opinion is, however, a background rather than a foreground influence. It is only one factor influencing the fluctuating political strengths of advocacy coalitions within the policy community. As Sabatier's work suggests, in analysing such coalitions, one should not focus just on interest groups, but also on legislators, legislative aides, agency officials and researchers. Within the policy community, there is a market for new ideas, particularly in a setting such as California where there is an expectation that legislators will introduce new measures. Which ideas survive and succeed depend on their relationship to core beliefs, their feasibility and the extent to which they threaten existing interests. In many respects, the political process in California is geared to preventing things happening, and it is only through the exploitation of windows of opportunity by policy entrepreneurs (such as Byron Sher of the 1988 Clean Air Act) that any change actually occurs.

FUTURE RESEARCH: INSTITUTION-BUILDING

One of the lessons to emerge from the Californian research was the willingness of a variety of actors in the policy process to engage in broadly based coalition building. Such coalitions were capable of helping to frame and define issues, building support for more effective policies, and assisting in the policy implementation process. In part, these networking activities were assisted by the relatively open character of the political process in California, and the existence of multiple points of access to the decision-making process. This does not mean, however, that Californian experience has no lessons for rather different political settings.

As part of the programme for European Cooperation in the Field of Scientific and Technical Research (generally referred to by the French acronym, COST), a management committee (COST 618) has been set up to promote social science research on urban air pollution with particular reference to information policy and institution-building. Drawing on the experience of the work in California, the author drafted a research design for a programme of cross-national European research in the area of institution-building. (The COST programme covers European countries which are not EU members such as Hungary.)

The proposed European research would attempt to assess the way in which a variety of institutional mechanisms contribute to urban air pollution control and abatement. Networks are seen as facilitating coalition-building between different actors, improving the chances of the identification and implementation of effective policy solutions. Institution-building is seen not in terms of the creation of new formal organizations or agencies, but as a network-building process in which networks stabilize and produce innovative policy solutions which are capable of adoption by institutional participants in the network. The process being analysed is thus one of shaping beliefs, creating coalitions, building networks and establishing institutions.

Following Sabatier, a key element in the analysis would be the examination of existing core belief systems, recognizing that these can be very resistant to change and that differences in core beliefs may be a source of conflict between network participants. Change factors leading to challenges to existing core beliefs would be analysed. The limits to that process, and the ways in which it is constrained by existing interests and perceptions, would form a central part of the analysis. The research would also identify key structural variables influencing the context in which network-building occurs, such as local government structures and competences and financial constraints. Network functions such as providing support, resolving conflicts, diffusing knowledge and monitoring policy implementation would be assessed. Finally, the research would analyse the way in which networks develop: how they are established and mobilized, and how they are maintained as entities which contribute to policy formation and implementation.

CONCLUSIONS

This book has shown that the formation and implementation of air pollution policy in California is a highly political process in which beliefs and interests play a crucial role. Analyses of policies for coping with the environmental impact of transport which focus simply on their feasibility, or their fit with economic models, are likely to be insufficient. The political dimension needs to be an integral part of the analysis. Policy discussions may focus on the more glamorous aspects of policy such as electric cars or subway-building (which are inevitably referred to in media discussions of California), but pay less attention to more mundane policies which might be more cost-effective, such as efforts to deal with the gross emitter problem.

The formation and implementation of air pollution policies in California is a more imperfect and flawed process than superficial accounts might lead us to believe. California has now had an air pollution problem for over 50 years. It has improved, but maintaining that improvement in the face of a continuing increase in vehicle miles travelled is not easy. The problem is unlikely to be overcome in the foreseeable future, but it may be contained. The underlying political constraint is that most cars are driven by voters, and most voters own a car. The best one can hope is that the cars on the road will continue to become cleaner.

Because California has been a car dominated society for so long, it provides a good test of which policy solutions are relatively feasible and effective and which are not. As countries like the People's Republic of China become more prosperous, car ownership will rise and they will experience problems of air pollution from motor vehicles. On a global scale, the challenge of air pollution from motor vehicles is likely to increase. California, as so often, has pointed to a future which we may not want but which we cannot easily prevent.

Bibliography

Air Quality Plan (1991), *Final Air Quality Management Plan, 1991 Revision*, Diamond Bar: South Coast Air Quality Management District.

Bannister, D. and Button, K. (1993), 'Environmental Policy and Transport: An Overview', in Banister, D. and Button, K. (eds), *Transport, the Environment and Sustainable Development*, London: E. & F.N. Spon.

Barber, M.B. (1993), 'Business Blues', *California Journal*, **XXIV** (5), 9–14.

Bernick, M.S. and Hall, P. (1991), *Land-Use Law and Policy for Maximising Use of California's New Interregional Rail Lines*, Berkely: California Policy Seminar.

Bottles, S.L. (1987), *Los Angeles and the Automobile*, Berkeley: University of California Press.

Briennes, M. (1975), 'The Fight Against Smog in Los Angeles, 1943–57', PhD thesis, University of California.

Bryner, G.C. (1993), *Blue Skies, Green Politics: The Clean Air Act of 1970*, Washington D.C.: Congressional Quarterly Press.

Button, K. (1993), *Transport, the Environment and Economic Policy*, Aldershot: Edward Elgar.

Button, K. and Rothengatter, W. (1993), 'Global Environmental Degradation: The Role of Transport', in Banister, D. and Button, K. (eds), *Transport, the Environment and Sustainable Development*, London: E. & F.N. Spon.

California Air Pollution Control Laws: 1993 edition, Sacramento: California Air Resources Board.

California Air Resources Board (1991), 'Facts about Air Pollution and Health', Sacramento: Air Resources Board Public Information Office.

California Air Resources Board (1993), 'Mobile Source Emission Reduction Credits', Sacramento: Stationary Source Division/Mobile Sources Division.

California I/M Review Committee (1993a), *Evaluation of the California Smog Check Program and Recommendations for Program Improvements: Executive Summary, Fourth Report to the Legislature*, Sacramento: Air Resources Board.

California I/M Review Committee (1993b), *Evaluation of the California Smog Check Program and Recommendations for Program Improvements: Fourth Report to the Legislature*, Sacramento: California Air Resources Board.

California Political Almanac 1991–92, Sacramento: California Journal Press.

California Political Almanac 1993–94, Sacramento: California Journal Press.

Caltrans (1991), *California Rail Passenger Development Plan 1991–96 Fiscal Years*, Sacramento: State of California Department of Transportation.

Caltrans (1993), *California Rail Passenger Program Report 1993/94 2002/03*, Sacramento: State of California Department of Transportation.

Cawson, A., Morgan, K., Webber, D., Holmes, P. and Stevens, A. (1990), *Hostile Brothers: Competition and Closure in the European Electronics Industry*, Oxford: Clarendon Press.

Cervero, R. (1989), *American's Suburban Centers: The Land-Use Transportation Link*, Boston: Unwin Hyman.

Cervero, R. (1993), 'Ridership Impacts of Transit-Focused Developments in California', University of California Transportation Center Working Paper No. 176, Berkeley.

Chu, X. and Fielding, G.J. (1994), 'Electronic Road Pricing in Southern California: Policy Obstacles to Congestion Pricing', University of California Transportation Center, Working Paper No. 189, Berkeley.

Cohen, R.E. (1992), *Washington at Work: Back Rooms and Clean Air*, New York: Macmillan.

Culver, J.H. and Syer, J.C. (1988), *Power and Politics in California, Third Edition*, New York: Macmillan.

Davie, M. (1972), *In the Future Now: A Report from California*, London: Hamish Hamilton.

Davis, M. (1990), *City of Quartz: Excavating the Future in Los Angeles*, London: Verso.

Deakin, E. (1988), *Transportation and Land Use Planning in California: Problems and Opportunities for Improved Performance*, Berkeley: California Policy Seminar.

Department of the Environment (1994), *Ozone in the United Kingdom 1993: Third Report of the United Kingdom Petrochemical Oxidants Review Group*, London: Air Quality Division, Department of the Environment.

Department of the Environment (1995), 'Air Quality: Meeting the Challenge', London: Department of the Environment.

Dowding, K. (1994a), 'Policy Networks: Don't Stretch a Good Idea Too Far', in Dunleavy, P. and Stanyer, J. (eds), *Contemporary Political Studies, Volume One*, Belfast: Political Studies Association.

Dowding, K. (1994b), 'Beyond Metaphor? Characteristic Explanation of Policy Networks', paper delivered at the American Political Science Association conference, New York.

Downs, A. (1992), *Stuck in Traffic: Coping with Peak-Hour Traffic Congestion*, Washington D.C.: The Brookings Institution.

Dudley, G. (1983), 'The Road Lobby: A Declining Force?', in Marsh, D. (ed.), *Pressure Politics*, London: Junction Books.

Environmental Protection Agency (1994), 'Fact Sheet: Federal Implementation Plans in California', United States Environmental Protection Agency Region IX, San Francisco.

Environmental Quality Laboratory (1972), *Smog: a Report to the People*, New York: Ward Ritchie.

European Commission (1994), 'Proposal for a Council Directive on Ambient Air Quality Assessment and Management', COM(94) 109 final, Brussels.

Friends of Kathleen Brown (1994), *Building a New California: The Kathleen Brown Economic Plan*, Los Angeles: Friends of Kathleen Brown.

Grant, W. (1989), *Government and Industry: A Comparative Analysis of the US, Canada and the UK*, Aldershot: Edward Elgar.

Grant, W. and Nath, S. (1984), *The Politics of Economic Policymaking*, Oxford: Basil Blackwell.

Grant, W., Paterson, W. and Whitston, C. (1988), *Government and the Chemical Industry: A Comparative Analysis of Britain and West Germany*, Oxford: Clarendon Press.

Grodin, J.R., Massey, C.R. and Cunningham, R.B. (1993), *The California State Constitution: A Reference Guide*, Westport: Greenwood Press.

Guiliano, G. and Wachs, M. (1992), 'A Comparative Analysis of Regulatory and Market-Based Transportation Demand Strategies', School of Urban and Regional Planning, University of Southern California.

Guiliano, G., Hwang, K. and Wachs, M. (1992), 'Employee Trip Reduction in Southern California: First Year Results', School of Urban and Regional Planning, University of Southern California.

Haagen-Smit, A.J. (1964), 'The Control of Air Pollution', *Scientific American*, **210** (1), 25–31.

Halberstam, D. (1979), *The Powers That Be*, London: Chatto and Windus.

Hall, J.V. (1993), 'The Atmosphere We Breathe', in Palmer, T. (ed.), *California's Threatened Environment: Restoring the Dream*, Washington D.C.: Island Press.

Hamley, H. and Block, A.G. (1990), 'Regional Government', *California Journal*, **XXI** (11), 530–34.

Harvey, R.B. (1991), *The Dynamics of California Government and Politics*: Fourth Edition, Dubuque: Kendall-Hunt.

Hempel, L.C. (1994), 'The Greening of IVHS: Integrating the Goals of Air Quality, Energy Conservation Mobility and Access in Intelligent Transportation Policy', paper presented at the National Conference on Transportation and the Environment, Washington D.C.

Hirsch, F. (1977), *Social Limits to Growth*, London: Routledge and Kegan Paul.

Hobbes, T. (1651), *Leviathan or the Matter, Forme and Power of a Commonwealth Eccleiasticall and Civil*, Oxford: Basil Blackwell.

Hughes, P. (1993), *Personal Transport and the Greenhouse Effect*, London: Earthscan.

Hulme, M. (1994), 'Can Predictions of Future Climate Change Be Made?' paper presented at the International Academic Conference on the Environment, Manchester.

Hurley, S. (1989), *Natural Reasons*, New York: Oxford University Press.

Ingram, H. and Schneider, A. (1990), 'Improving Implementation. Through Framing Smarter Statutes', *Journal of Public Policy*, **10** (1), 67–88.

Jenkins-Smith, H.C. and Sabatier, P.A. (1993), 'The Study of Public Policy Processes', in Sabatier, P.A. and Jenkins-Smith, H.C. (eds), *Policy Change and Learning: An Advocacy Coalition Approach* Boulder: Westview.

Jordan, G. (1990), 'Sub-Governments, Policy Communities and Networks: Refilling the Old Bottles?', *Journal of Theoretical Politics*, **2** (3), 319–38.

Jordan, G., Maloney, W.A. and McLaughlin, A.M. (1992), 'Assumptions About the Role of Groups in the Policy Process: The British Policy Community Approach', University of Aberdeen British Interest Group Project Working Paper No. 4.

Judge, D. (1993), *The Parliamentary State*, London: Sage.

Kingdon, J.W. (1984), *Agendas, Alternatives and Public Policies*, New York: Harper Collins.

Kirlin, J.J. (1990), 'Commands or Incentives to Improve Air Quality', in Kirlin, J.J. and Winkler, D.R. (eds), *California Policy Choices, Volume Six*, Los Angeles: University of Southern California.

Kunstler, J.H. (1993), *The Geography of Nowhere: The Rise and Decline of America's Man-Made Landscape*, New York: Simon and Schuster.

Kurani, K., Turrentine, T. and Sperling, D. (1994), 'The Zero Emissions Vehicle Market: A Diary Survey of New Car Buyers in California', Institution of Transportation Studies, Davis.

Lamare, J.W. (1994), *California Politics: Economics, Power and Policy*, Minneapolis/St Paul: West Publishing.

Landis, J.D. (1992), 'How Shall We Grow? Alternative Futures for the Greater San Francisco Bay Region', California Policy Seminar, University of California.

Lange, L.E. (1993), 'Transportation and the Environmental Costs of Auto Dependency', in Palmer, T. (ed.), *California's Threatened Environment*, Washington D.C.: Island Press.

Law, R.M., Wolch, J.R. and Takahashi, L.M. (1993), 'Defense-less Territory: Workers, Communities and the Decline of Military Production in Los Angeles', *Environment and Planning C: Government and Policy*, **11**, 291–315.

Lazzareschi, C. (1977), 'The Pressure Tactics of Smog Boss Tom Quinn', *California Journal*, **8**, July.

Lester, J.P. and Bowman, A.O'M. (1989), 'Implementing Environmental Policy in a Federal System: A Test of the Sabatier-Mazmanian Model', *Polity*, **XXI** (4), 731–53.

Lloyd, A.C., Wuebben, P. and Leonard, J.H. (1991), 'Electric Vehicles and Future Air Quality in the Los Angeles Basin', paper presented at the 84th Annual Meeting, Air and Waste Management Association, Vancouver.

Macdonald, C. (1993), 'Water Supply: A New Era for a Scarce Resource', in Palmer, T. (ed.), *California's Threatened Environment: Restoring the Dream*, Washington D.C.: Island Press.

Marsh, D. (1992), 'Youth Employment Policy 1970–1990: Towards the

Exclusion of the Trade Unions', in Marsh, D. and Rhodes, R.A.W. (eds), *Policy Networks in British Government*, Oxford: Clarendon Press.

Marsh, D. and Rhodes, R.A.W. (1992), 'Policy Communities and Issue Networks: Beyond Typology', in Marsh, D. and Rhodes, R.A.W. (eds), *Policy Networks in British Government*, Oxford: Clarendon Press.

Nadis, S. and MacKenzie, J.J. (1993), *Car Trouble*, Boston: Beacon Press.

Niven, R. (1994), 'Air Pollution and Asthma', paper presented at the International Academic Conference on the Environment, Manchester.

Nivola, P.S. and Crandall, R.W. (1993), 'Still Crazy After All These Years? The Political Economy of U.S. Energy Policy for Automotive Transportation', paper presented at the annual meeting of the Western Political Science Association, Pasadena.

OECD (1992), *Market and Government Failures in Environmental Management: The Case of Transport*, Paris: Organization for Economic Cooperation and Development.

Paquette, P. (1993), 'The Green Tide', *California Journal*, **XXIV** (2), 15–18.

Pressman, J.L. and Wildavsky, A.B. (1973), *Implementation*, Berkeley: University of California Press.

Price, C.A. (1993), 'Lobbying, post-140', *California Journal*, **XXIV** (10), 31–4.

Public Utilities Commission (1993), 'Progress Report of the California Public Utilities Commission Concerning Policies on Rates, Equipment and Infrastructure Implemented to Facilitate the Use of Electric Power and Natural Gas to Fuel Low-Emission Vehicles', prepared for the California State Legislature.

Rand, C. (1967), *Los Angeles: The Ultimate City*, New York: Oxford University Press.

Reisner, M. (1986), *Cadillac Desert: The American West and its Disappearing Water*, New York: Penguin.

Rhodes, R.A.W. and Marsh, D. (1992), 'Policy Networks in British Politics: A Critique of Existing Approaches', in Marsh, D. and Rhodes, R.A.W. (eds), *Policy Networks in British Government*, Oxford: Clarendon Press.

Rhodes, R.A.W. and Marsh, D. (1994), 'Policy Networks: "Defensive" Comments, Modest Claims and Plausible Research Strategies', paper presented to the Political Studies Association annual conference, Swansea.

Rieff, D. (1991), *Los Angeles: Capital of the Third World*, New York: Simon and Schuster.

Ringquist, E.J. (1993), *Environmental Protection at the State Level: Politics and Progress in Controlling Pollution*, Armonk: M.E. Sharpe.

Rose, R. (1993), *Lesson-Drawing in Public Policy*, Chatham, N.J.: Chatham House Publishers.

Royal Commission on Environmental Pollution (1994), Eighteenth Report, Transport and the Environment, London: HMSO.

Sabatier, P.A. (1986), 'Top-Down and Bottom-Up Approaches to Implementation Research: A Critical Analysis and Suggested Synthesis', *Journal of Public Policy*, **6** (1), 21–48.

Sabatier, P.A. (1988), 'An Advocacy Coalition Framework of Policy Change and the Role of Policy-Oriented Learning Therein', *Policy Sciences*, **21**, 129–68.

Sabatier, P.A. (1991), 'Towards Better Theories of the Policy Process', *Political Science and Politics*, **XXIV** (2), 147–56.

Sabatier, P.A. (1993a), 'Policy Change Over a Decade or More', in Sabatier, P.A. and Jenkins-Smith, H.C. (eds), *Policy Change and Learning: An Advocacy Coalition Approach*, Boulder: Westview.

Sabatier, P.A. (1993b), 'The Suitability of Several Models for Comparative Analysis of the Policy Process', paper given at the Conference on Comparative Observation of Governmental Activity, Université Laval, Quebec.

Sabatier, P.A. and Jenkins-Smith, H.C. (1993), 'The Dynamics of Policy-Oriented Learning', in Sabatier, P.A. and Jenkins-Smith, H.C. (eds), *Policy Change and Learning: An Advocacy Coalition Approach*, Boulder: Westview.

Sabatier, P.A. and Mazmanian, D. (1980), 'The Implementation of Public Policy: A Framework of Analysis', *Policy Studies Journal*, **8**, 538–60.

Sacramento Air Quality Management District (1991), *Sacramento Air Quality Attainment Plan*, Sacramento: Sacramento Air Quality Management District.

Sacramento Air Quality Management District (1993), 'Concept Paper: Employer Commute Alternative Rules 1001', Sacramento Air Quality Management District.

Schlager, E. (1994), 'Policy Making and Collective Action: Defining

Coalitions Within the Advocacy Coalition Framework', School of Public Administration and Policy, University of Arizona, Tucson.

Schneider, K.D. and Capo, P. (1991), *California Transit Guide*, Davis: California Transit Publications.

Schwartz, J. (1992), 'Business Flight: Myths and Realities', Coalition for Clean Air, Venice Ca.

Schwartz, J. and Little, T. (1992), 'Comments Regarding the SCAQMD RECLAIM Pollution Trading Programme', Coalition for Clean Air, Venice Ca.

Secretary of State (1992), *California Ballot Pamphlet: General Election, November 3, 1992*, Sacramento: Secretary of State.

Secretary of State (1994), 'Lobbying Expenditures and the Top Lobbying Firms October 1–December 31 1993 and Cumulative Totals for 1993', Secretary of State, State of California, Sacramento.

Shoup, D.C. (1992), 'Cashing Out Employer-Paid Parking', University of California Transportation Center Working Paper No. 140, Berkeley.

Shoup, D.C. (1994), 'Cashing Out Employer-Paid Parking: An Opportunity to Reduce Minimum Parking Requirements', University of California Transportation Center Working Paper No. 204, Berkeley.

South Coast Air Quality Management District (1992a), 'Amendment to the 1991 Air Quality Management Plan'.

South Coast Air Quality Management District (Technology Advancement Office) (1992b), *1992 Progress Report, Volume II: Project and Technology Status*, Diamond Bar: South Coast Air Quality Management District.

Sperling, D. and Turrentine, T. (1991), 'The Market for Electric Vehicles', paper submitted to the Subcommittee on International Trade and Business Development, Los Angeles, 16 December.

Sperling, D., DeLuchi, M.A. and Wang, Q. (1991), *Toward Alternative Transportation Fuels and Incentive-Based Regulation of Vehicle Fuels and Emissions*, Berkeley: California Policy Seminar.

SRI International (1994), *The Economic Impact of an Enhanced Test-Only Automotive Inspection and Maintenance Program in California*, SRI Project 5535, Menlo Park: SRI International.

Superintendent of Documents (1991), *Intermodal Surface Transportation Efficiency Act of 1991*, Washington: Government Printing Office.

Teitz, M.B. (1990), 'California Growth: Hard Questions, Few Answers', in Kirlin, J.J. and Winkler, D.R. (eds), *California Policy Choices: Volume Six*, Los Angeles: University of Southern California.

Thompson, B.H. Jr (1993), 'Institutional Perspectives on Water Policy and Markets', *California Law Review*, **81** (3), 673–764.

Transport Committee (1994), Sixth Report from the House of Commons Transport Committee, *Transport-Related Air Pollution in London*, London: HMSO.

Turrentine, T., Lee-Gosselin, D., Kurani, K. and Sperling, D. (1993), 'The Pre-Conditions for Preferences for Electric Vehicles', Transportation Research Board Annual Meeting, Washington D.C.

Wachs, M. (1990), 'Regulating Traffic by Controlling Land Use: The Southern Californian Experience', *Transportation*, **16**, 241–56.

Wachs, M. and Guiliano, G. (1992), 'Employee Transportation Coordinators: A New Profession in Southern California', *Transportation Quarterly*, **46** (3), 411–27.

Waldman, T. (1990), 'South Coast Air Quality Management District: Bringing Supergovernment to Southern California', in Hoeber, T.R. and Price, C.M. (eds), *California Government and Politics Annual 1990–91*, Sacramento, California: Journal Press.

Waldman, T. (1991), 'L.A. Air Board Starts a Fresh Wind Blowing', in Hoeber, T.R. and Price, C.M. (eds), *California Government and Politics Annual 1991–92*, Sacramento: California Journal Press.

Walters, D. (1992), *The New California, 2nd edition*, Sacramento: California Journal Press.

Weale, A. (1992), *The New Politics of Pollution*, Manchester: Manchester University Press.

Wuebben, P., Lloyd A.C. and Leonard, J.H. (1990), 'The Future of Electric Vehicles in Meeting the Air Quality Challenges in Southern California', Society of Automotive Engineers Technical Paper Series 900580.

Zane, D. and Schwartz, J. (1993), 'Cleaning the Air with an Improved Smog Check Program', testimony to the California Senate Transportation Committee.

Index